I0810426

IMAGES
of America

FULTON

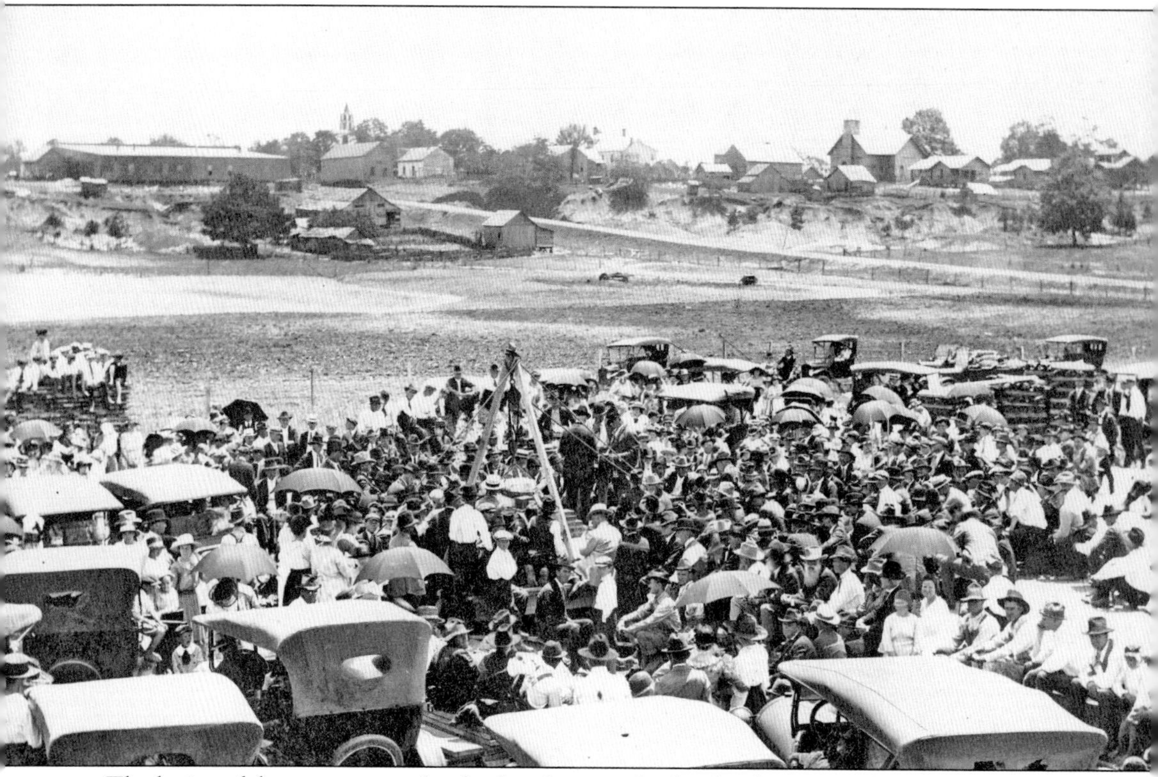

The laying of the cornerstone for the first four-year high school in Itawamba County took place on May 19, 1921, just east of Fulton's court square. The cornerstone, located on the northeastern corner of the two-story Administration Building, was put in place during a ceremony conducted by members of the Masonic lodge and contained a Bible, a statement from the Fulton Bank, and a copy of the *Itawamba County News*. When the building was torn down in 1966 to make room for new classrooms for the community college, the cornerstone was removed. (Courtesy of Janie Alexander.)

On the Cover: Fulton Furniture Company was Fulton's first exclusive furniture store when it opened in 1951. Owned by Manuel Gorden, the store was managed for many years by H.G. "Grady" Betts, pictured in front of the store's delivery truck in 1951. At this time, the store was in the original location of the Dixie Theatre building on the south side of the square; the theater's marquee sign can be seen here, still being used by the furniture store. (Courtesy of the Delmus Harden collection.)

IMAGES
of America

FULTON

Bob Franks and Mona Robinson Mills

ARCADIA
PUBLISHING

ISBN 978-1-4671-2379-2

Published by Arcadia Publishing
Charleston, South Carolina

Printed in the United States of America

Library of Congress Control Number: 2016958669

For all general information, please contact Arcadia Publishing:
Telephone 843-853-2070
Fax 843-853-0044
E-mail sales@arcadiapublishing.com
For customer service and orders:
Toll-Free 1-888-313-2665

Visit us on the Internet at www.arcadiapublishing.com

We dedicate this book to the hardworking and industrious founders of our community. Their legacy continues with the photographs portrayed in Images of America: Fulton, *and we owe a debt of gratitude for their struggles and perseverance.*

Contents

Acknowledgments		6
Introduction		7
1.	Around Town	11
2.	Courthouse Square, the Hub of Fulton	35
3.	Business and Industry	45
4.	School Time	73
5.	Fairs, Parades, and Other Fun Stuff	93
6.	Faces from the Past	113

ACKNOWLEDGMENTS

We are indebted to many people who took the time to share their collections of old photographs of the people, businesses, and organizations of our wonderful little town of Fulton. Our community is blessed to have so many who work to preserve its history.

Special thanks and appreciation go to Rubye Del Harden, who generously allowed us access to her father's collection of negatives from the "Only Newspaper in the World That Cares Anything about Itawamba County." No one loved his town and community more than Delmus Harden, editor and publisher of the *Itawamba County Times*. Delmus and his camera spent many days, evenings, and weekends photographing special events. From parades, dairy shows, and picnics to family reunions, weddings, and beauty pageants, Delmus rarely turned down a request for photographic coverage of an event in his home county. Unless otherwise noted, the photographs in this book come from the Harden collection.

The authors' royalties from the sale of this book will benefit the Itawamba Historical Society, a nonprofit organization created by grassroots volunteers in 1982.

INTRODUCTION

Fulton, the seat of county government, is one of the oldest towns in northeast Mississippi. Itawamba County was organized in 1836 as one of the original Chickasaw Cession counties of northern Mississippi. On February 9, 1836, the Mississippi legislature divided the Chickasaw Cession land into counties, and five days later, the same body appointed commissioners in each of the 10 organized counties. James Rowland, William Coats, Lewis Gideon, and David Walker were appointed commissioners for Itawamba County. As instructed by the legislature, these commissioners called for a vote, and five men were elected to the board of police: James Spears Bourland, Alfred G. Lane, John Beene, Elijah S. Spearman, and Eliba Allen. This body held an election, and the following men were elected as officers of the new county of Itawamba: Charles Warren (sheriff), C.H. Richie (probate judge), Lewis Gideon (probate clerk), and Russell O. Beene (circuit clerk).

At this time Fulton had not yet been established, and the county's business was transacted west of the Tombigbee at the store house of Elisha Thomas and the home of James Spears Bourland in the present-day Cardsville community. The board of police was empowered by the state legislature to select the site of county government, which was to be in the center of the county, if suitable, and to acquire this location either by purchase or donation.

A deed recorded in Deed Book 1, Page 53, shows Section 25, Township 9 South, Range 8 East was purchased by land speculators Kenneth Clark, John Miller, and Robert Miller. This group donated 50 acres of this land to the board of police for the site of county government. The town of Fulton was established on this donation by an act of the Mississippi legislature on May 11, 1837, with the corporate limits of the town set. The first post office was established in July, and John Thompson was selected as the first postmaster for Fulton, the northernmost town established on the Tombigbee River. By 1838, the town had been mapped, with the county board of police selling lots. Some of the first lot buyers in town were Edward Moore, William Peacock, the firm of Eckford & Clifton, John Walker, James C. Wright, Lemuel Beene, Wiley Gaither, Joseph G. Clarke, Samuel Vaughn, Joshua Toomer, John Beene, Charles Anderson, Burt G. Moore, John Kemp, Reuben Warren, and D.N. Cayce.

Northeast Mississippi in the 1840s was known as "the old southwest." Shortly before the establishment of Fulton, this area was a virtual wilderness. John Tannahill, an early settler, wrote in January 1842: "After having been tossed about the world for about four months, I have at last found a home in the wilderness. . . . The country here is but thinly settled as it is only six years since the Indians left it. The land is not so rich as it is in other parts of the States where I have been but I am told it is very healthy."

Pioneer Malachai C. Cummings has often been referred to as the "Father of Fulton." David Johnson, the editor of the *Fulton Reporter*, wrote in 1888 that "a history of Fulton could not be written without a history of Cummings." Johnson noted that Cummings settled near the future town of Fulton in the early part of 1836, when the area was covered by a thick growth of large pine trees. Cummings, wrote Johnson, was involved in "nearly every enterprise in the interest of Fulton from its beginning to the present time [1888]" and served the county in the state legislature for many years. Cummings is also credited with building a "nice and commodious" church house as well as providing "ample means" to build a school for the town.

During the 1840s, Fulton saw some growth but never had the development of its sister towns of Aberdeen and Columbus downriver. Two reasons were the lack of steamboat navigation on the waters of the upper Tombigbee River and the lack of fertile soil as seen in the Black Belt region to the south. However, Fulton was establishing itself as the center of commerce for Itawamba County. During the 1840s, the Fulton Female Academy (located on North Cummings Street) and the Fulton Male Academy (located adjacent to the Fulton Cemetery) were established, and by 1844, Fulton had a temperance society with Josiah Hinds, a Mr. Ellis, E.G. Thomas, Jeptha Robins, and Will Cage as officers.

In the early years, special events were held in the town, including Independence Day celebrations and countywide candidate speeches during election years. On October 21, 1843, pioneer Josiah Hinds wrote in his diary: "Two of our candidates for representative took a little too much fire water at court last week and one of them concluded to call off the dogs and quit the drive and has left the field in disgust. One of the drunken candidates took the stand in the courthouse on Monday, and after abusing one of our preachers at a dreadful rate, left the courthouse and made his way to the doggery and got as drunk as Bacchus."

An 1845 issue of the *Fulton Herald* newspaper tells of a celebration on the town square honoring the memory of Gen. Andrew Jackson on July 4. Jackson had died that June. More than 2,000 county citizens were present. All the stores were closed until late afternoon, and their doors were hung with mourning wreaths. After speeches were given, the flag was then stripped of its mourning and a celebration of the Fourth was held, featuring a speech by Fulton mayor D.N. Cayce.

Fulton continued to slowly grow through the 1850s, and by 1860, the town had a population of a little more than 500 citizens. However, the Civil War had disastrous effects upon the town. In 1909, Mollie Gaither of Fulton submitted a 19th-century newspaper clipping to the *Itawamba County News* for republication. It details quite vividly the loss Fulton suffered during the war. The article reads in part: "At the breaking out of the Civil War in 1861, there were about 40 voters within the corporate limits of the town of Fulton, and 5 or 6 boys who were under age. Of that number, 18 were killed in battle and died of disease contracted in the army." This article illustrates the fact that Fulton lost nearly half of the town's adult male citizens during the war.

Two years after the war, Itawamba County lost nearly half its population when Lee County was formed from Itawamba's western borders and portions of northern Itawamba were given to Prentiss and Tishomingo Counties. Former citizens who were in the areas removed from Itawamba County now traveled and conducted commerce and governmental affairs in other counties. Adding to Fulton's woes was the construction and completion of the Mobile & Ohio Railroad, which was now running through the new county of Lee. New towns sprang up along the railroad, including Verona, Tupelo, Saltillo, Guntown, and Baldwyn. At this time, since the railroad did not come into Itawamba County, citizens of Itawamba had no mode of efficient transportation of goods. Many Fulton merchants moved west to the growing towns along the railroad, especially to Tupelo.

By 1900, the census counted only 171 people living in Fulton. When Zereda Greene moved to town in 1900 with her parents, there were a mere 30 homes. Just a few years earlier, when W.G. Orr moved to Fulton and opened a mercantile business, there were only five "store houses" in town. City streets did not get officially named until 1891. When the 1920 census was completed, only 227 citizens were living in Fulton.

Progress bypassed Fulton until the early 1920s, when Fulton finally saw a renaissance thanks to four factors: the construction and completion of the Bankhead Highway through the county, the establishment and construction of Itawamba Agricultural High School, the construction and completion of the Mississippian Railway, and the development of the timber industry. By the end of the decade, Fulton's population had nearly quadrupled to 937 citizens. Many African Americans moved to Fulton during the decade, largely due to jobs in the lumber mills in town.

Prior to the 1920s, the roads of Itawamba County were maintained primarily for horse and wagon travel. Many of the old roads had been used for generations and were usually named for the settlements they connected, such as the Fulton and Pikeville Road and the Aberdeen and Jacinto Road. Other roads were named for families and settlements. During the early years of the 20th century, more and more Americans were traveling by automobile, and a need for better roads was voiced by many citizens. Thanks to John Hollis Bankhead, congressman from neighboring Alabama (and grandfather of actress Tallulah Bankhead), a major national concrete road was built through the entire width of Itawamba County, connecting previously isolated Fulton to major cities.

The Good Roads Movement came out of concern by many citizens for better highways, and in 1916, the Federal Aid Road Act was passed. Congressman Bankhead was ready with his plan for a national road that would link the older states of the south and east with the new ones in the west. The Bankhead Highway was a cross-country automobile highway connecting Washington, DC, and San Diego, California. It was part of the National Auto Trail system. The Itawamba portion of the national highway, built during the early 1920s, transformed travel in the county. Although the progress of the road was slowed by World War I, construction continued, and by the late 1920s, the national road was complete. Considered the "Broadway of America," this national highway brought prosperity and commerce to many towns along its route, including Fulton, where it was completed in 1923, the same year the Mississippian Railroad was incorporated in Amory. It was during this time that the major timber industry was developed in the county.

A 1923 newspaper article from the *Tupelo Journal* reads: "Our neighbor on the east, Fulton, saw more building during the last six months of the year than has taken place within the ten years previous. Two new schools, the public school of Fulton and the Itawamba County Agricultural High School, and the new Baptist church there were built previous to 1923, but with the completion of the Bankhead concrete road an impetus was given the spirit of improvement which is bringing the town up to the point of being one of the most progressive towns in this part of the state."

The beginnings of the Itawamba Agricultural High School can be traced back to shortly after 1910, when a county tax levy raised $1,354.67 for the purpose of "maintaining an Agricultural High School." However, actual construction of the facility did not begin for more than 10 years.

In 1919, the trustees of the Itawamba Agricultural High School began acquiring property for the new school, to be located west of the town square of Fulton under the hill. In June 1919, the trustees received properties from the W.L. Gaither estate, Isaac Lewis Sheffield, J.A. Senter, and W.G. Orr. In December of that year, properties were received from Annie Gaither and M.C. Benson for a total of nearly 100 acres for the new school campus.

The first contractor who signed on to build the school backed down, so a new contract was let. By May 1921, construction was underway, and on May 19 of that year, a cornerstone ceremony was held at the Administration Building site attended by hundreds of Itawambians. Only two buildings were completed before the school opened in September 1921: the Administration Building and the Girls' Dormitory. The Itawamba Agricultural High school officially opened at 10:00 a.m. on September 19, 1921, with registration and opening exercises for nearly 150 students.

It was during this time of great expectations that Fulton experienced growth like it had never seen before. Several new businesses opened in the little town, including a new hardware store from Amory (Staub-Stewart), a new automobile dealership, groceries, and other businesses. With the opening of the Mississippian Railway, the timber industry in Itawamba County expanded, becoming the largest industry in the county with lumber mills opening up all around Fulton.

The Mississippian Railway was organized in Amory in 1923. The *Itawamba County News* published an article from the *Commercial Appeal* in Memphis on August 9, 1923, stating:

> Incorporation and organization of the Mississippian Railway, a proposed line to extend from Amory, Monroe County, to Fulton, Itawamba County, were completed yesterday at a meeting held in Amory, Miss., and actual construction on the project will go forward rapidly. Itawamba County has heretofore had no railroad facilities and the new line will open up a territory along the valley of the Tombigbee of hardwood and pine timber, various farm products and cotton. The railroad when completed will be about 20 miles in length, connecting with the Frisco at Amory.

By the following September, this new railroad was already finished to White Springs in Itawamba County, and it was due to be completed to Fulton by October. On September 16, 1924, an article in the *Itawamba County News* told of progress:

> The progress of the new construction now under way on the railroad project running from Amory through Itawamba County is progressing even beyond expectations of those interested in the movement. The work of track grading has been completed to Fulton and steel has been laid approximately a mile beyond White Springs. The promoters are of the opinion that the road will be completed to Fulton by the first of October and trains will be running on schedule time in this once inland county. That Itawamba is forging ahead and is keeping abreast of the times is evidenced by the number of homes that are being built and the best sign of the progress is that they are all neatly built bungalows or nicely furnished buildings in modern designs. The new railroad, The Mississippian, will be continued thru the county and will open up one of the richest counties of lumber in the state. Gilmore & Puckett own fifteen hundred acres north of Fulton in virgin pine as fine as ever grew in the county and in which an axe has never been struck. The lumber industry alone is bringing many thousands of dollars into the county.

Shortly after 1920, the lumber industry saw tremendous growth in Itawamba County. The Kilpatrick family of Carrollton, Alabama, and the Gibbs family from Hardin County, Tennessee, opened mills at Fulton. Additionally, there were the lumber companies of Haynes-Walker, Propst and Howell, McAdams, Mattox, Berthold-Jennings, and others. In 1925, the Memphis *Commercial Appeal* wrote, "Fulton is a booming town in a thriving timber district," and noted that the mills of Fulton shipped out 20 railroad cars of lumber daily, creating a monthly payroll of $48,000 in Fulton alone.

In 1927, Mississippi Power & Light Company built a power plant to provide electricity to Fulton, and two years later, a water and sewerage system was installed by the town.

The Bankhead Highway, Itawamba Agricultural High School, the Mississippian Railway, and the development of the timber industry were perhaps the greatest factors to the growth and improvements in the town of Fulton, all taking place in the 1920s.

From that era to the present, Fulton has continued to grow and prosper thanks to the seeds sewn during the 1920s. Itawamba Agricultural High School was expanded during the 1940s, adding a two-year college known as Itawamba Junior College—now Itawamba Community College. Today, the college serves a five-county area and is known as one of the most dynamic community colleges in the state.

The 1970s marked the completion of the Tennessee-Tombigbee Waterway, marking the western boundary of the town of Fulton. This waterway, connecting the Gulf of Mexico with the Tennessee River, not only affords shipping capabilities to area industries but also serves as a major recreation destination.

Fulton's history spans three centuries. The "can-do" spirit of the early trans-Appalachian settlers who entered this territory during the 1830s and who forged a nation out of the wilderness continues to be alive and well in Fulton.

One

Around Town

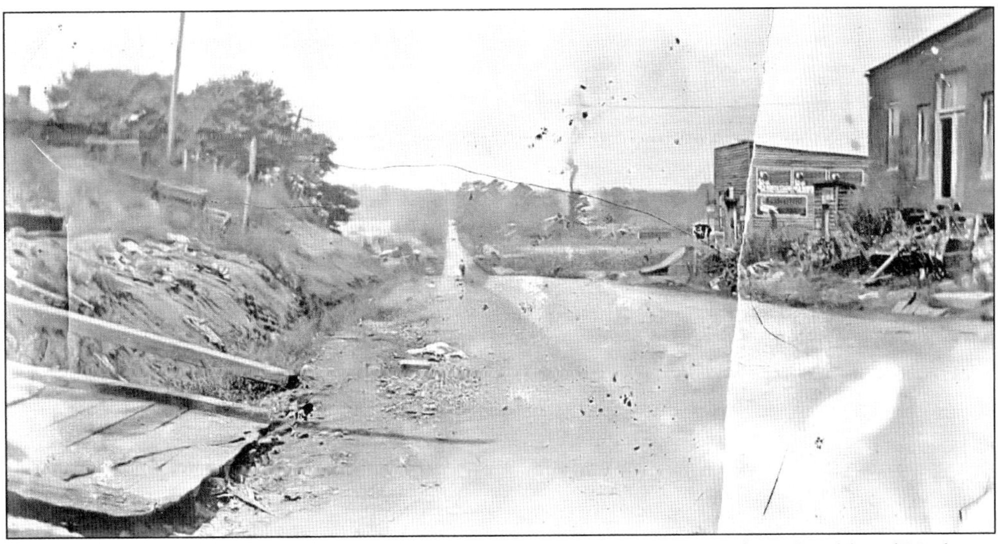

Standing at the crest of the hill at the Fulton square and looking west along Bankhead Highway around 1921, smoke can be seen rising from one of the many sawmills west of town, as well as the fields that would later become home to Itawamba Agricultural High School and Itawamba Community College. (Courtesy of Margo Mize Marlin.)

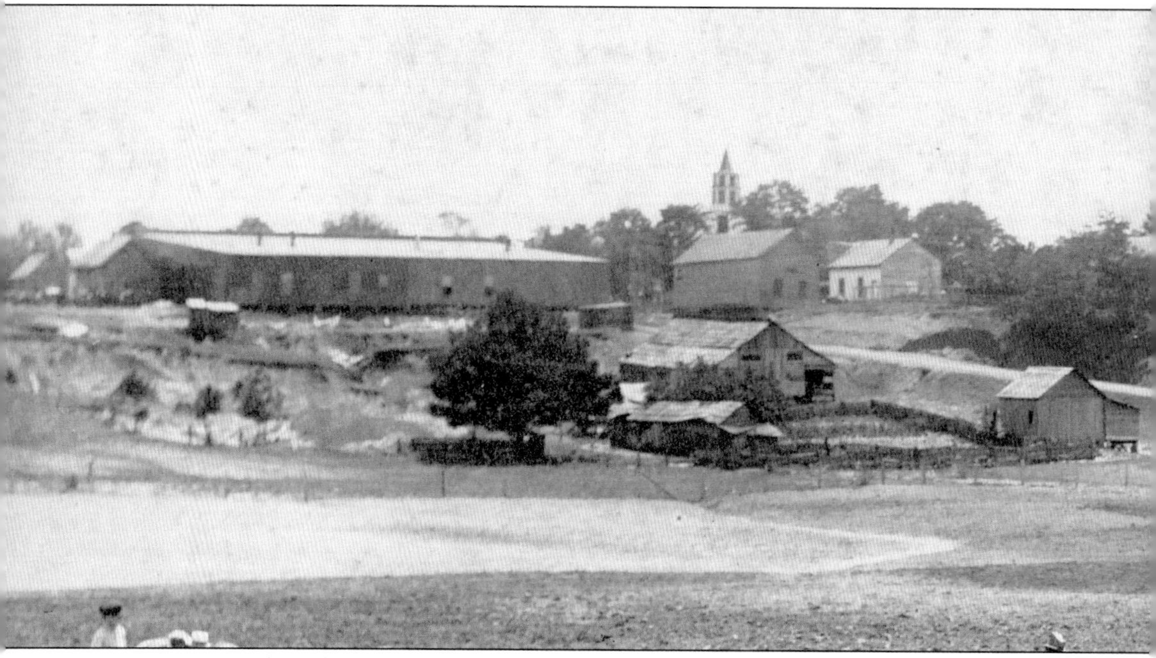

In May 1921, when this scene was photographed from the western edge of town, Fulton was a village of just over 200 people. Until the timber industry and lumber manufacturing came along in the 1920s, causing an economic boom in the area, the town's main activity centered around the courthouse. Completion of the Bankhead Highway and the opening of Itawamba Agricultural High School provided additional stimulus for growth in the 1920s, and by the end of the decade,

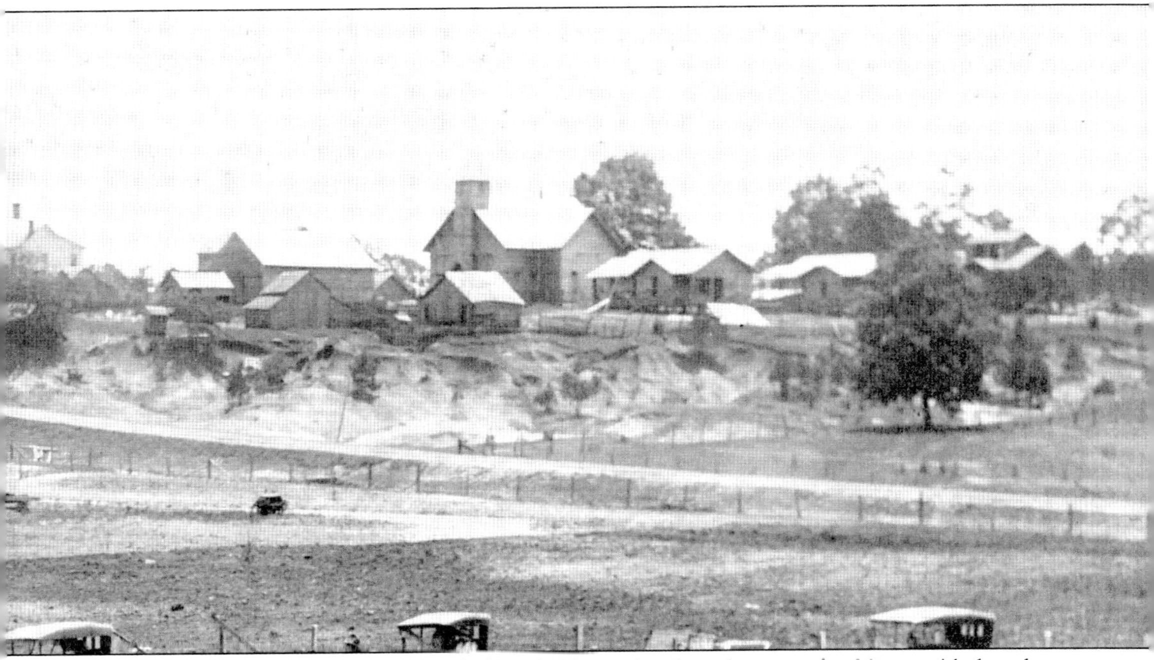

Fulton's population had nearly quadrupled, with 20 new brick and cement buildings added to the landscape. In this photograph, the cupola of the county courthouse can be seen above the trees to the left. The courthouse itself is obscured from view by a building housing Fulton Bank. At far left is a mule barn that was located on the northwest corner of what would become Main and Cummings Streets. (Courtesy of Janie Alexander.)

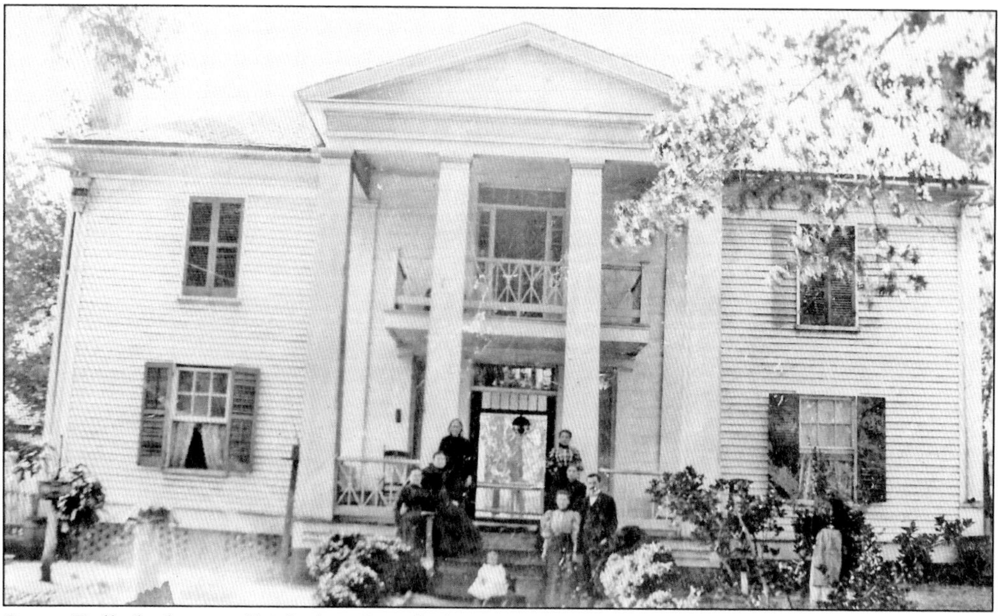

Sunny Dell, the home of Malachai Crawford Cummings, the "Father of Fulton," was located north of Fulton on a hill overlooking Cummings Creek. The old antebellum home was destroyed by fire around 1920. It was considered one of the most beautiful private dwellings in northern Mississippi. This 12-room house had 18 windows, each composed of 12 glasses and measuring 18 by 20 inches. The window glass was cut by hand. Six rooms were 20 feet square. There were 12 fireplaces in the house, and all lumber used in its construction was ripsawed and dressed by hand.

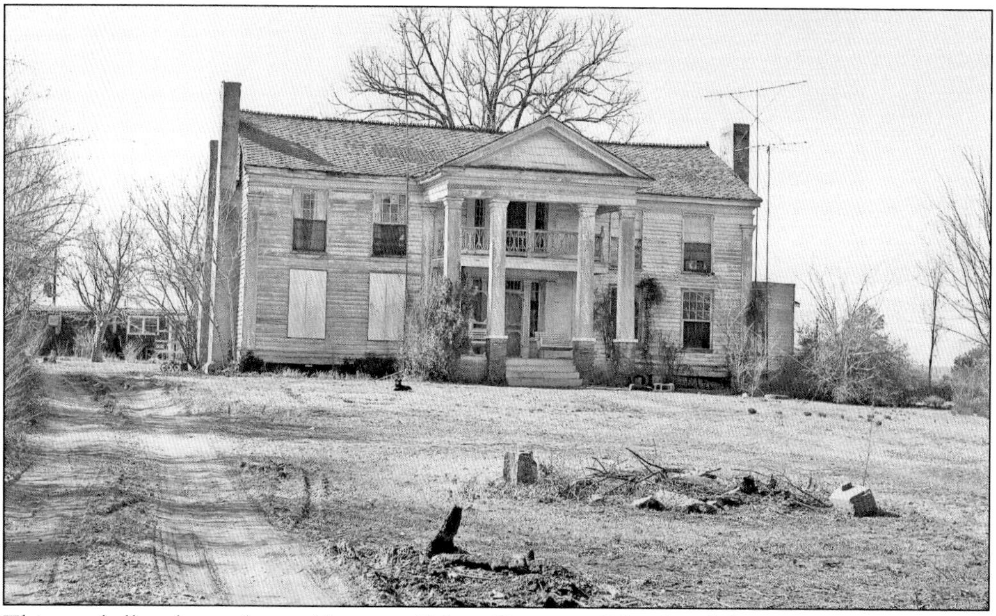

This antebellum home, located between Fulton Grammar School and the court square, was built in 1856 by Dr. A.J. McWilliams using lumber from trees that were felled in the clearing of land for the town of Fulton. Dr. M.W. Howard purchased the home in 1872, and Leonard N. Robison purchased it from the Harden family in 1924, becoming the home's last owner. Robison sold lots surrounding the property to home builders.

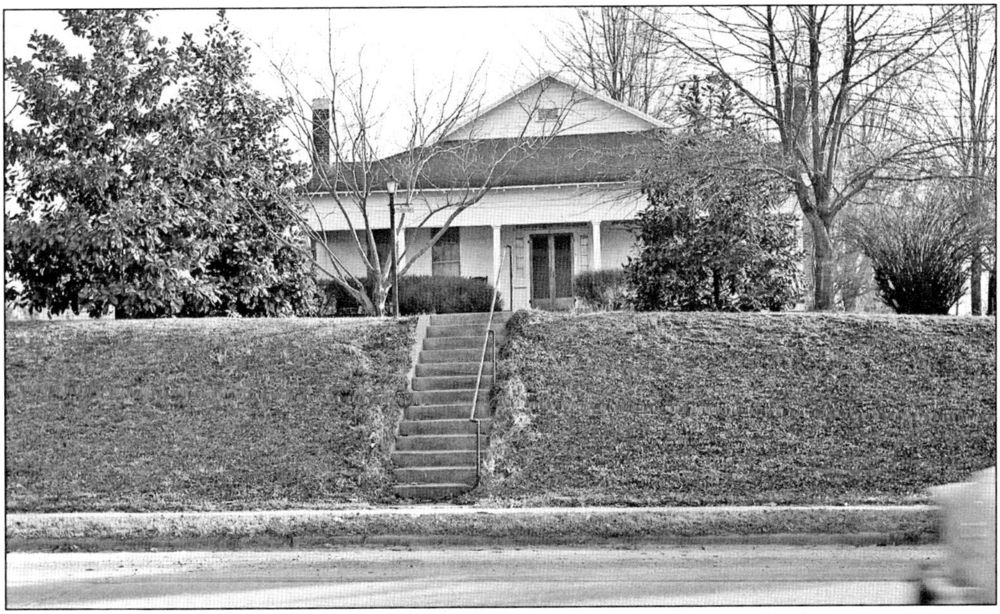

Known today as the Cates-Gaither home or the Cedars, this home was built in the 1860s and later expanded by Pleasant Cates. Pleasant's son Luke Cates sold the home to William L. Gaither in 1901, and it remained in the Gaither family until 2009, when the Methodist church donated the house for removal to an adjacent lot and subsequent restoration.

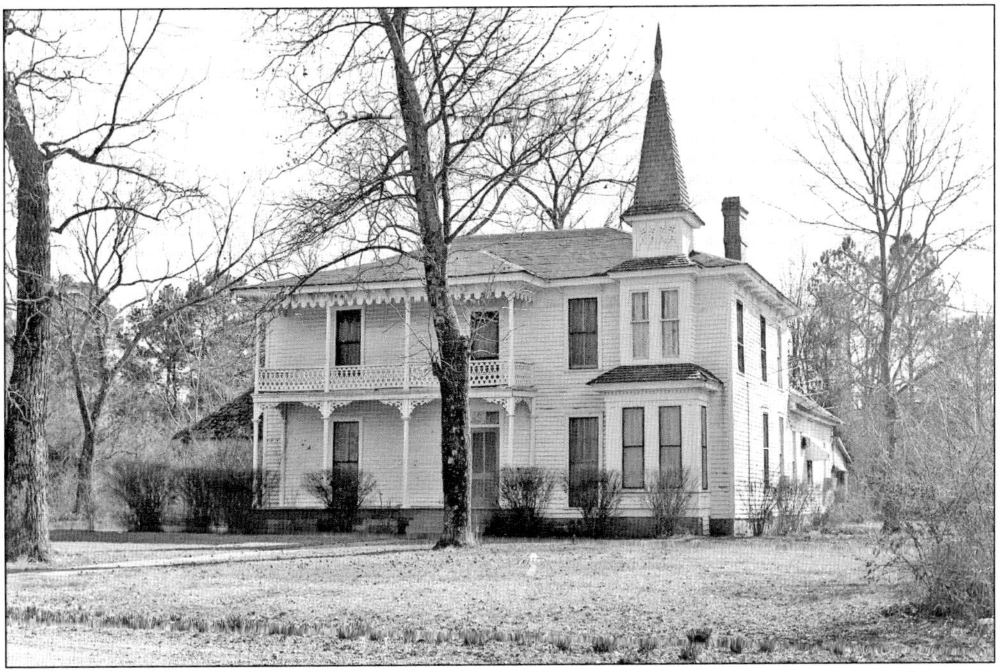

Aeolian Grove was built around 1840 and is one of Fulton's oldest surviving residences. Pleasant Cates purchased the home in the 1860s but later sold it to his son-in-law J.P. Baldridge, who added rooms and a second story. In 1903, his widow, Elizabeth Cates Baldridge, sold the house and all its furniture to W.G. Orr, a local merchant. Lovingly restored, the home is now owned by Mary and Phil Morris.

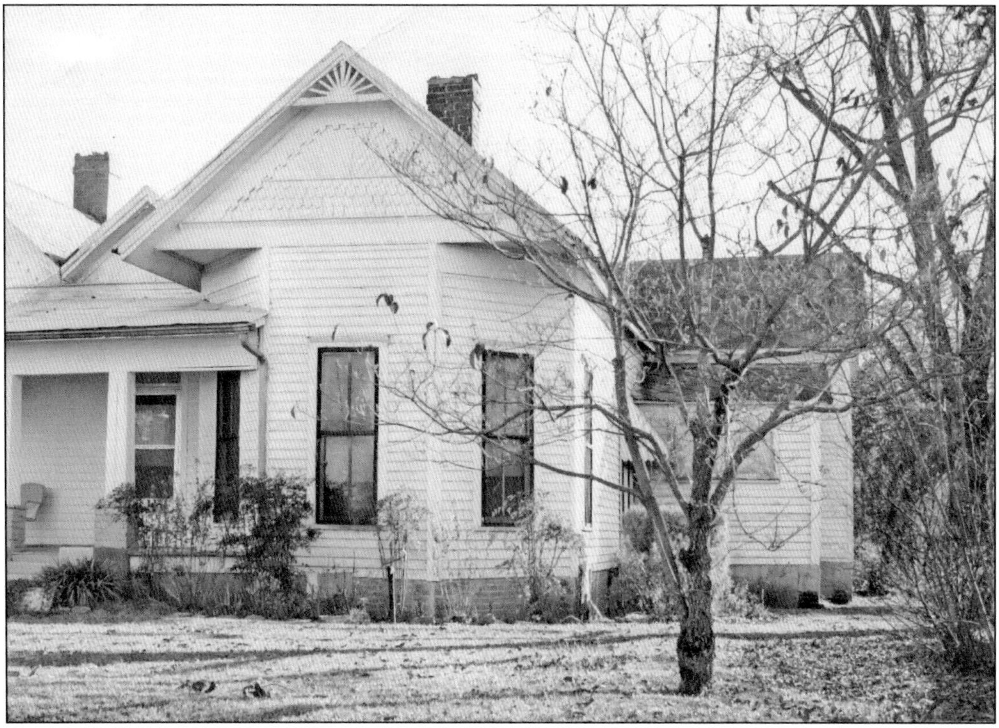

Standing on the lot where the Fulton post office is today, this home was owned for many years by the Senter family. The lot was originally owned by pioneer Reuben Wiygul and was sold by his daughters to J.W. Hudson, who had a house built upon the lot in 1901. Owners included Thomas A. Senter (1908), Jim Senter (1919), and Bob Senter (1920), whose family owned it until it was torn down in 1976.

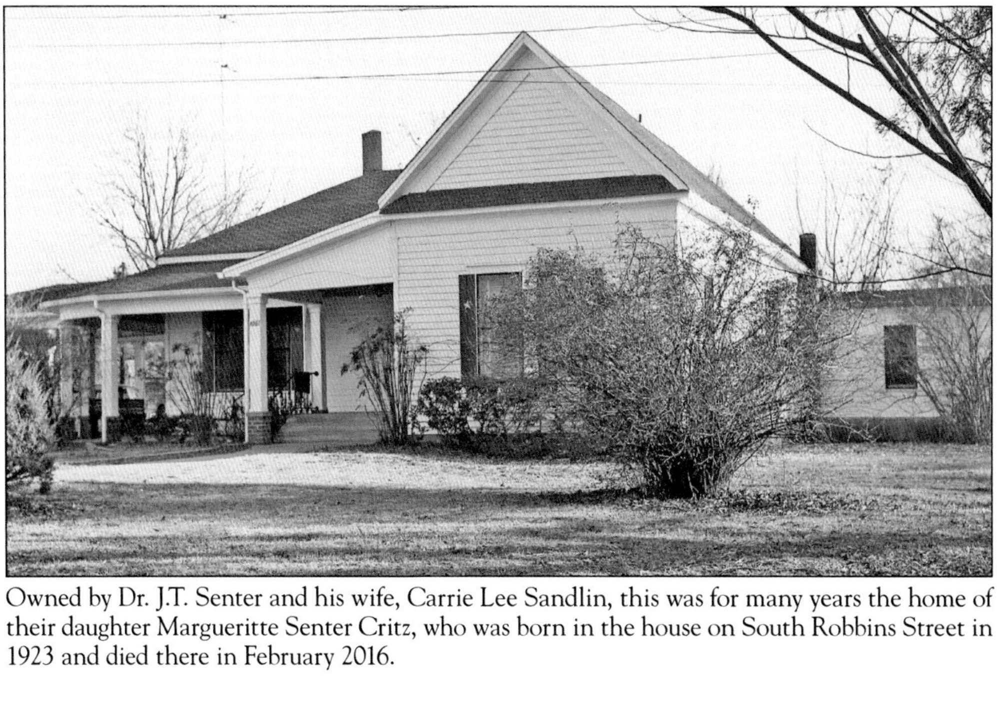

Owned by Dr. J.T. Senter and his wife, Carrie Lee Sandlin, this was for many years the home of their daughter Margueritte Senter Critz, who was born in the house on South Robbins Street in 1923 and died there in February 2016.

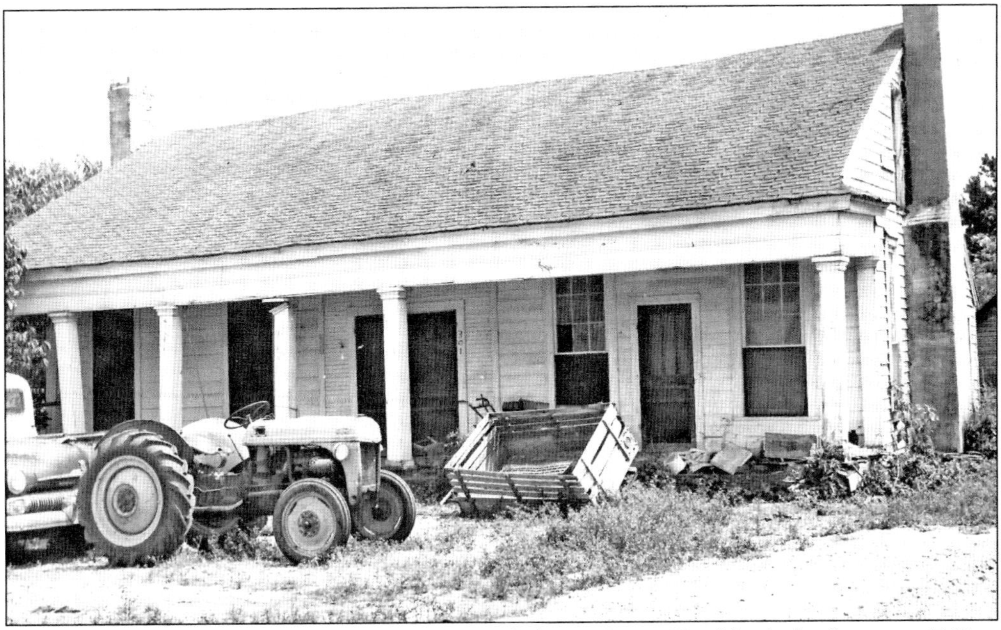

William Harvey Keys (son of Itawamba judge and planter James Keys) built this home in 1861 at the corner of South Cummings and Cedar Streets in Fulton and lived here until 1878, when he sold the home to Dr. J.M. Walker and moved back to the old Keys plantation across the Tombigbee River. In later years, the home was known as the Benson House. It burned down in the 1960s during the construction of a medical office (the current Fulton Police Department building).

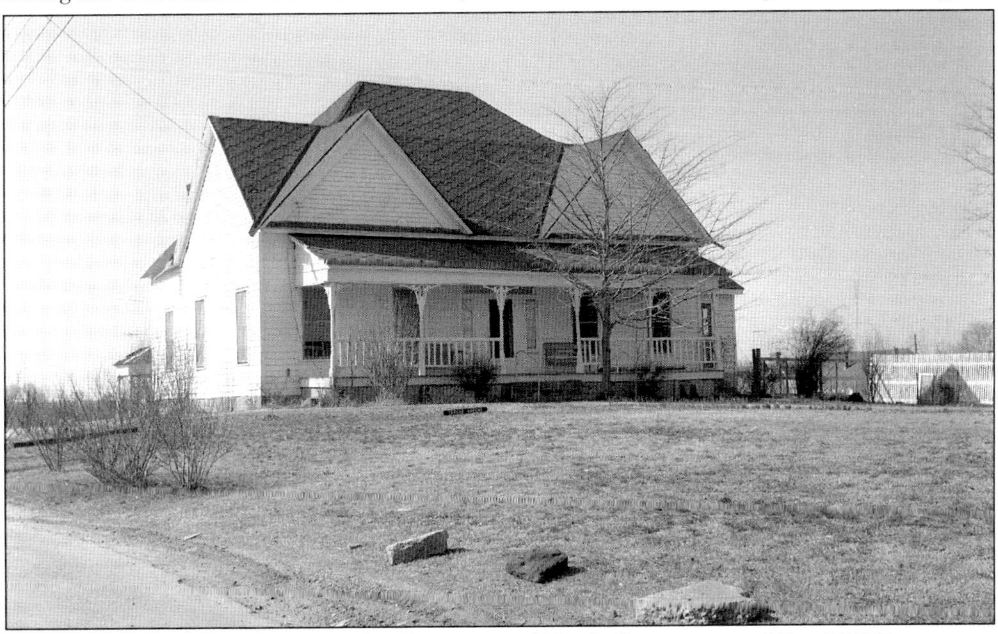

The Zereda Greene House, located at the corner of North Cummings and East Hill Streets, was built around 1849 by Robert O. and Louisa Maupin. Robert was a Fulton attorney, and Louisa operated the Fulton Female Academy, a boarding school located near the corner of Main and South Cummings Streets, two blocks south of the home. Zereda Greene's father bought the house in 1901.

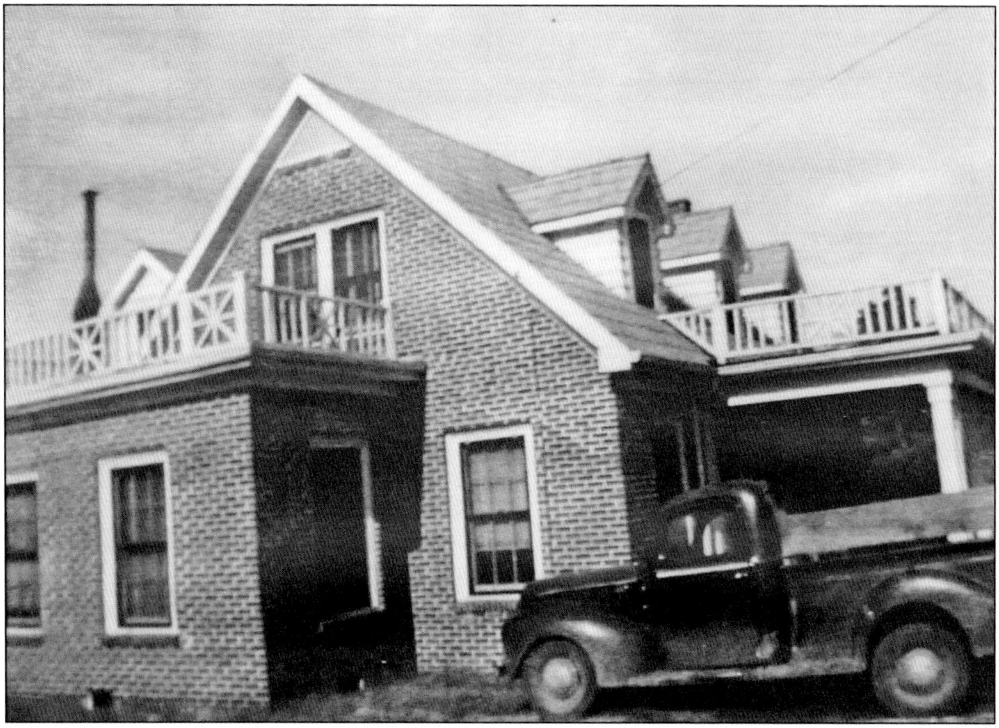

This is a 1940s view of the Gibbs House, located at the corner of Cedar and South Clifton Streets and built by Fulton lumberman James Miles Gibbs. The Gibbs family came to Fulton in the 1920s and was instrumental in building the sawmill industry in Itawamba County, causing a boom in the local economy. Over the years, the family was involved in several local businesses.

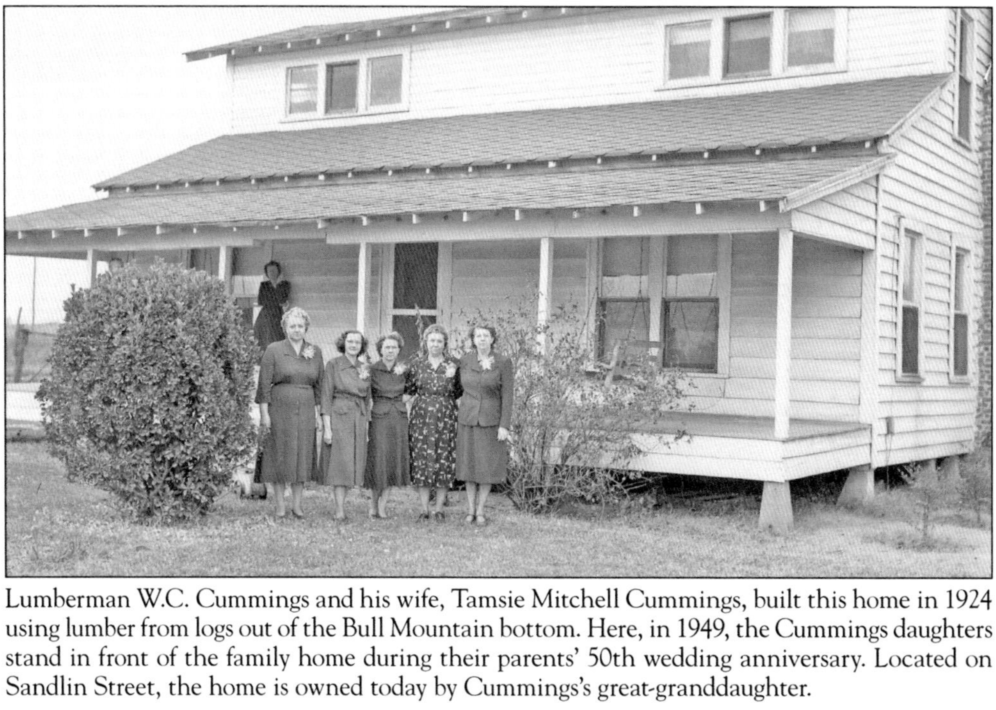

Lumberman W.C. Cummings and his wife, Tamsie Mitchell Cummings, built this home in 1924 using lumber from logs out of the Bull Mountain bottom. Here, in 1949, the Cummings daughters stand in front of the family home during their parents' 50th wedding anniversary. Located on Sandlin Street, the home is owned today by Cummings's great-granddaughter.

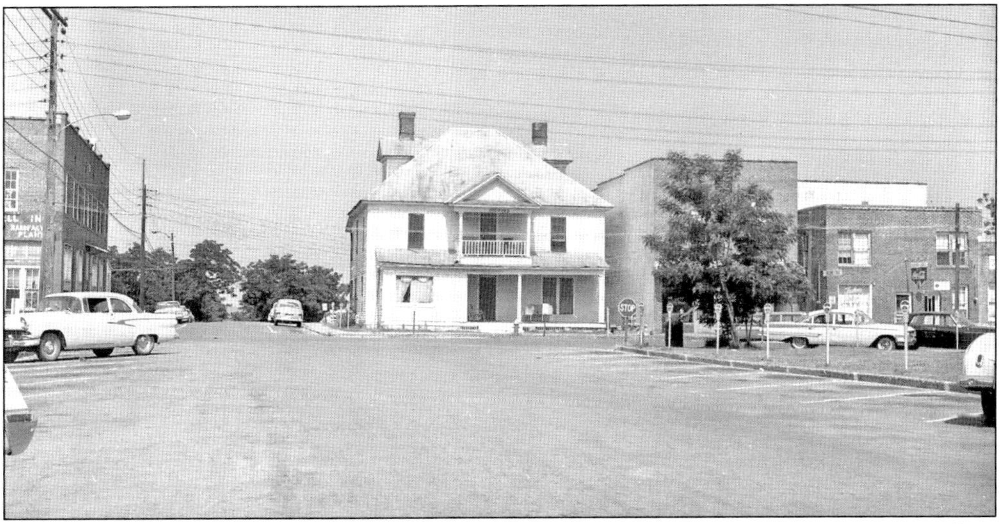

Known in later years as the Bennett Hotel (owned by Rodney Bennett), this former antebellum home of Fulton pioneer Eli Phillips was torn down in 1962 to make room for a parking lot for White's Super Market and later as the site of S&W Pharmacy. Phillips served as Fulton mayor, county probate judge, and state representative.

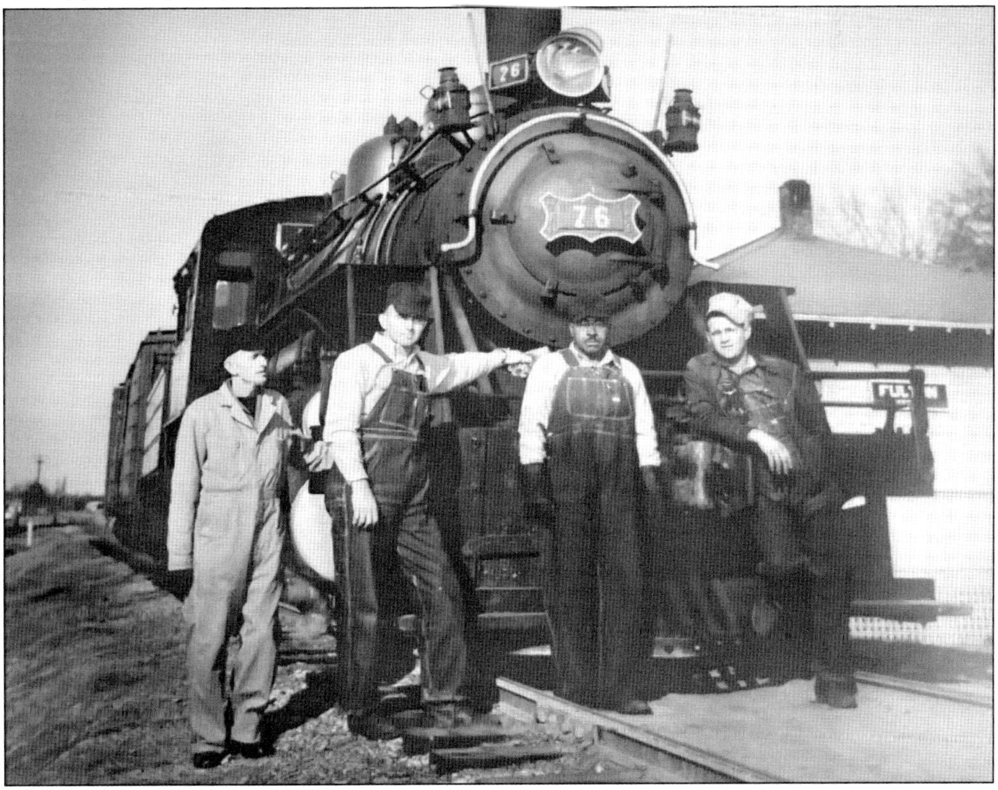

The "Old 76" train pulls into the Fulton depot on a winter afternoon in the 1950s. Since 1923, the Mississippian Railway has connected Fulton to the BNSF Railway in Amory. For years, this locomotive hauled timber products south along the track behind Itawamba Agricultural High School, with its coal smoke billowing into the sky.

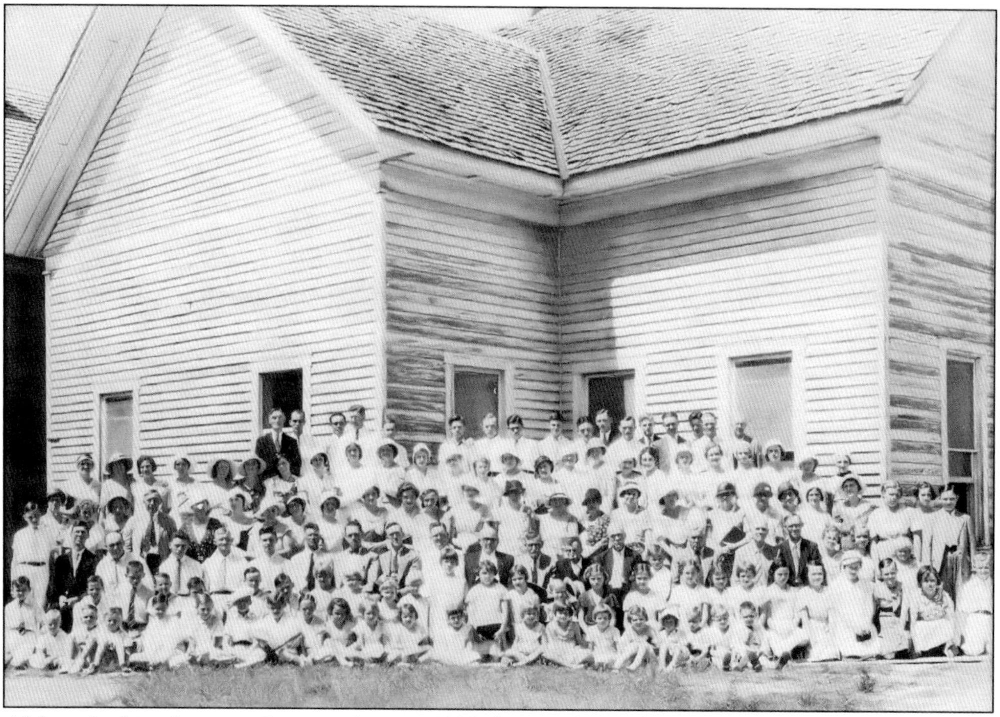

Although this photograph was taken in 1933 during the dedication of an annex, First Baptist Church was organized in Fulton in 1909 and initially met in the Methodist church. A wood-frame building was built in 1921 on a lot purchased from M.C. Benson, and in 1942, brick was added to the building. Today, First Christian Church occupies it.

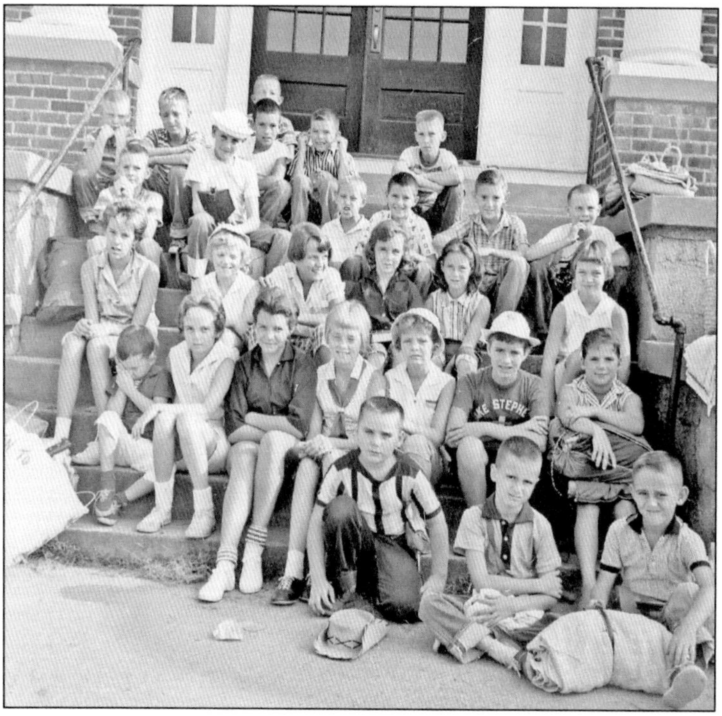

Youth attending the Fulton Methodist Church day camp in 1959 include Tim Wiygul, Rick Carter, Stanley Joe Spradling, Genie Mize, Beth Jamieson, Mitzi Anthony, Carrie Ann Senter, Kathy Senter, Suzanne Stubblefield, Myra Oliver, Henry Paula Mize, Martha Lewis Gibbs, Dena Sheffield, Sammy Kilpatrick, Bill Stubblefield, Steve Pate, Larry Pate, Denny Crockett, Gary Davis, and Frank Brown.

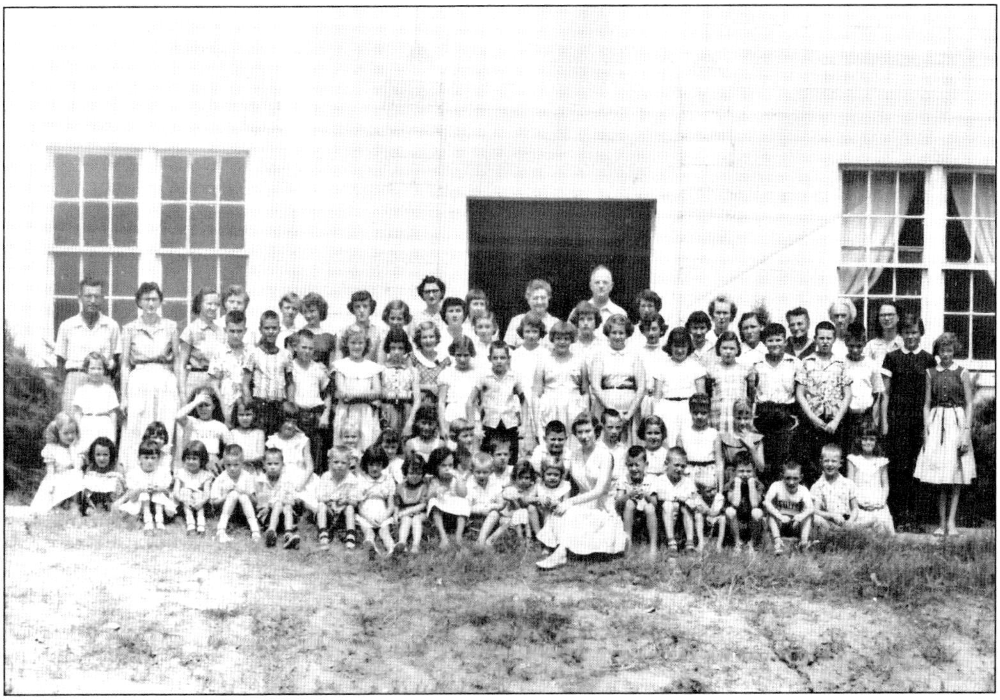

Children enjoy vacation Bible school at Trinity Baptist Church in 1954. The church was organized in 1943 with 15 charter members; a concrete block building was completed in 1949, and an additional auditorium was built in 1954. Each summer, the various churches in town held vacation Bible schools where local children attended from all the different churches.

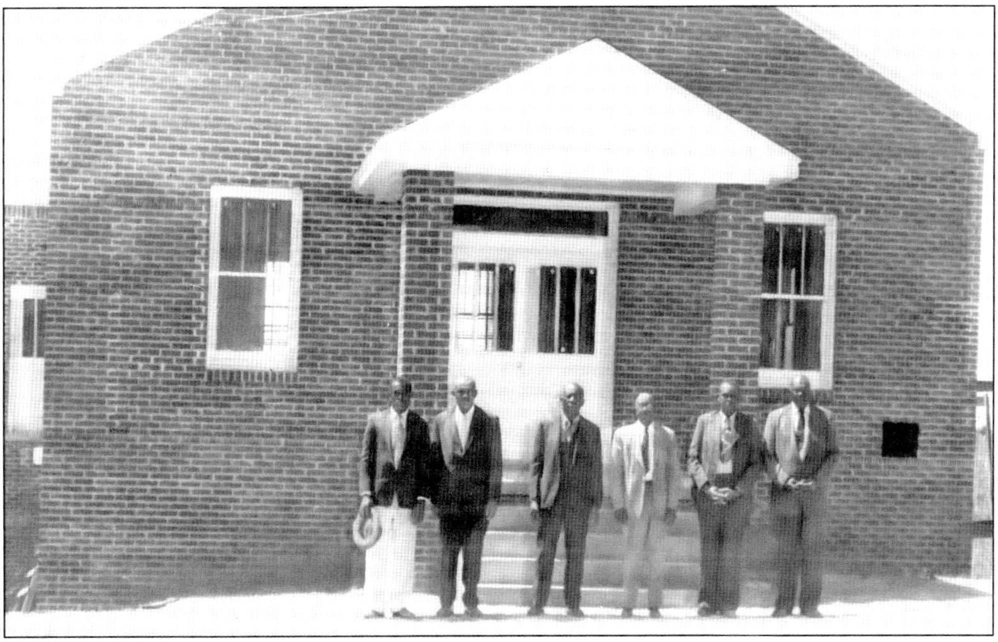

Leaders of St. Matthew Missionary Baptist Church stand in front of their church building in Fulton. The church was organized in 1863 and moved to its present location in 1919. Identified members of the church in this photograph are Dabb Ferguson, Earnest Hughes, and George Gibson.

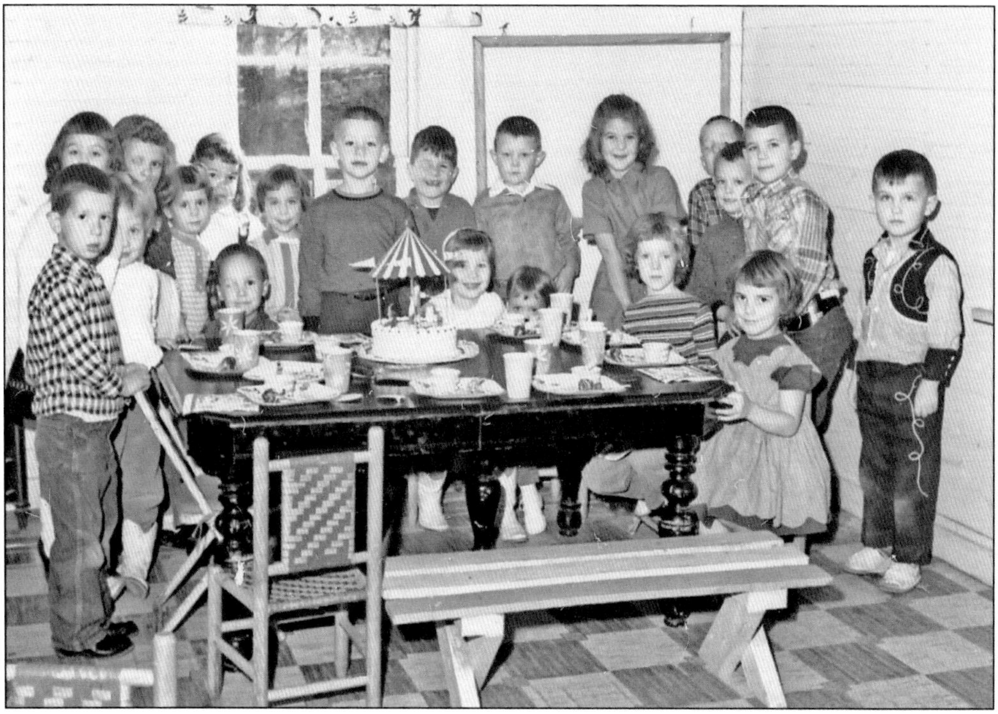

In 1961, little Jimmy Chism (standing behind cake) and his friends enjoy a birthday celebration at his home in Fulton. Jimmy's parents were Johnnie Chism and Virginia "Jennie" Senter.

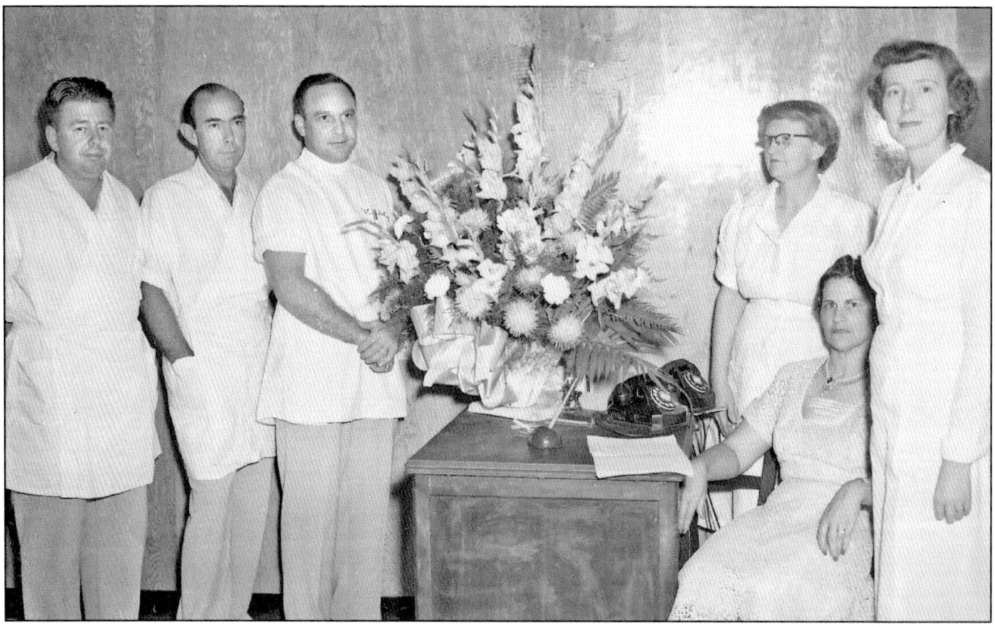

In 1954, the first hospital opened in Fulton, and more than 250 people attended the open house. Standing from left to right are Dr. Denton Crockett and Dr. William J. Daniel, owners; Dr. Victor Rather, dentist; Mrs. Jeff Brinkley, nurse; and Sybil Carter, medical technologist. Seated is Verna Haynes Rogers of the Fulton Civic Club, sponsor of the open house.

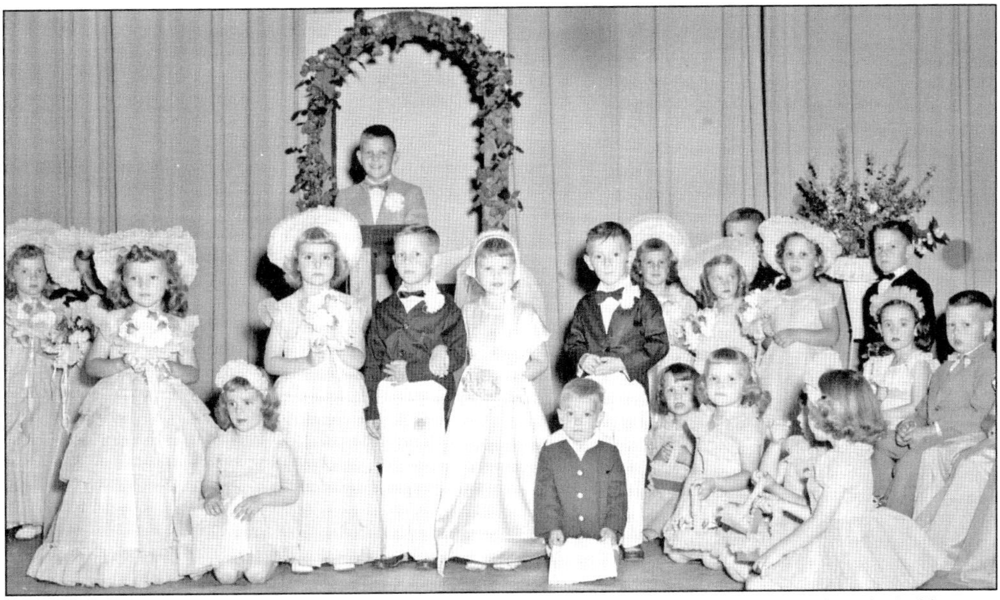

Some of the most popular community events held at the Fulton Grammar School included beauty pageants, operettas, Halloween carnivals, and Tom Thumb weddings. This "wedding" took place in 1953, featuring a preacher, bride, groom, and attendants, and was sponsored by the American Legion Auxiliary as a fundraiser for the Legion Hut building fund.

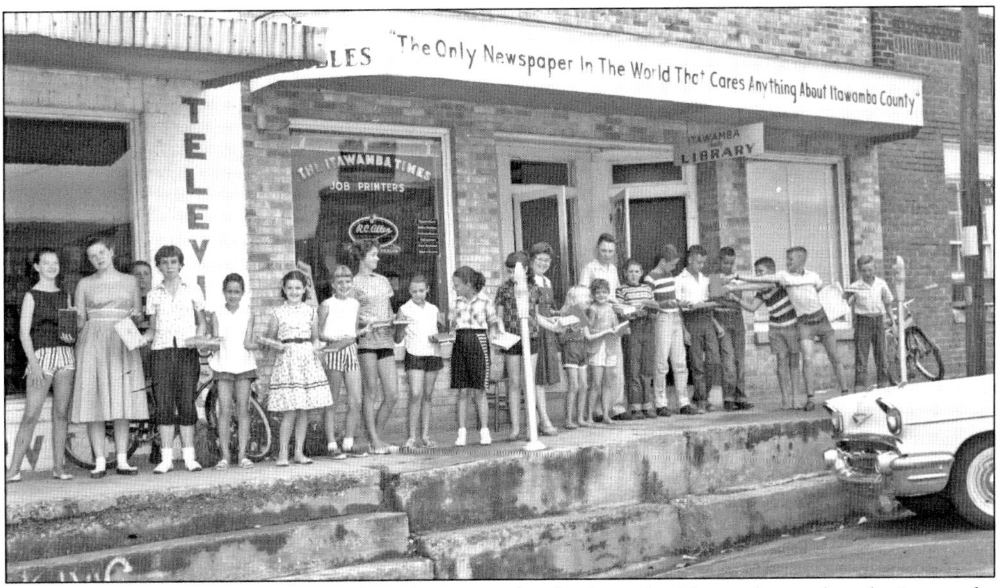

Children form a book brigade in July 1957 to carry books from the library, located in the *Itawamba County Times* building on North Gaither Street, to a new location practically next door. The library was created as a result of the untiring efforts of Rubye Harden, wife of Delmus Harden, the newspaper publisher. Fulton Grammar School sponsored walking field trips from the school to the library, where schoolchildren could obtain books to read.

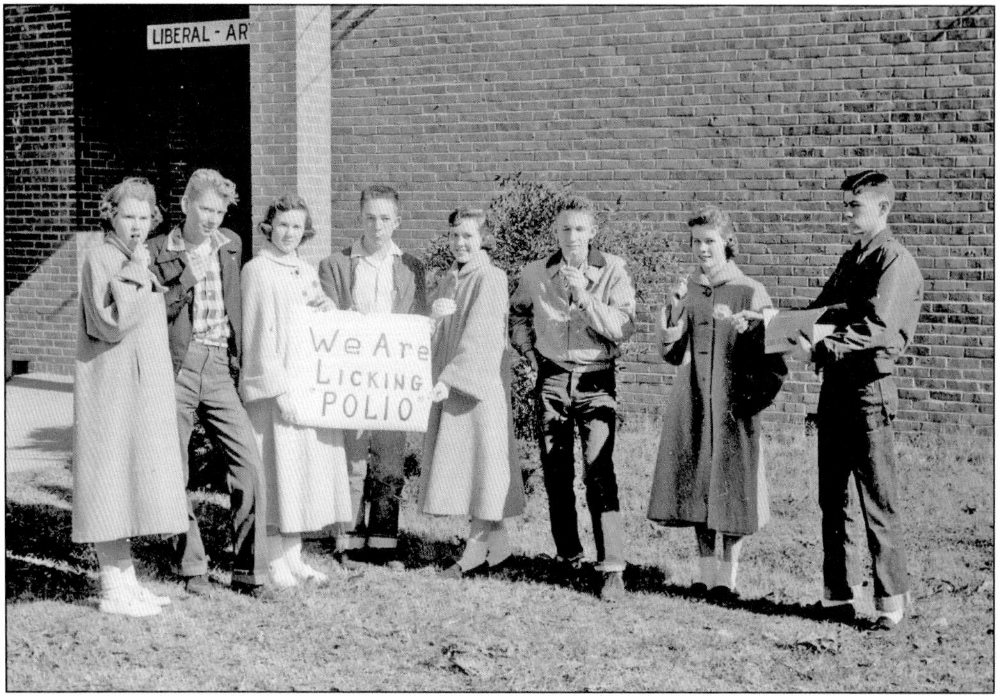

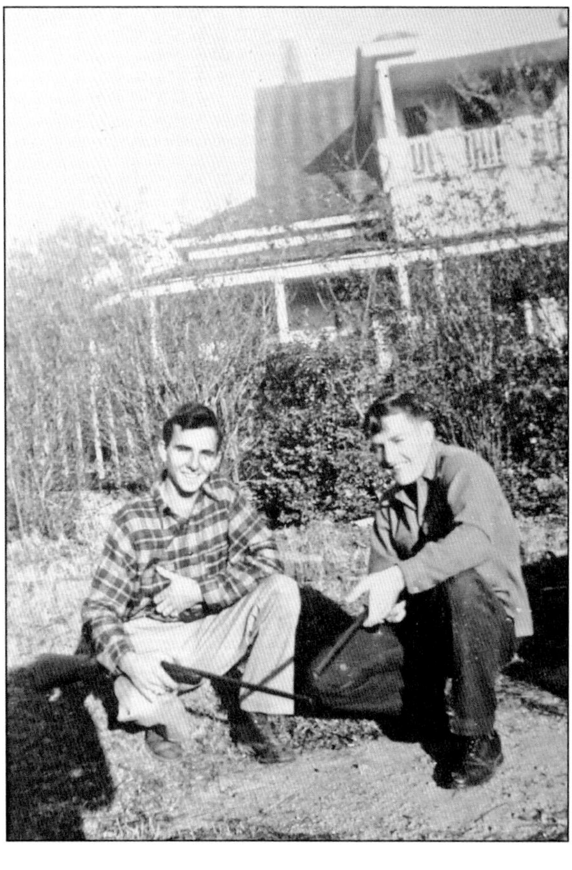

The 1952 polio epidemic became the worst outbreak in the United States' history. Of approximately 58,000 cases reported during that year alone, 3,145 people died and more than 21,000 were left with paralysis. Students at Itawamba Agricultural High School, as at many schools across the nation, held a polio drive that year, collecting donations to cure this dreaded disease.

Friends Buddy Sheffield (left) and A.C. "Butch" Lambert kneel in front of the Isaac Lewis Sheffield home, located off South Cummings Street. I.L. Sheffield, son of Isaac Judson Sheffield and Fannie McBride, was a prominent attorney in Fulton. His wife was Anna Rogers Walker, daughter of Dr. J.M. Walker and Anna Rogers. (Courtesy of Margo Mize Marlin.)

In the front yard of the Benson house on West Cedar Street looking north toward the present-day BancorpSouth building, houses on South Robbins Street can be seen in the background, as well as the old smoke house in the foreground probably dating to 1861 when William Harvey Keys built the house. This photograph was taken around 1929 after the timber industry boom of the 1920s with newer houses being built around town, including along South Robbins Street.

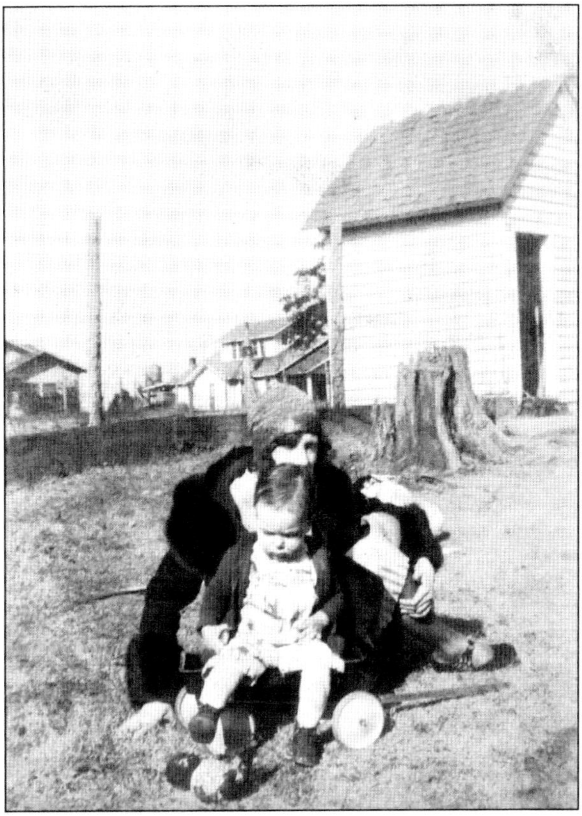

Members of the Fulton Lions Club shown in this 1950s photograph are, from left to right, (first row) Bill White, Jimmy Stone, Larry Quinn, and Butch Lambert; (second row) F.G. "Red" Wiygul, Dan McElroy, Brice Prestage, D.W. Crockett, and Rex Brown.

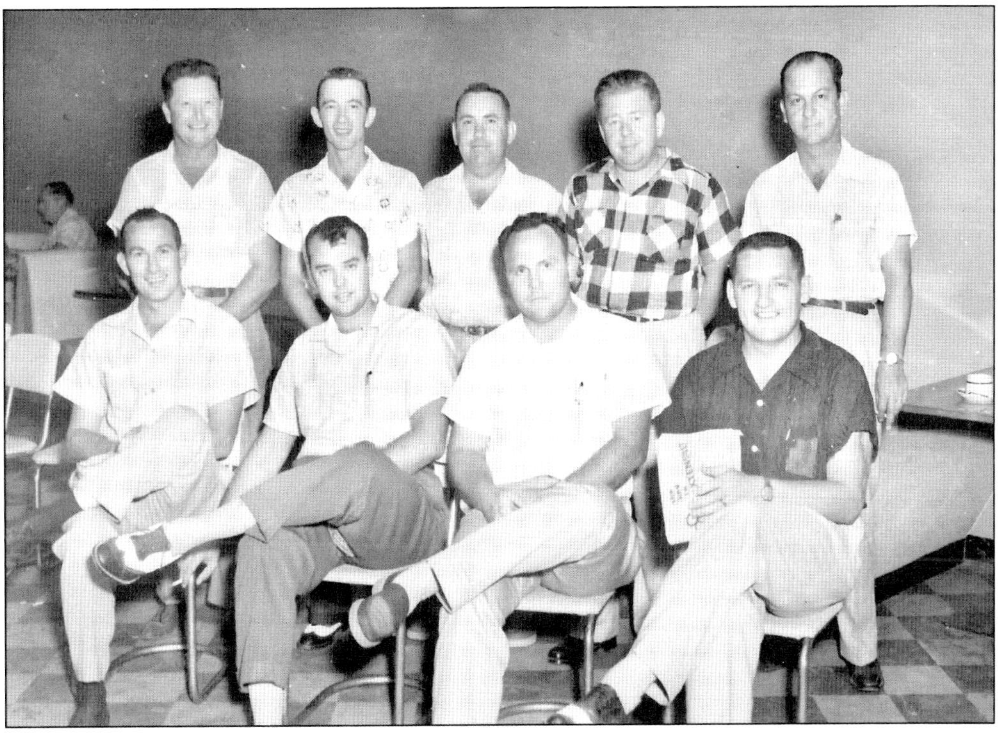

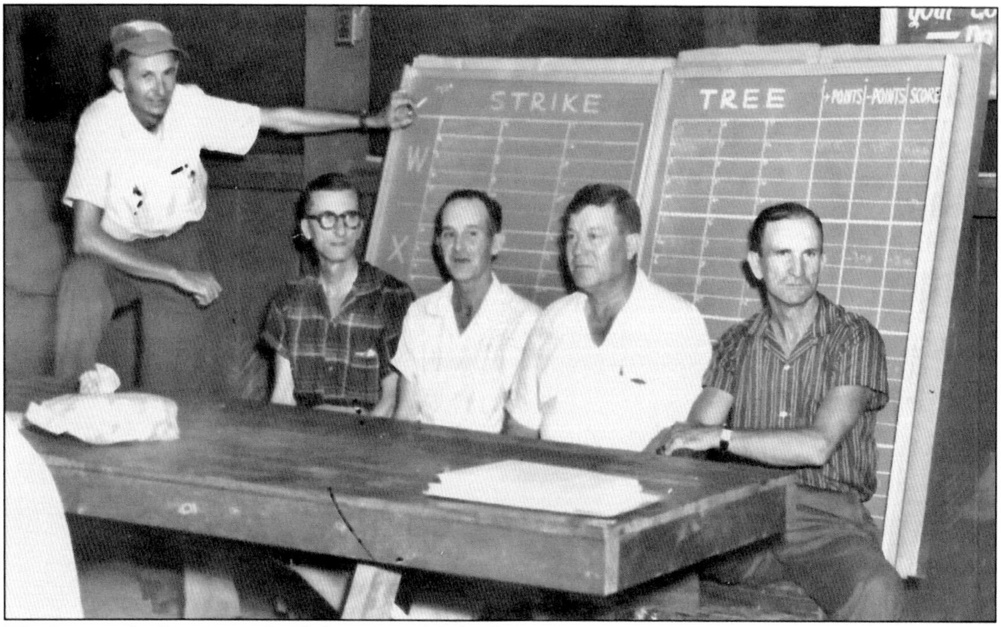

The Itawamba Sportsmen's Club was established on property just north of East Wiygul Street and featured a large bass lake, picnic tables, and a lodge that was constructed in 1951. Pictured are members at an event at the lodge. The lake was home to the annual Coon on the Log competition, which was held for many years on the Fourth of July, attracting over 2,000 people.

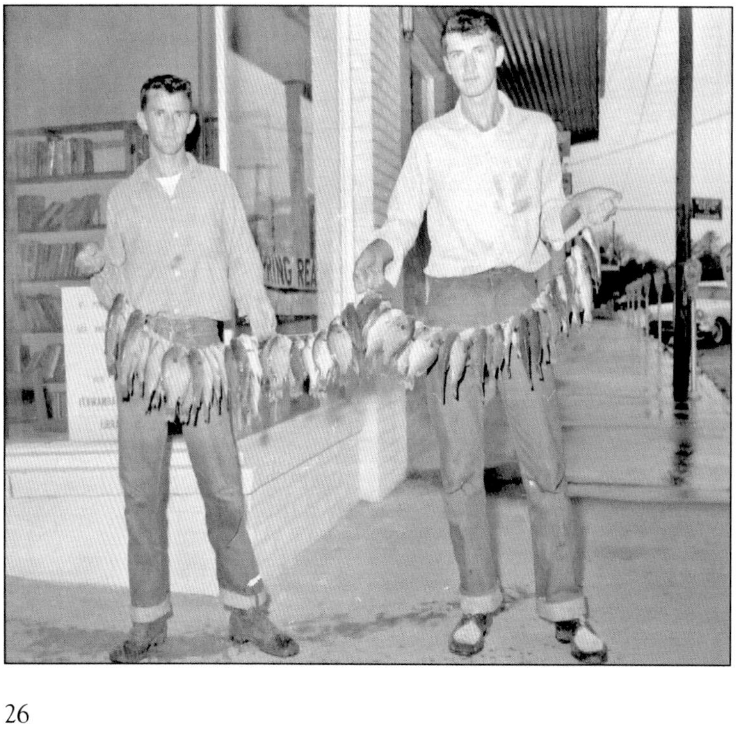

Bill Wallace (left) and Bobby Beard are posing with fish they caught on Lick Skillet Branch on a summer day in 1958. A common sight in Fulton was a *Times* camera, usually held by publisher Delmus Harden, photographing people with their dead snakes, fish, deer, unusual vegetables, and other interesting items.

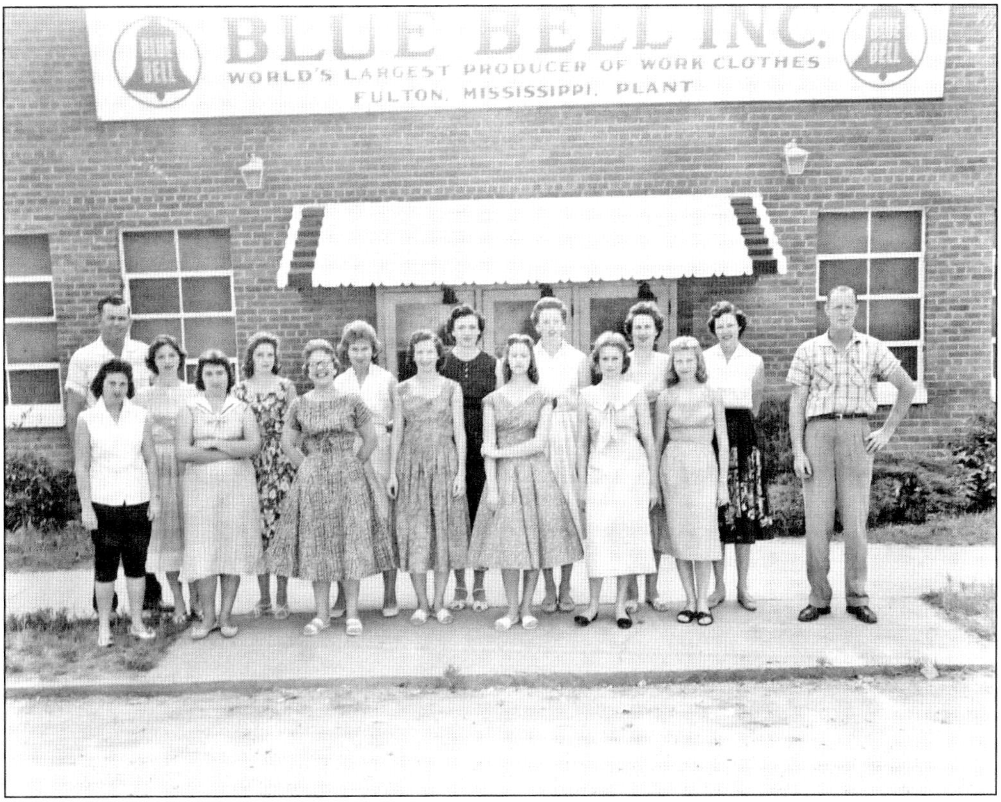

The Blue Bell plant on North Gaither Street in Fulton employed many county citizens manufacturing denim jeans. Legend has it that in 1919 at the company's first plant, a group of railroad workers who bought overalls at the founder's store gave the company founder a bell, and after spending time in the factory, the bell became covered in denim dust, thus the name Blue Bell. Pictured is the Fulton factory's softball team in the early 1950s.

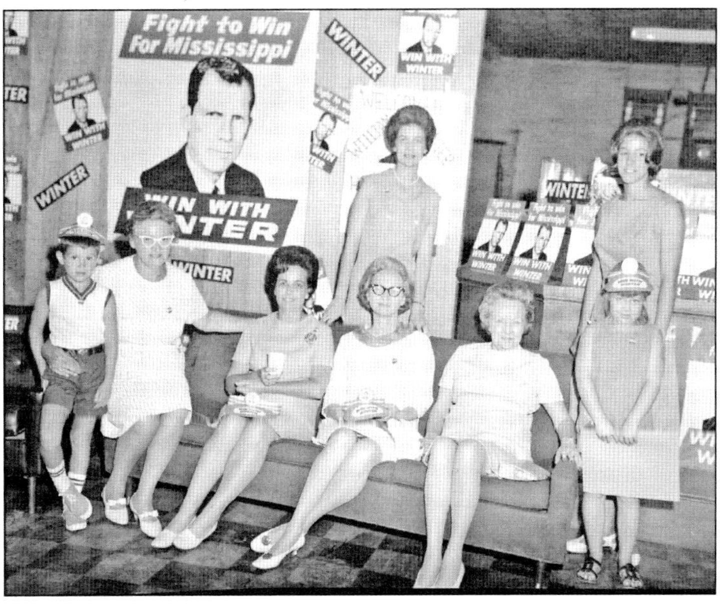

Fulton, being the seat of county government, has seen many political events over its 150-year history. In 1967, these women sponsored a tea in honor of Elise Winter, wife of gubernatorial candidate William Winter. Pictured from left to right are (seated) Jeanette Gordon, Ann Stubblefield, Barbara Daniel, and Billie Staub; (standing) Elise Winter and Karen Camp. The children are unidentified.

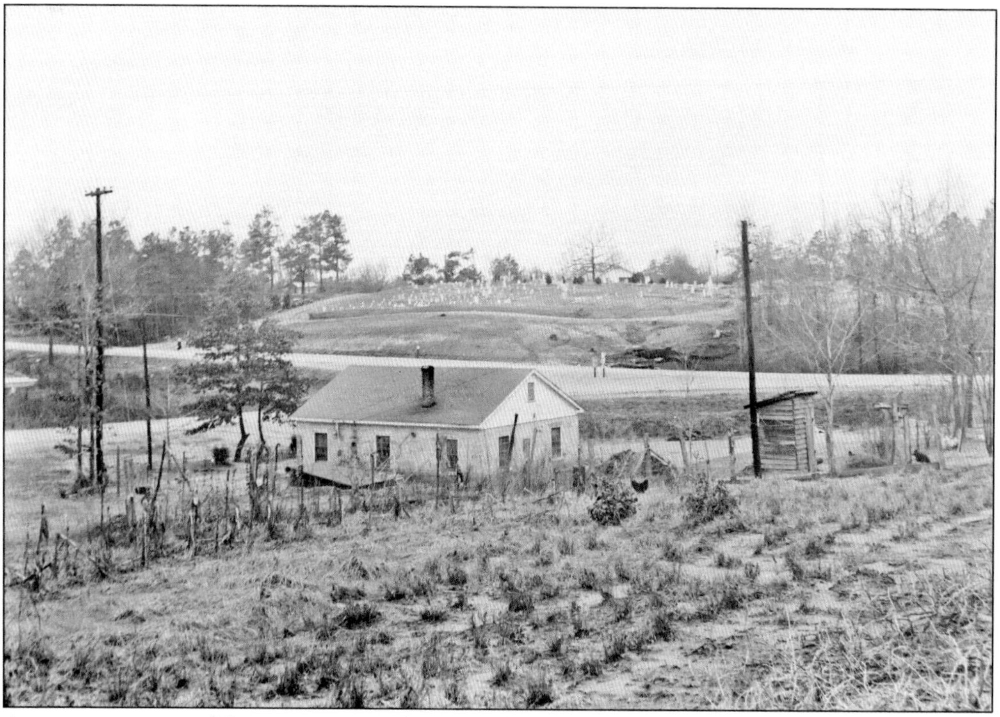

A panoramic view of the intersection of State Highway 25 and US Highway 78 in the 1950s shows the Fulton Cemetery in the background. The photograph was taken from the edge of the garden behind Wiley Matthews's house. Matthews ran a taxi service in Fulton.

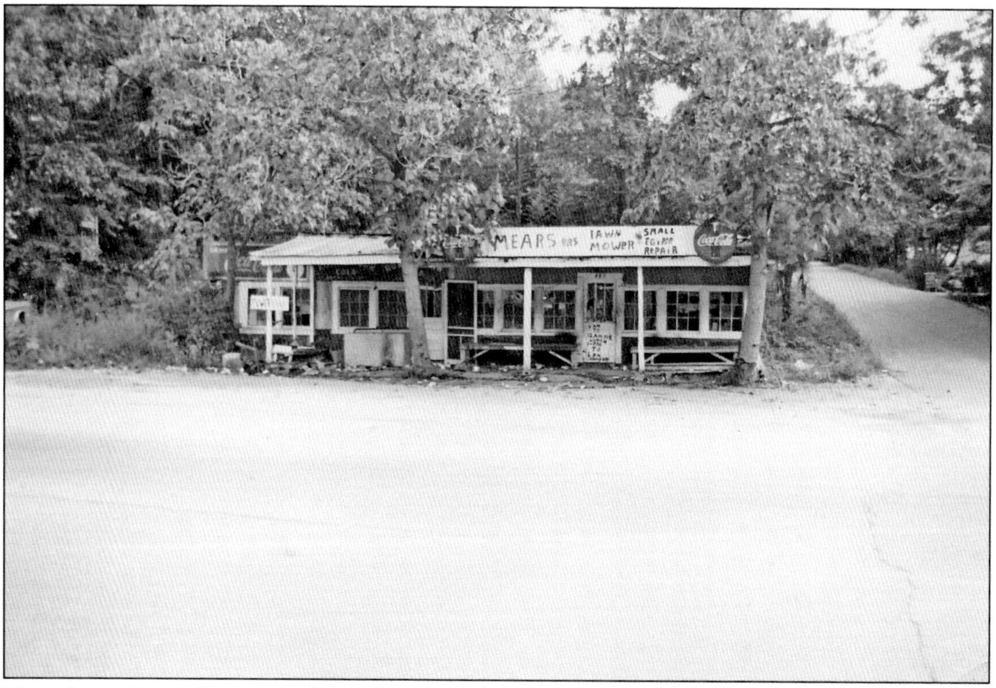

Mears Lawn Mower Repair was located on East Main Street just east of Matthews Grocery during the early 1970s. Before housing a lawn mower repair shop, the building was Bert Norton's Garage.

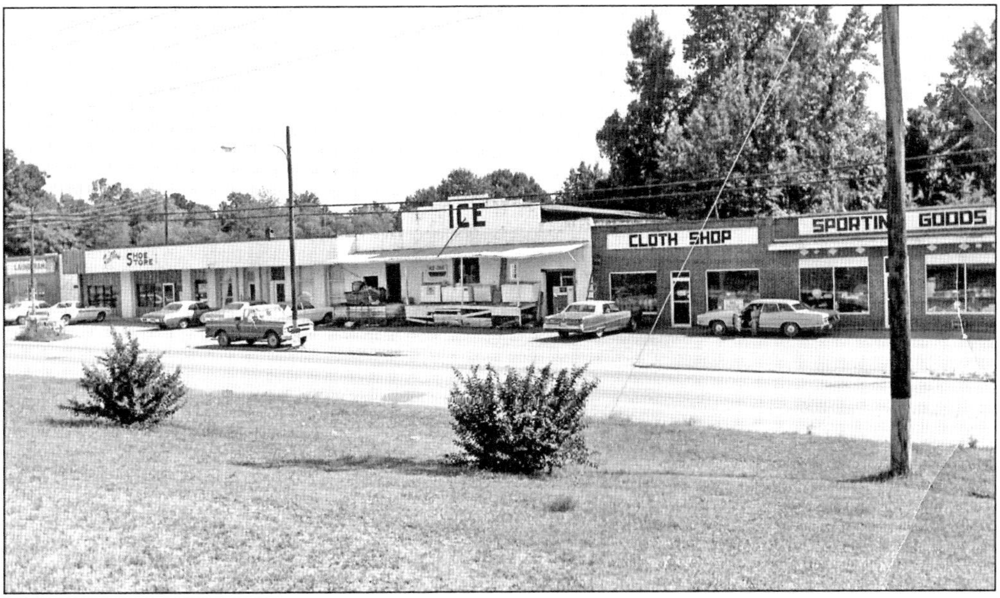

Located west of town "under the hill," this shopping area was owned by the Gaither family, and individual buildings were leased to various businesses. Considered the precursor of shopping centers in Fulton, this line of buildings in the 1950s and early 1960s included a laundry, a Sinclair service station, an ice plant, a fabric shop, and a sporting goods store.

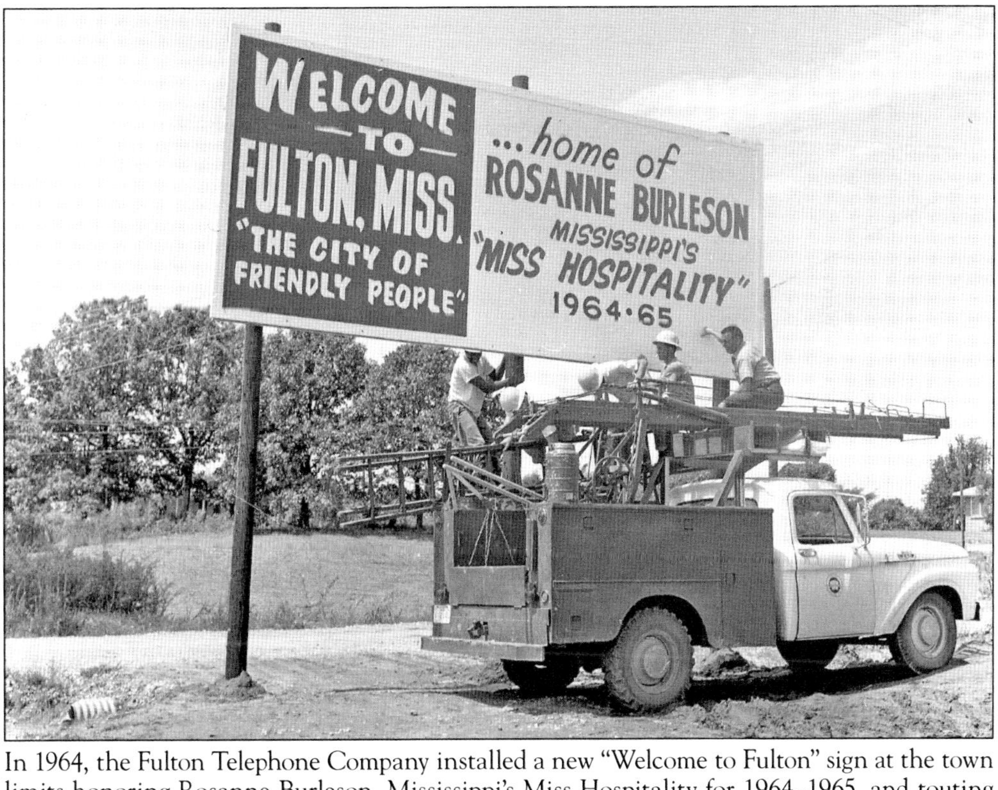

In 1964, the Fulton Telephone Company installed a new "Welcome to Fulton" sign at the town limits honoring Rosanne Burleson, Mississippi's Miss Hospitality for 1964–1965, and touting Fulton as "The City of Friendly People."

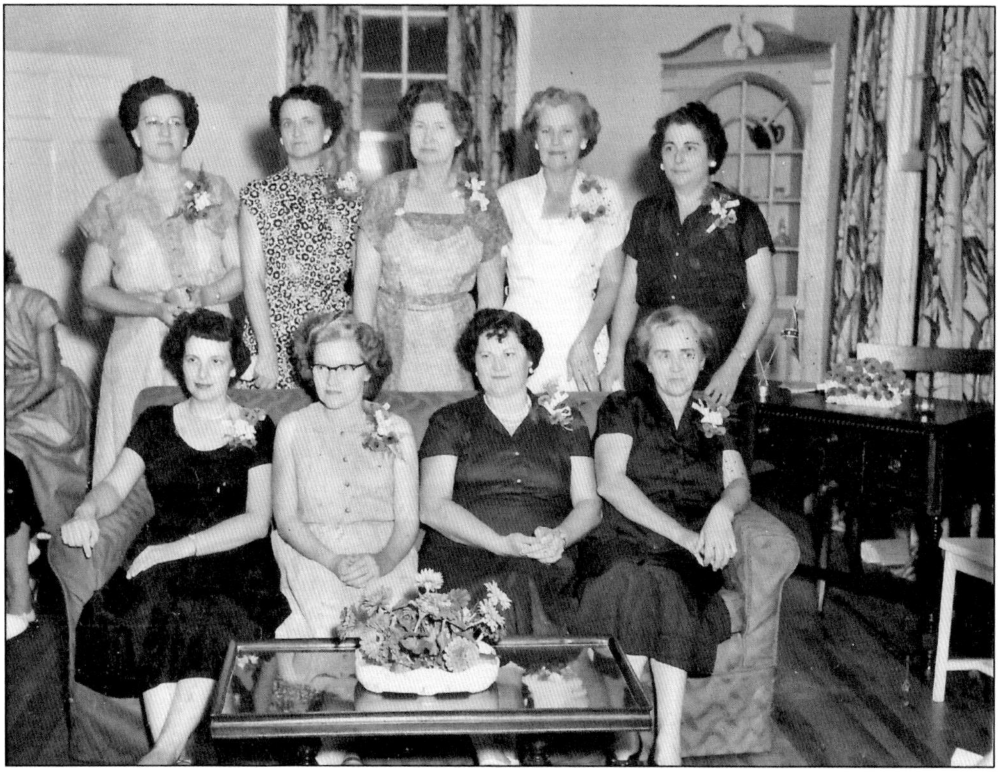

Members of the American Legion Auxiliary pose for a group photograph at a reception at a member's house in Fulton during the 1950s. The auxiliary was one of the many organizations active in Fulton throughout the years, and it continues to be an important organization.

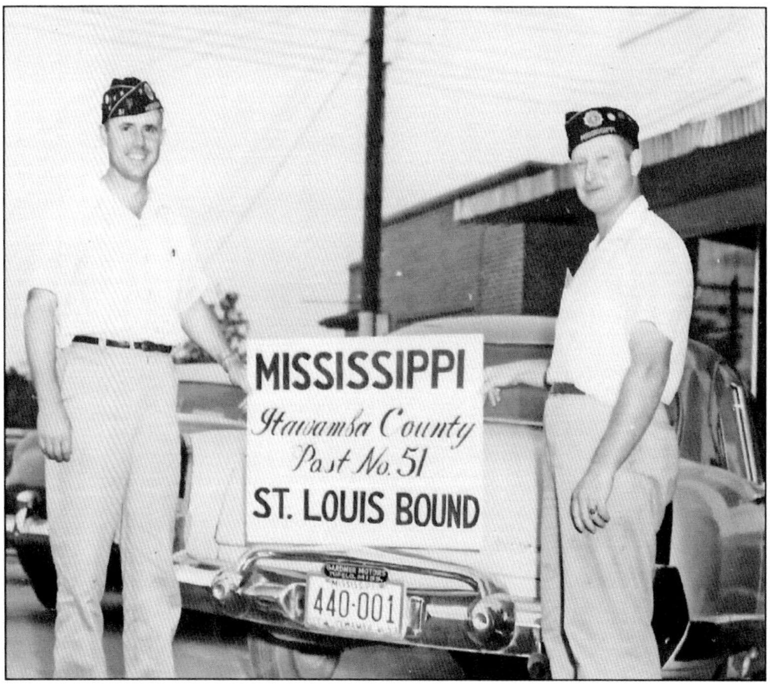

American Legion Post 51 members Herman Camp (left) and F.G. "Red" Wiygul are seen getting ready for a trip to the national convention in St. Louis in 1953.

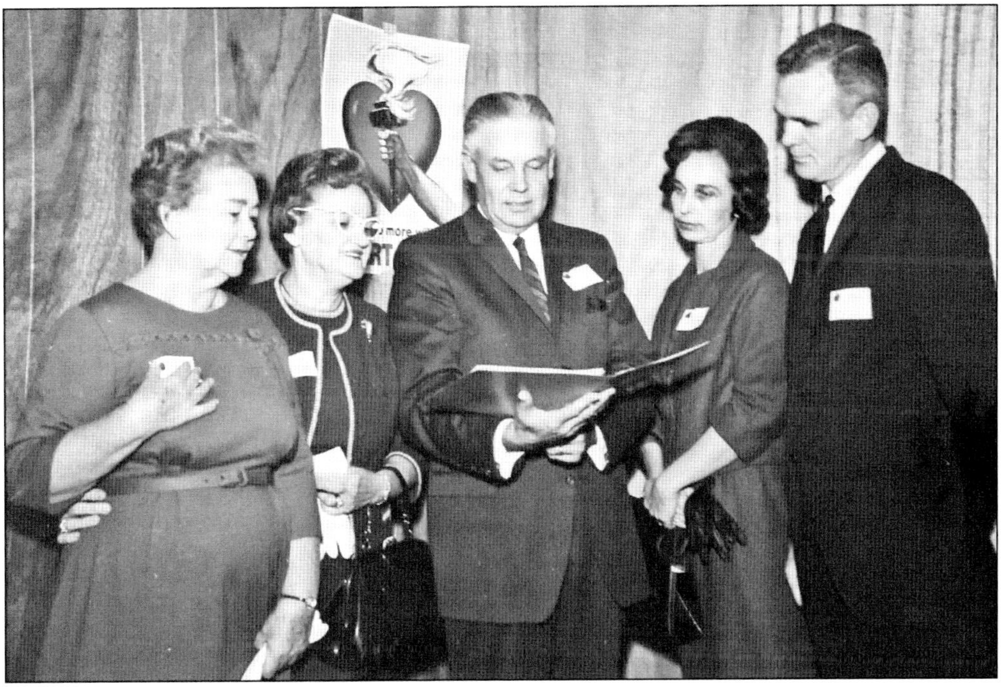

Heart Association volunteers for a 1960s Heart Fund Drive in Fulton include, from left to right, Fannie Yawn and Jeanette Gorden, a Heart Associate representative, and Hazel and Paul Mize.

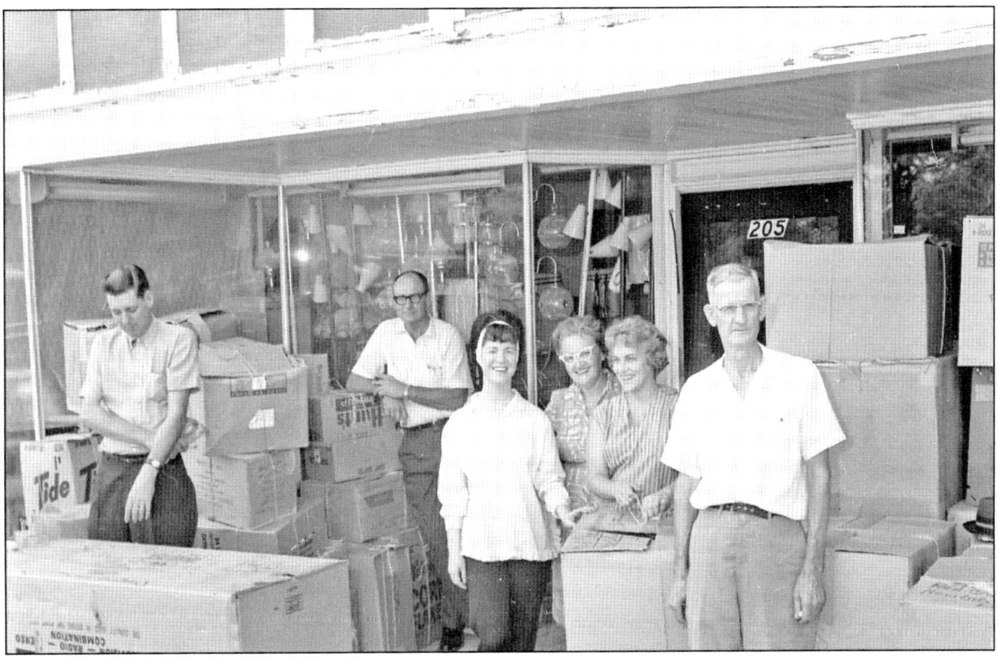

Fulton citizens came to the aid of New Orleans victims of Hurricane Betsy in September 1965 by donating goods collected at the Coggins & Nabors Furniture store on the town square. Hurricane Betsy roared ashore near New Orleans on the evening of September 9 after already pounding Florida as a Category 3 storm with wind gusts of 145 miles per hour. Fulton has always come to the aid of those in need.

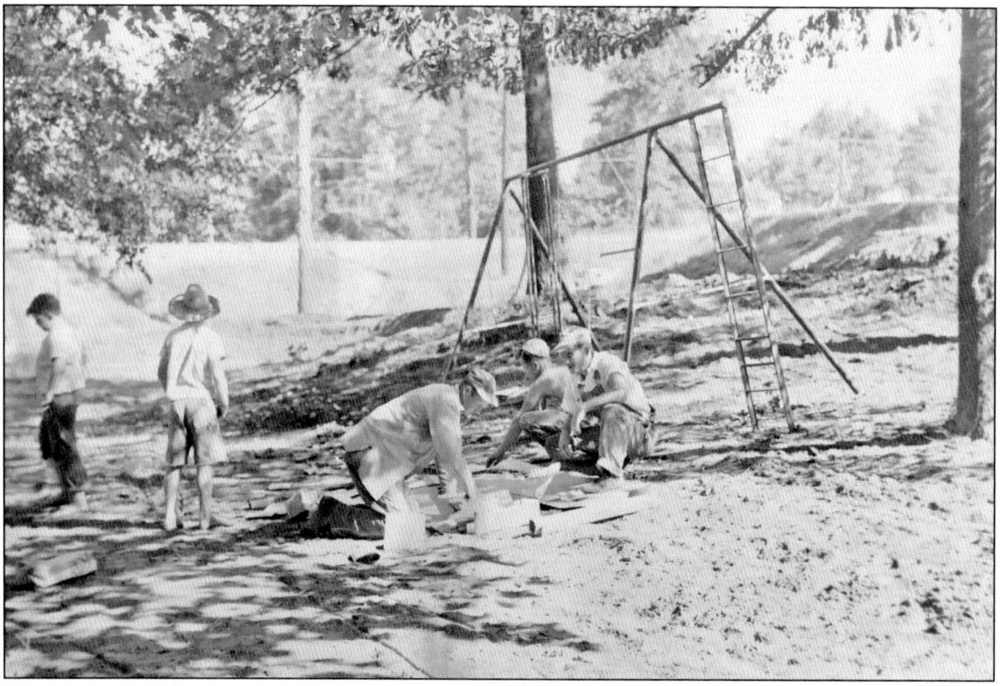

For many years, Fireman's Park was Fulton's only park. The park was created by members of the Fulton Fire Department and constructed in the 1950s. Shown is the construction of the playground equipment. The park featured a wading pool and a small clubhouse where many special events were held, including birthday parties, family reunions, and vacation Bible school picnics.

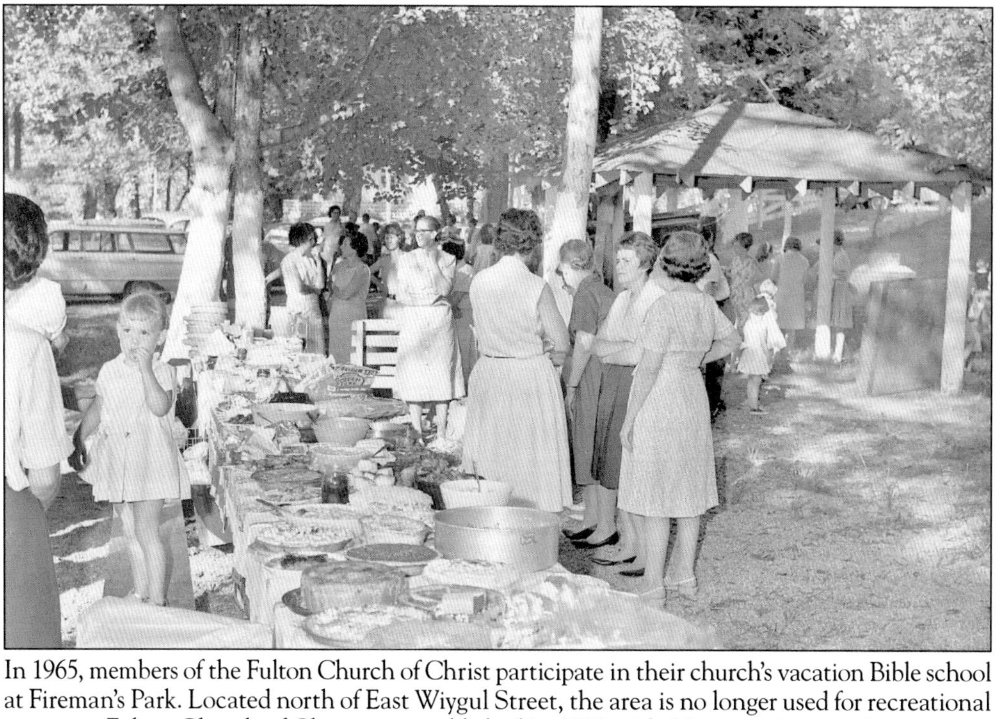

In 1965, members of the Fulton Church of Christ participate in their church's vacation Bible school at Fireman's Park. Located north of East Wiygul Street, the area is no longer used for recreational purposes. Fulton Church of Christ was established in 1923 with 30 organizing members.

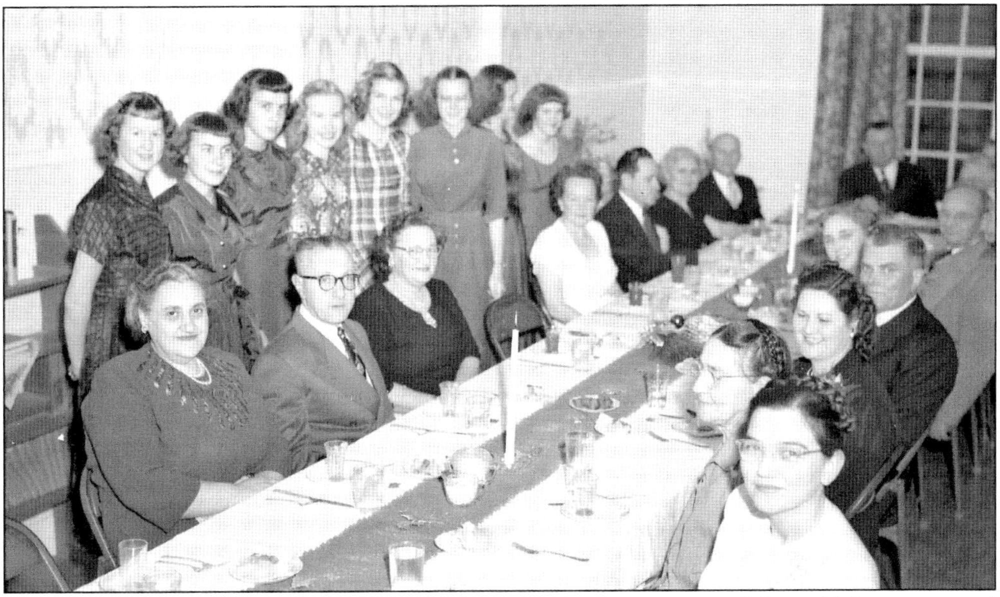

The Fulton Civic Club was one of numerous service organizations in Fulton. Club women and their husbands are seen enjoying their 1949 Christmas party. Young ladies serving the meal are, standing from left to right, Phyllis Gorden, Robbie Lewis Alverson, Jo Gaither, Fannie Ann Mayhall, Betty McNeece, Geraldine Burns, Ann Maples, and Hildreth Crane.

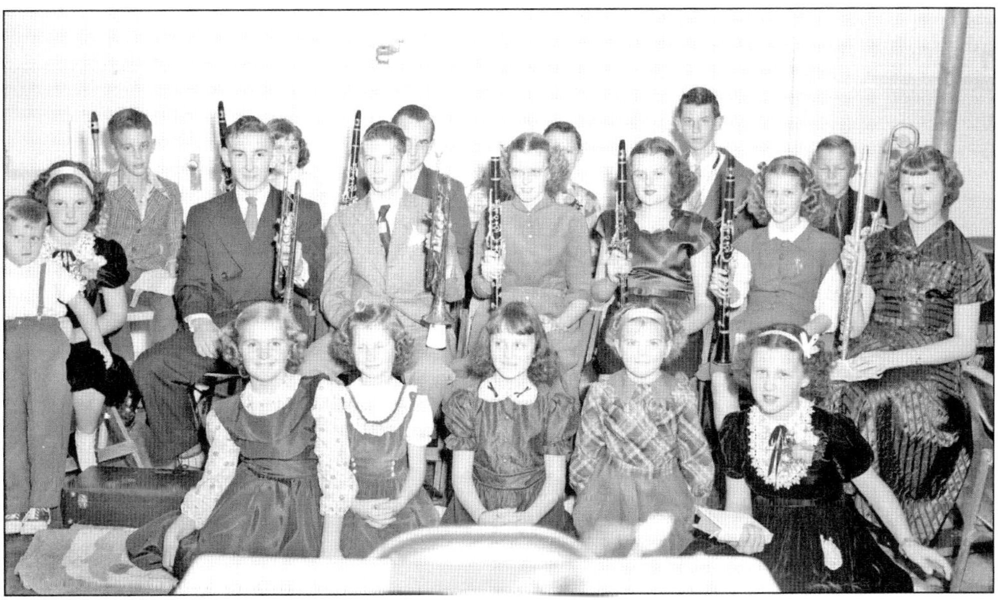

Members of the Fulton Grammar School band performed at the Fulton Civic Club's annual Christmas party in 1949. From left to right are (first row) Betty Stringfellow, Janice Overton, Martha Ellen Gibbs, Rubye Del Harden, and Nanette Holcomb; (second row) Barry Holcomb, Hilda Holcomb, David Mattox, Billy Bonds McElroy, Geraldine Burns, Ann Maples, Carolyn Overton, and Phyllis Gorden; (third row) James Whitehead, Carolyn Prestage, Travis Staub, Jimmie Gibbs, Bobby Overton, and Lloyd Burns.

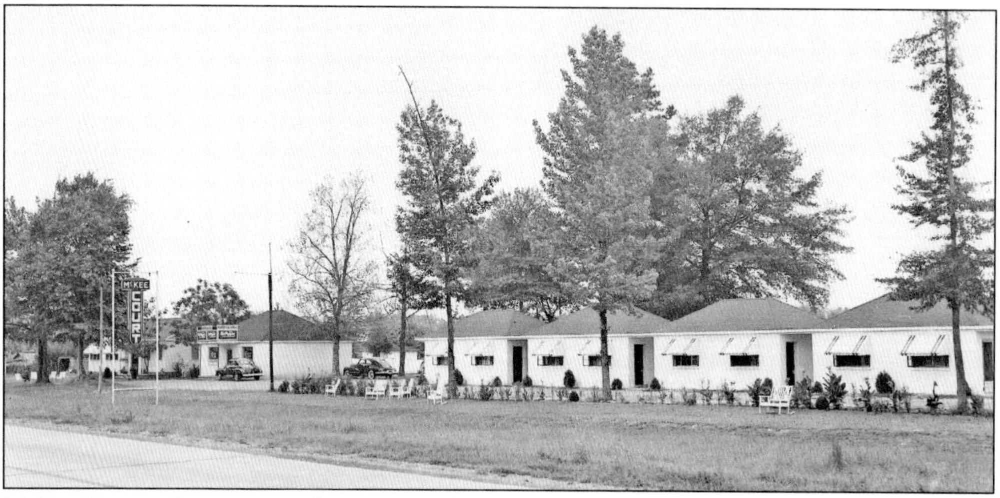

McKee Tourist Courts opened in 1949 with four duplex cabins that featured modern showers, venetian blinds, and inlaid tile floors. An adjacent café was added later. Built by Nolan McKee, Fulton's first modern lodging for travelers was located west of town on US Highway 78, where Davis Ford Company is today.

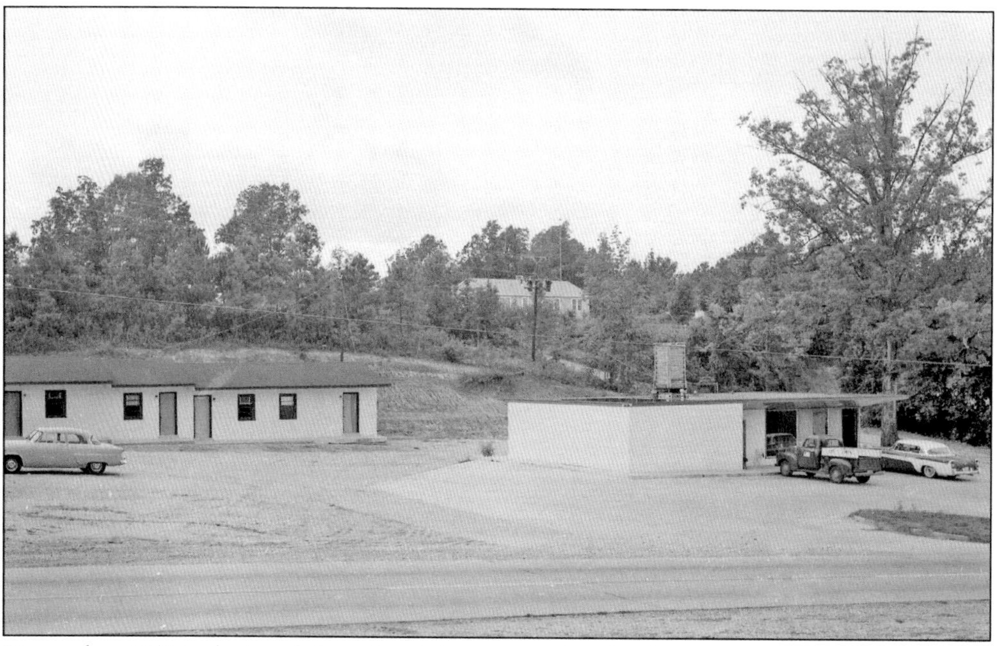

Pictured in 1958 is the Sands Motel and Restaurant shortly after it was completed by Mr. and Mrs. Tommy Strawhorn. This was the second "modern tourist motel" in Fulton and at the time was considered the east edge of town fronting the busy US Highway 78. The motel was probably named for the famous Sands in Las Vegas, built six years earlier.

Two

Courthouse Square, the Hub of Fulton

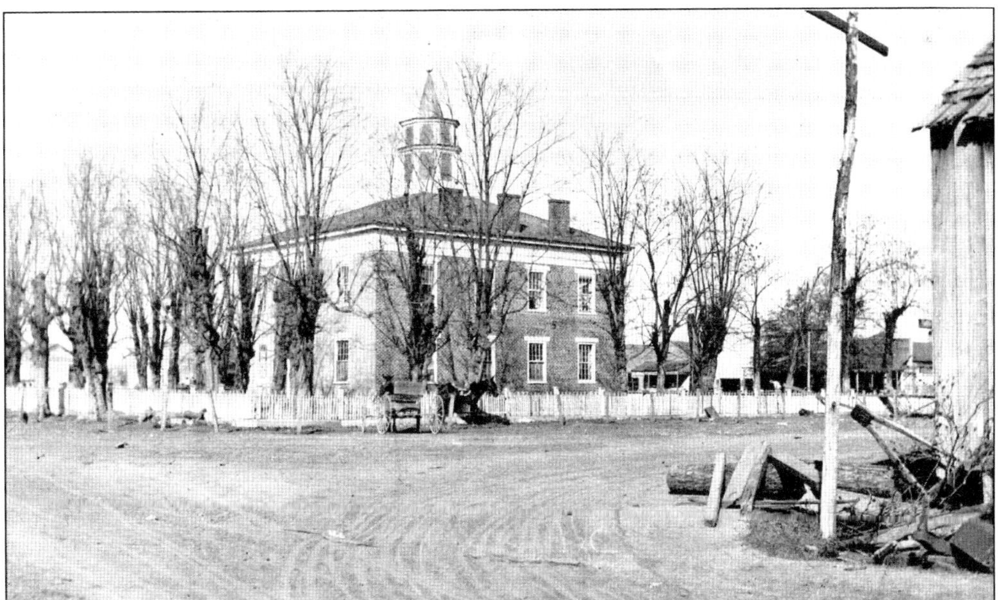

The Itawamba County Courthouse has anchored Fulton's downtown square for over 150 years, serving as a hub for the town's activities. County business was originally held in a log structure, but about 1853, a redbrick building was constructed that was topped by an octagonal cupola and a weather vane. This c. 1917 photograph, taken from the southeastern corner of the court square, shows the courthouse surrounded by black locust trees. Note the crude telephone pole at the corner of what is now Carl's Cleaners.

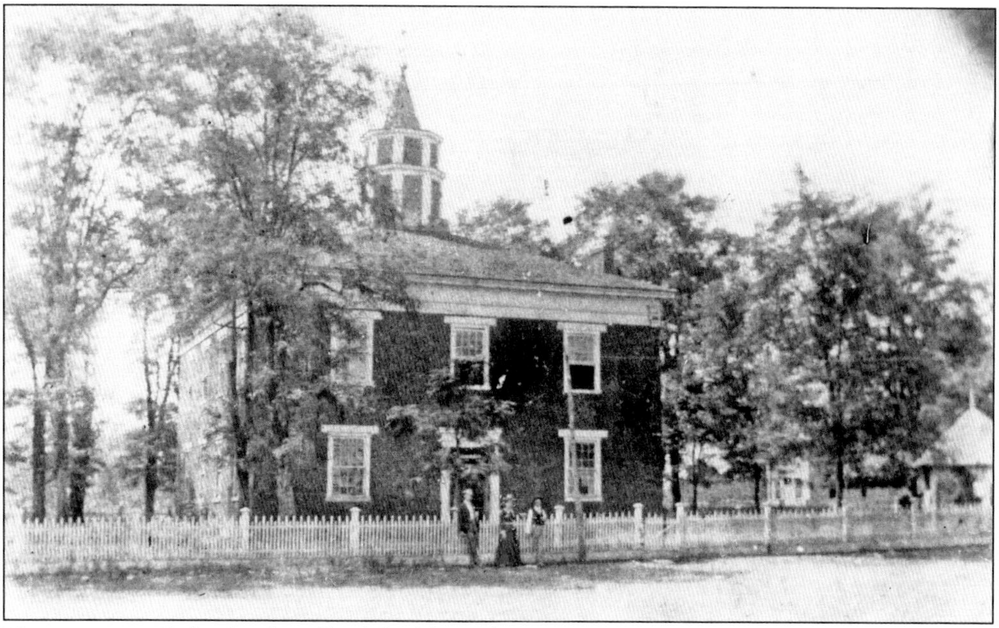

This two-story, Federal-style redbrick building, photographed about 1900 by E.A. Harbor, replaced the log structure that was Itawamba County's first courthouse. Three chimneys stood on the east and west sides, each with fireplaces on both floors. Heavy double doors opened to a central hall that ran north-south, while large windows adorned each exterior wall. A wood fence, with gates centered on all four sides, surrounded the courthouse. Standing at the gate, from left to right, are Tony Pierce, Lula Boatright Pearce, and Mr. Hester.

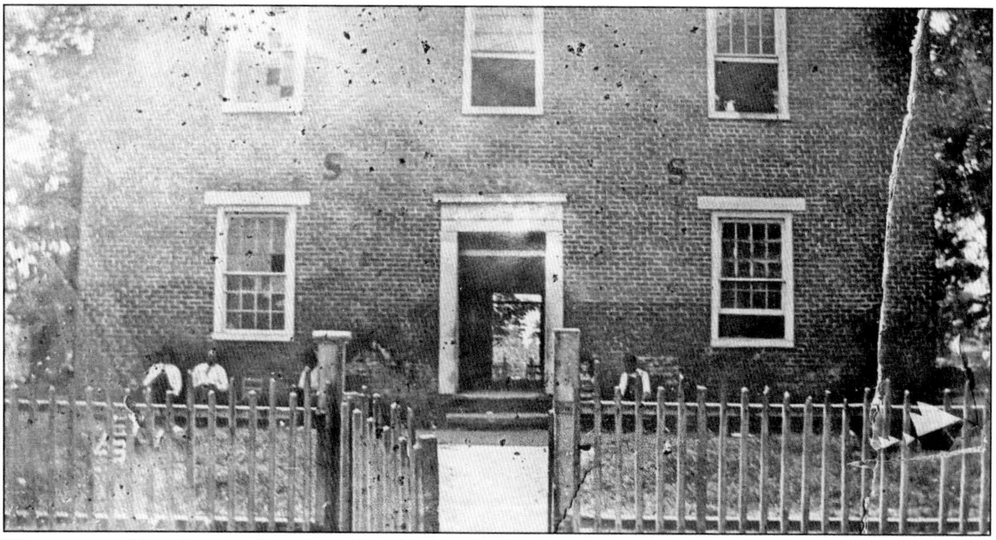

The original brick courthouse had a double stairway in the front of the center hall that went up to a second-floor courtroom with four fireplaces. Local historian Zereda Greene recalled the courtroom being used for candidate speeches, teachers' examinations, and even funerals. In this close-up photograph of the courthouse, probably made before 1920, the straight-shot view to the other side is interesting, as are the broken window panes, the fence and open gate, the seated men, and the water pitcher sitting in the open window. (Courtesy of Margo Mize Marlin.)

To accommodate the growing number of vehicles in the 1920s, the town of Fulton took steps in 1924 to install concrete curbs and pave the streets surrounding the courthouse. The courthouse, however, was beginning to show its age, and in 1936, an extensive remodeling was undertaken as a project of the Works Progress Administration in which the south side of the building was expanded 42 feet. The cost of the project was about $24,000, with the WPA contributing $17,000 of the needed funds.

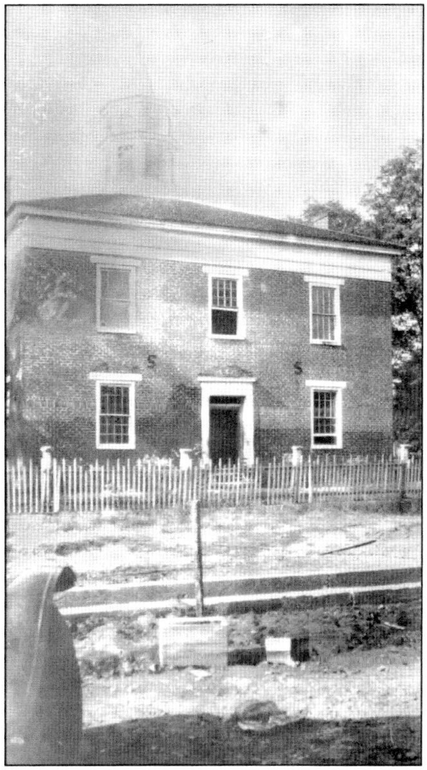

Black locust trees, planted around 1875, completely surrounded the old courthouse and provided a shaded courtyard for the town's citizens. A few of these early trees can be seen in this c. 1930 photograph. As late as 1936, seventeen locust trees remained, many with four-foot circumferences. The sign in the right window at top says "Homer Benson, Attorney at Law," while the sign on the left states "Public Library." Nailed to a tree is a sign providing details of a beauty contest. The gazebo at right once housed a public well.

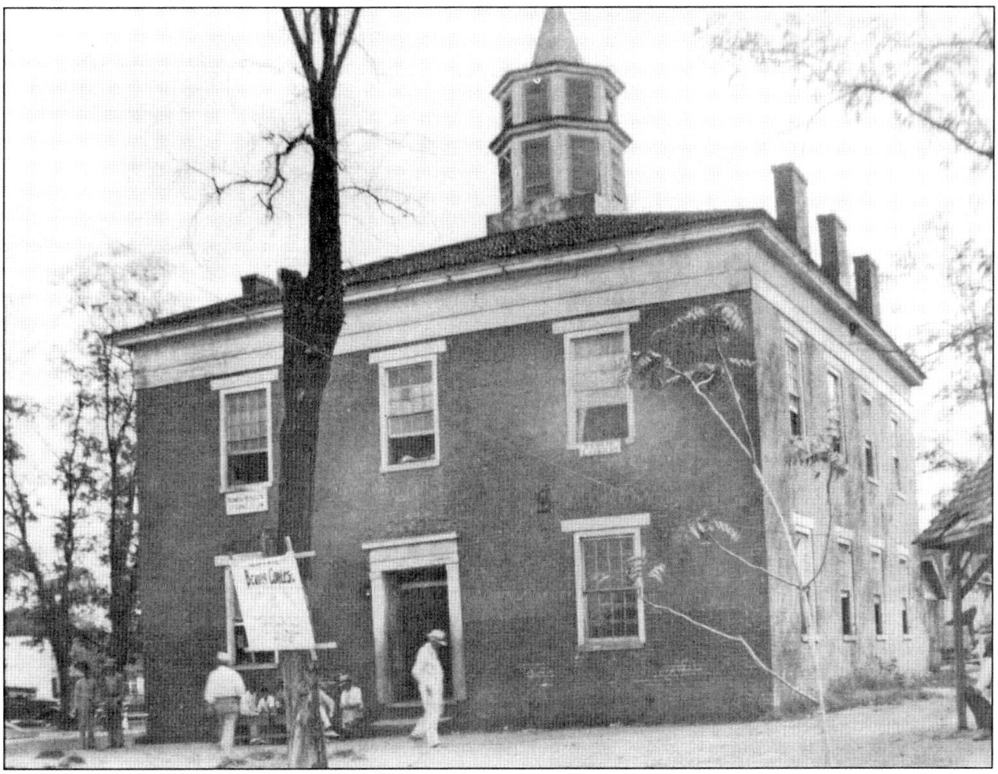

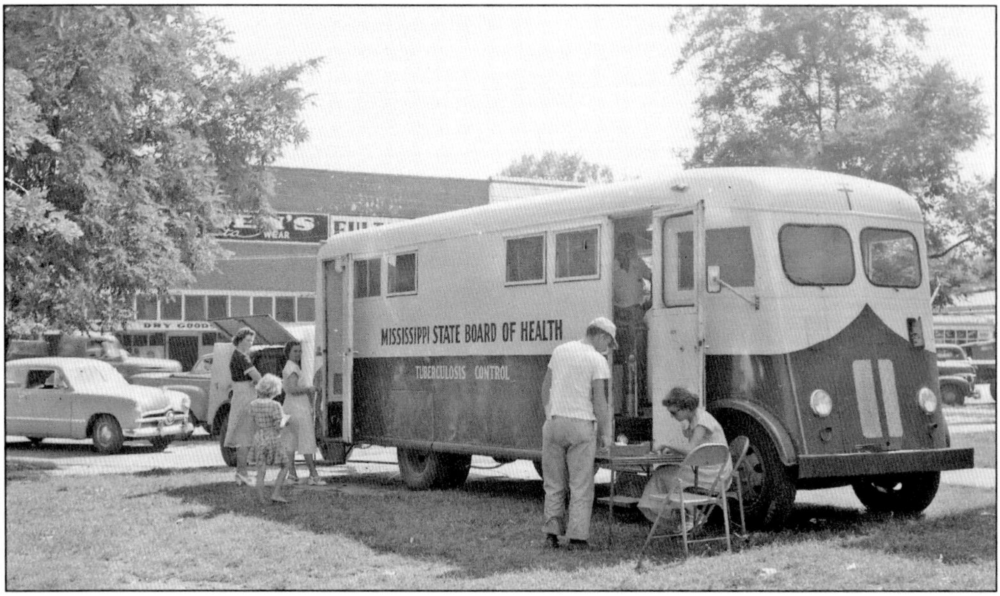

Fulton residents in 1949 were able to be screened for tuberculosis when the mobile bus from the Mississippi State Board of Health visited the south side of the court square. Behind the bus is the sign for Gorden's Dry Goods Store, opened in 1935 by Manuel and Jeanette Gorden, Russian immigrants who were the only Jewish family in Fulton.

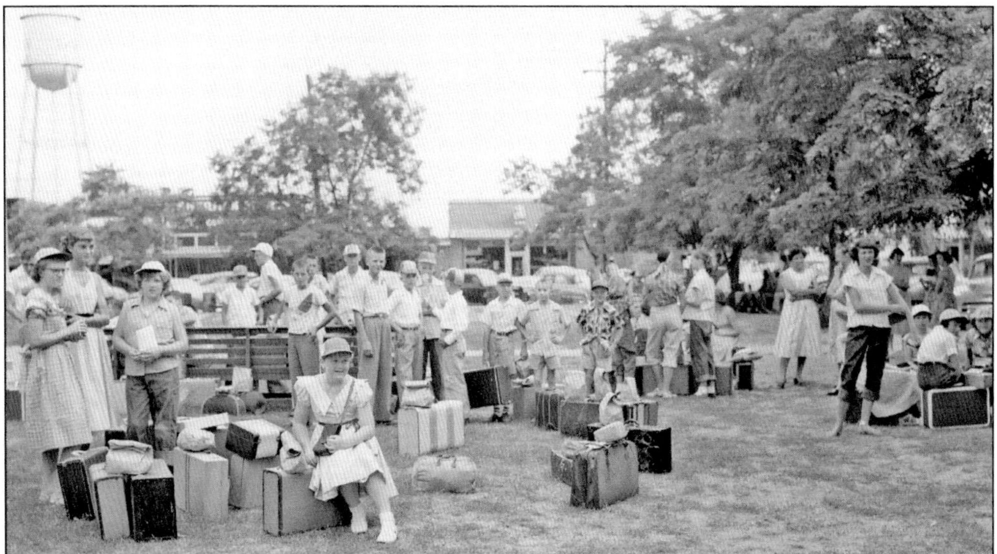

The highlight of summer for a 4-H member was the trip to camp. In this 1952 scene, campers with their luggage gather on the court square with their families to wait for buses and departure for camp.

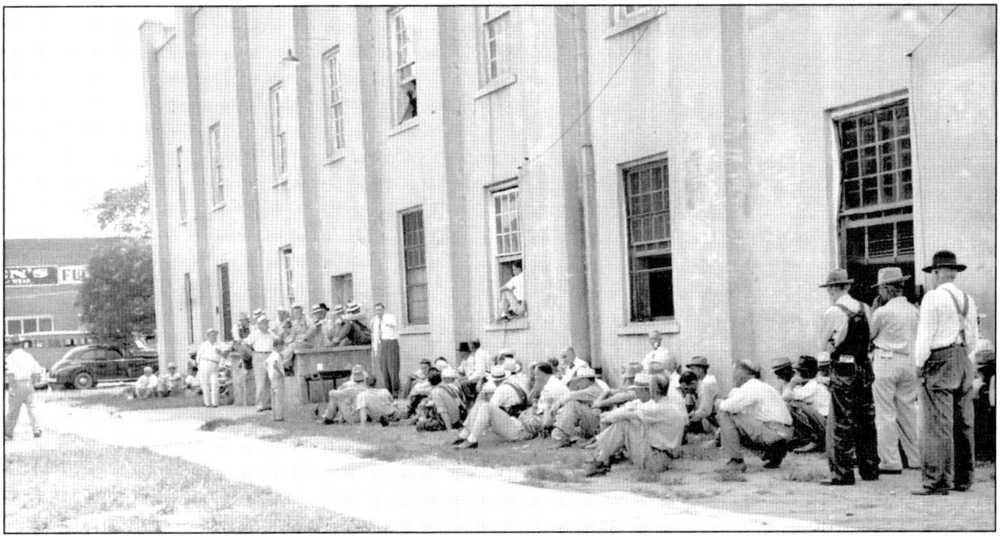

Political "speakings" were frequent and popular occurrences on the Fulton courthouse lawn. In this scene, Congressman Thomas G. Abernethy speaks to a crowd gathered on the east side of the courthouse in July 1951. Congressman Abernethy defeated Itawamba native John E. Rankin when their congressional districts were combined due to redistricting. This speech appears to have been impromptu; scheduled political gatherings attracted much larger crowds.

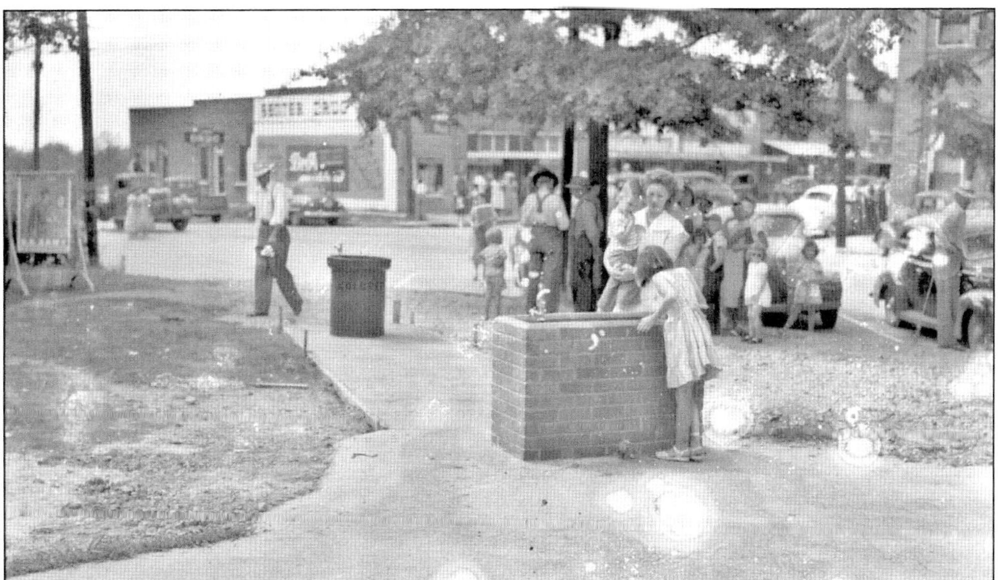

Separate drinking fountains for "colored" and "whites" were installed on the courthouse lawn in 1950 by the board of supervisors. Saturday was a very busy time for downtown Fulton—many people came to town to trade, watch a movie matinee, or just visit around the square.

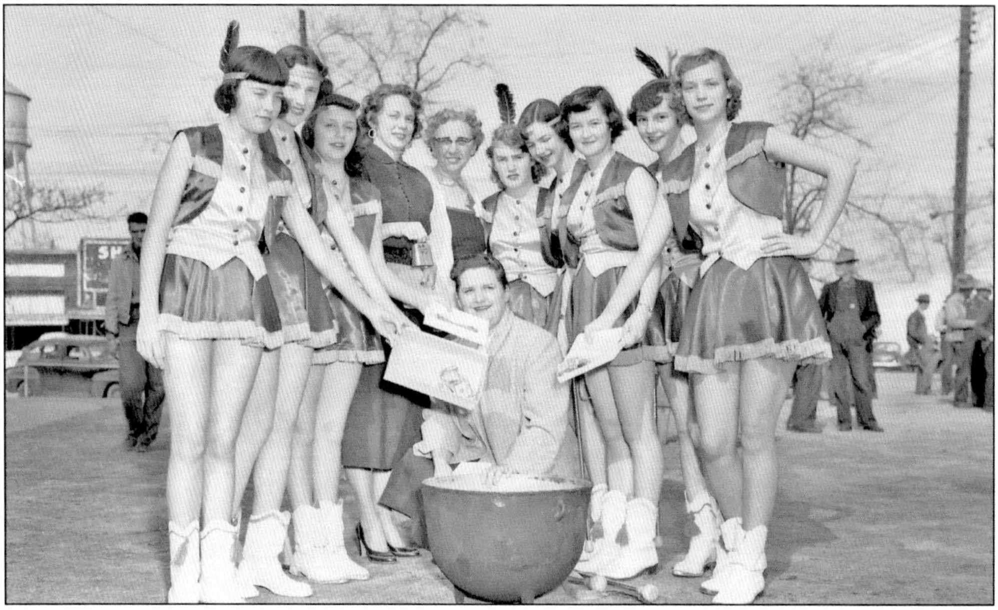

Fundraising events often took place around the court square. Bonnie Ruth Gibbs Owings, kneeling, is surrounded by Fulton Indianettes during a Town Day event to raise funds for the county polio fund drive in 1954. Also pictured is Vera Jane Whiteside Mattox (center, with glasses), and to the left of her, Grace Mae Coleman holds the cowbell.

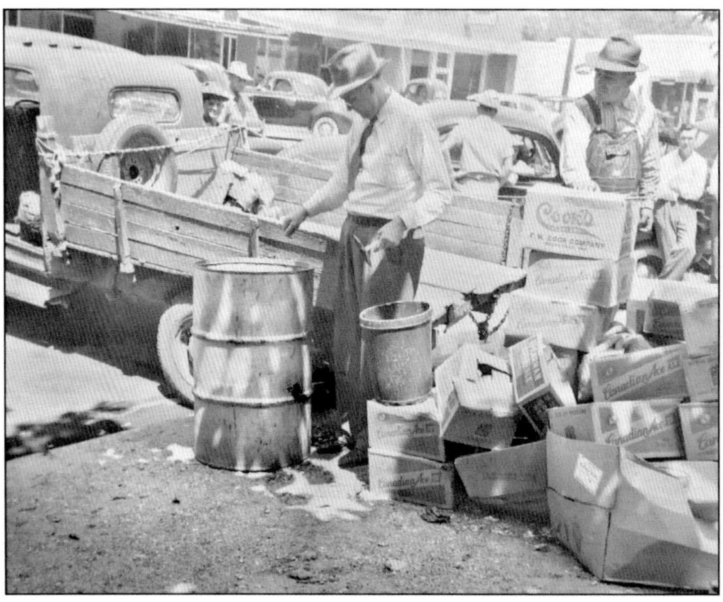

Mississippi was the last state to repeal Prohibition, in 1966, but many counties such as Itawamba continued to remain dry. Scenes such as this one were not uncommon, especially during election years. Here, Bill Fields (right) watches as Sheriff Jim Gilliland pours out bootlegged beer and whiskey on the courthouse square. In 2014, the voters of Fulton approved the sale of beer and liquor in their town.

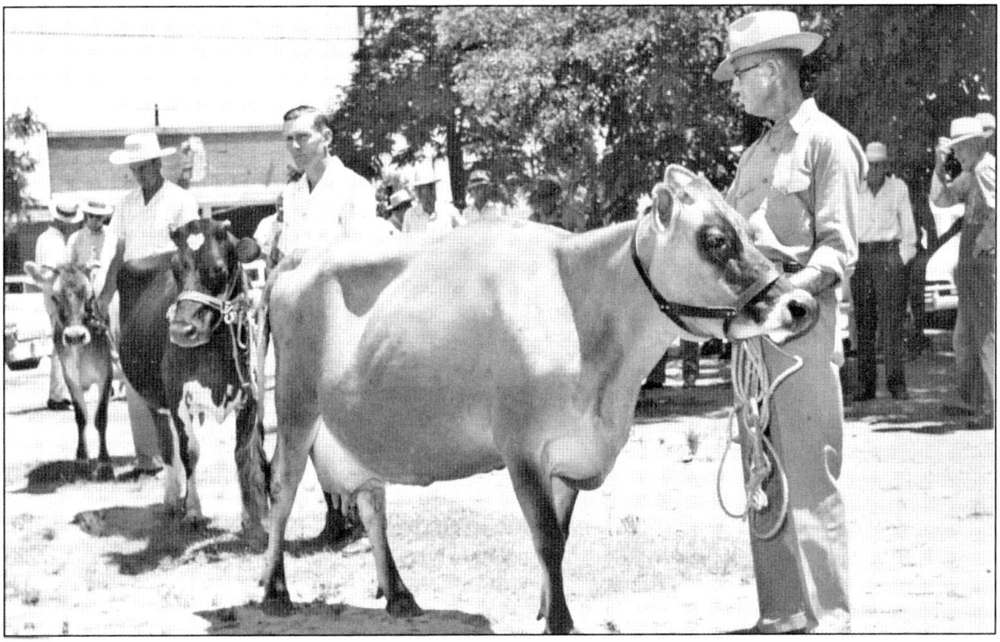

It was not unusual to see livestock around the court square. Above, cattle are being judged as part of the observance of Dairy Day, held in Fulton in June 1960 on the east lawn. Pictured with their winning cows are, from left to right, Simeon Holley, J.D. Wilson, and R.F. Henderson. Behind them, the Rexall sign on the Fulton Drug Store building can be seen. Below, a poultry sale was conducted in 1969 on the west side of the courthouse. This was an annual event, sponsored by Sears, in which poultry raised by 4-H members was sold. Note the City Café sign on the former Dixie Theatre facade.

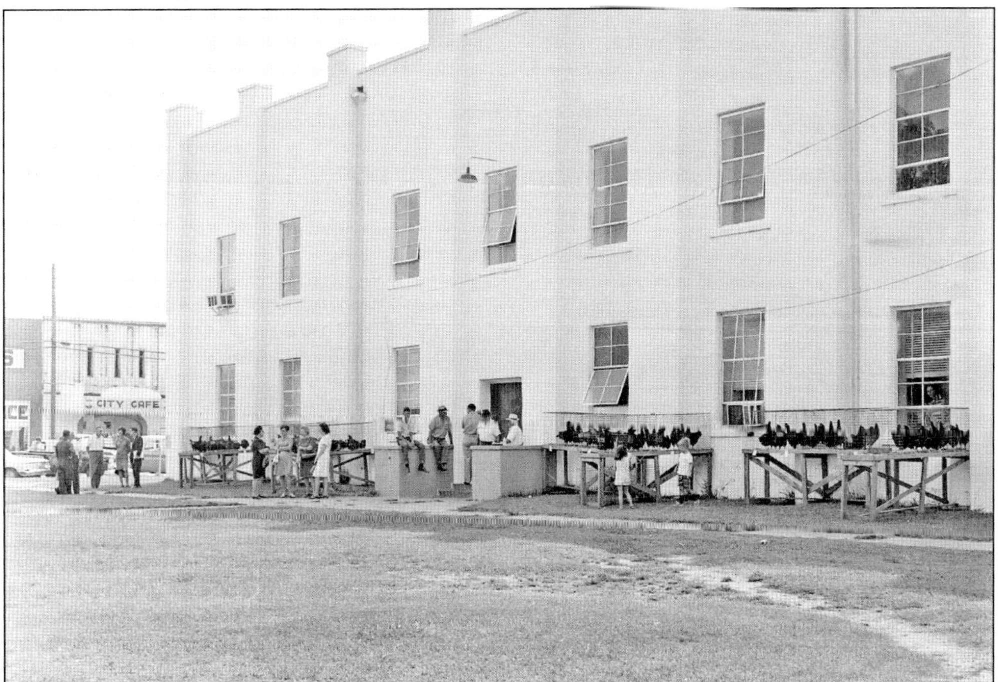

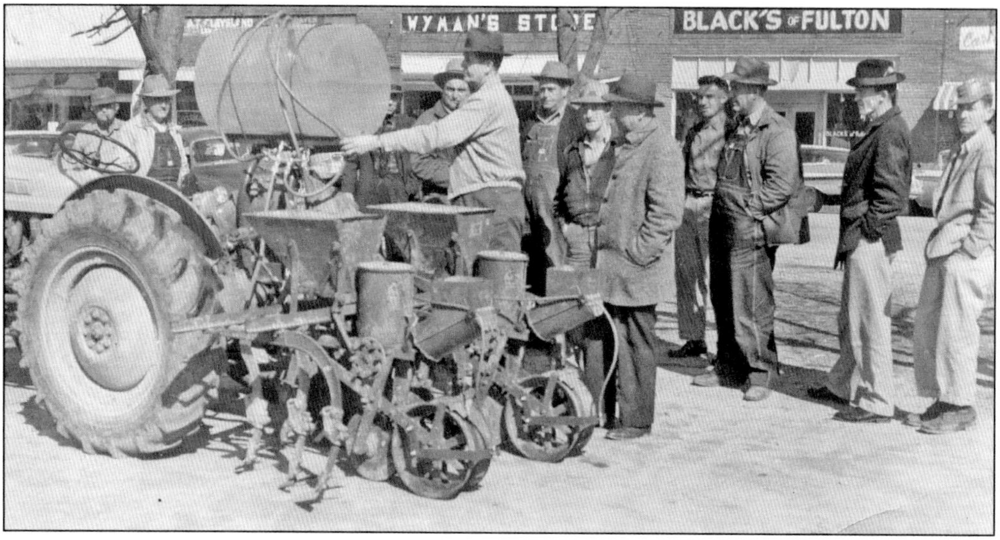

The courthouse lawn was frequently used as a gathering spot for a variety of events. In the 1920s, a croquet court on the east lawn was enjoyed by lawyers, merchants, and other town residents. Above, J.R. Duncan, manager of the Itawamba Farm Improvement Association, shows a group of farmers how to set up a tractor for a spray to control weeds. Below, the annual art exhibit sponsored by the Fulton Civic Club attracted many visitors to the court square. Artwork by schoolchildren from across the county was on display, as well as art done by adult citizens. The Civic Club often served lemonade to those who came to see the art.

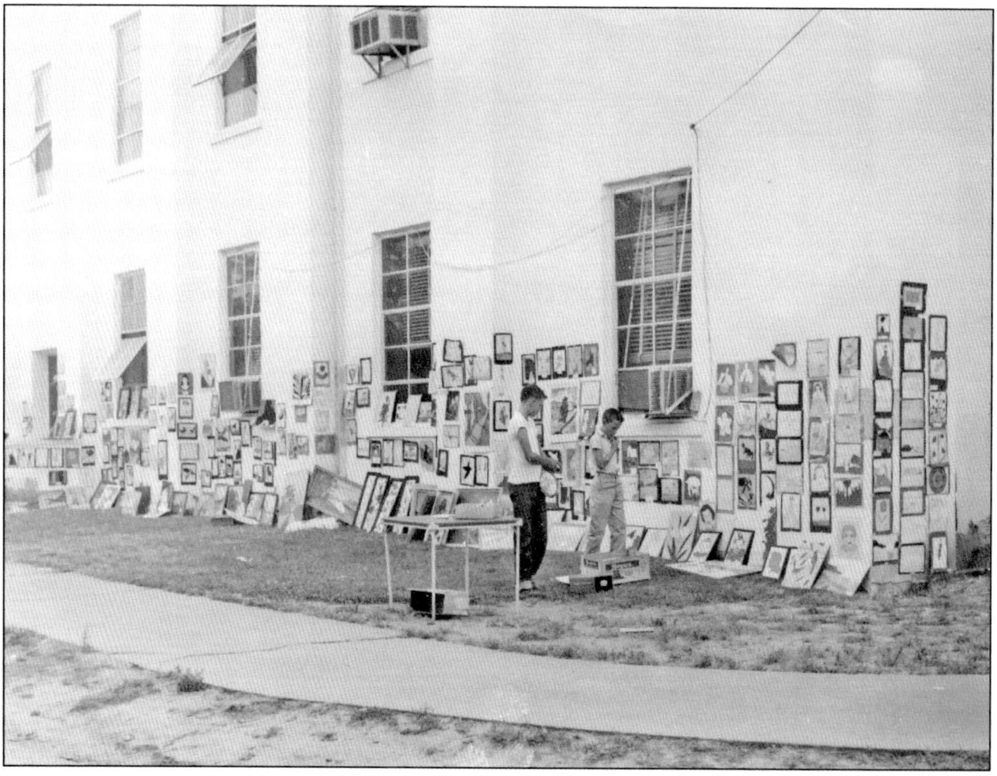

Before the county established a fairground east of Fulton, the court square served as a location for carnival rides as well as demonstrations of farm produce, arts and crafts, flowers, and other exhibits. In this 1958 photograph, brothers Jerry (left) and Bob Franks enjoy a spin in the boats at a carnival on the courthouse lawn. The brothers are sons of Cleveland Franks and Ernie Marie Cockrell.

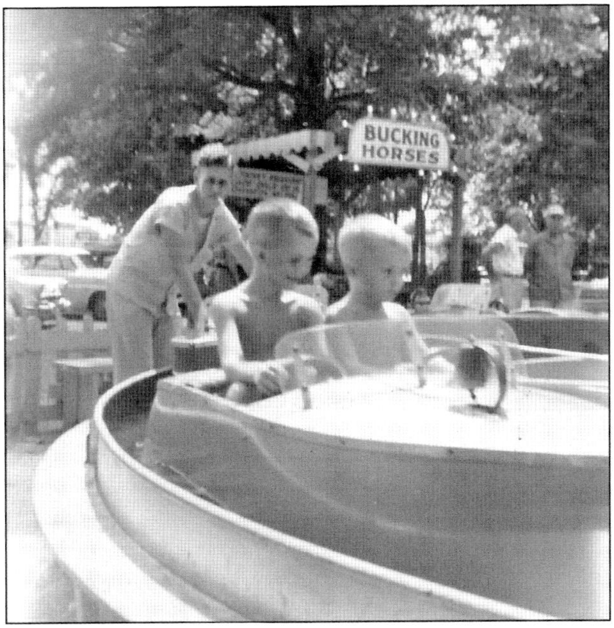

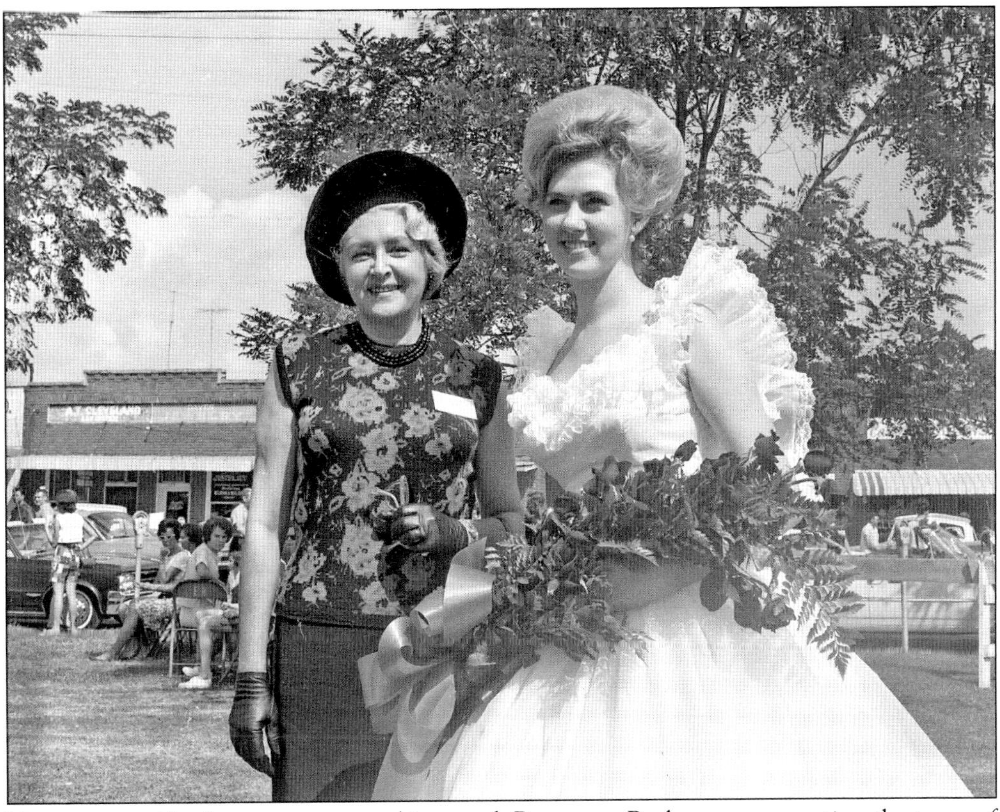

Hometown pride always turns out a big crowd. Roseanne Burleson, representing the town of Fulton, was crowned Miss Hospitality for the state of Mississippi in July 1964, and Fulton honored Burleson with a parade and street party. She is pictured on the courthouse lawn with Dorothy Johnson, Gov. Paul B. Johnson's wife, who was in town for the festivities.

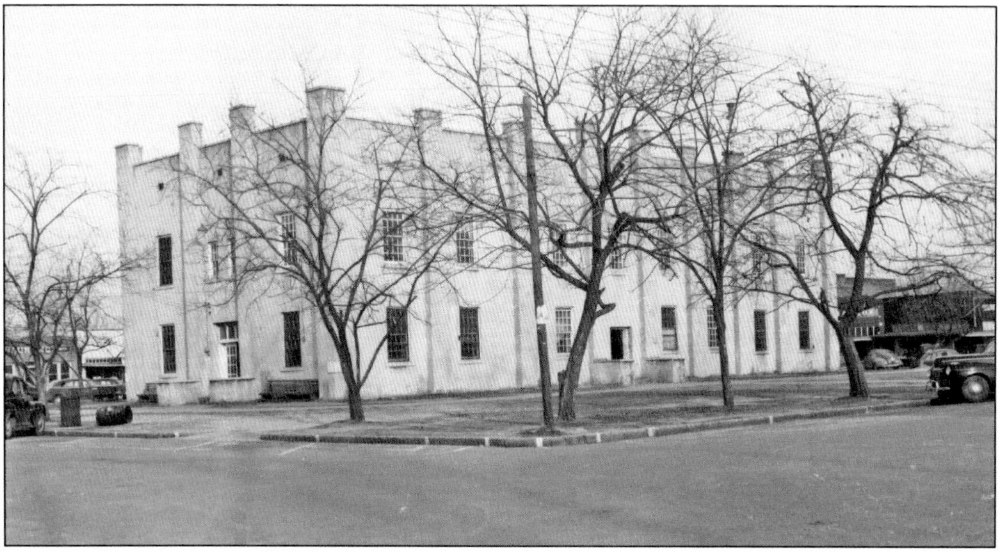

In 1957, the original brick of the courthouse was painted white following the addition of a two-story redbrick annex to the west side of the building in 1952. After several decades of maintaining the white facade, the county undertook a significant renovation, the first since the 1930s, when the Works Progress Administration completely remodeled the then-80-year-old structure.

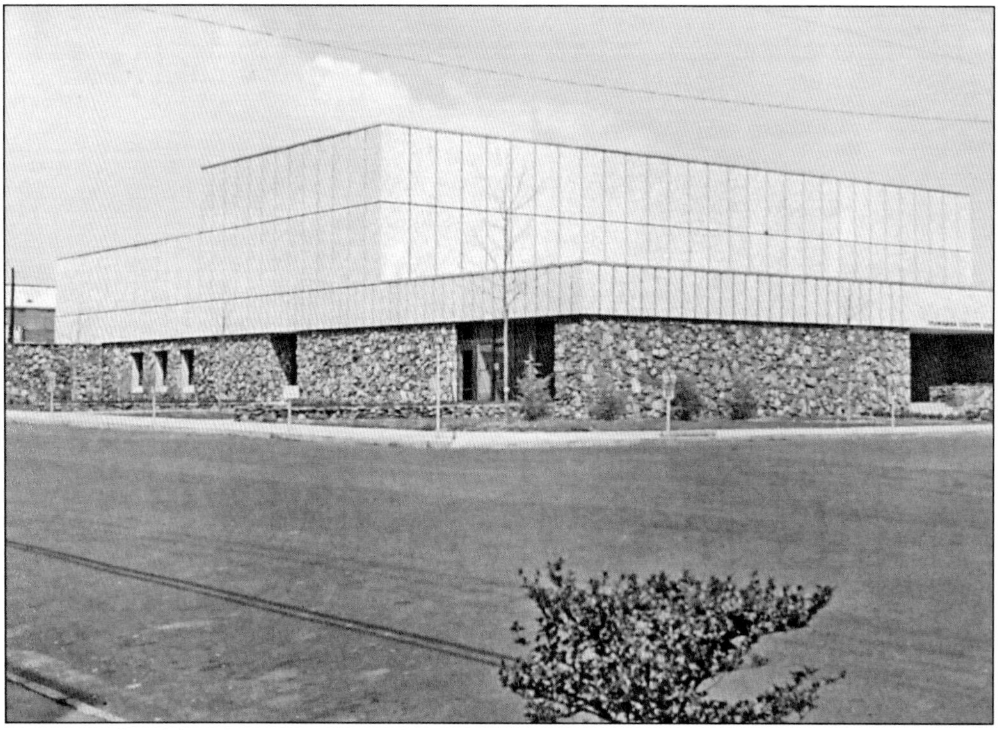

In 1968, a local bond issue was passed to remodel the existing courthouse, and the landscape of the hub of Fulton was forever changed. The "new" courthouse was designed by architect A.J. Staub, a Fulton native, and J.E. Staub and Company performed the construction work, which included a new wing on the east side of the courthouse. The work was completed in 1971, and this was the last major renovation to the building.

Three

Business and Industry

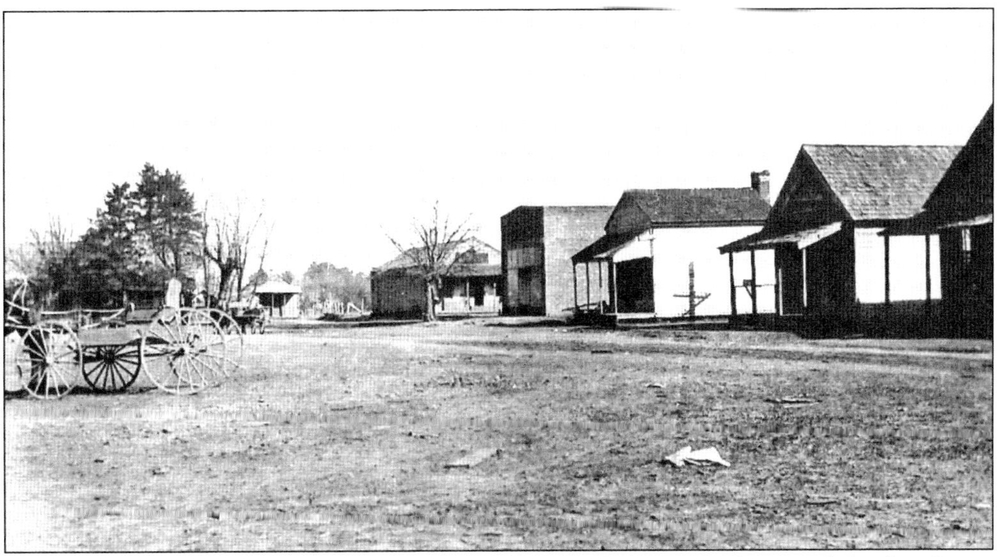

Standing at the southeast corner of the courthouse and facing north toward Gaither Street around 1921, one could see Gaither Brothers Store, the first commercial brick building in Fulton. Left of this brick store was William G. Orr's mercantile business, which he began in 1891 in a different location. The two buildings to the right later housed sandwich shops, while the small building at rear was Greene's Coffin Shop. (Courtesy of Itawamba Historical Society.)

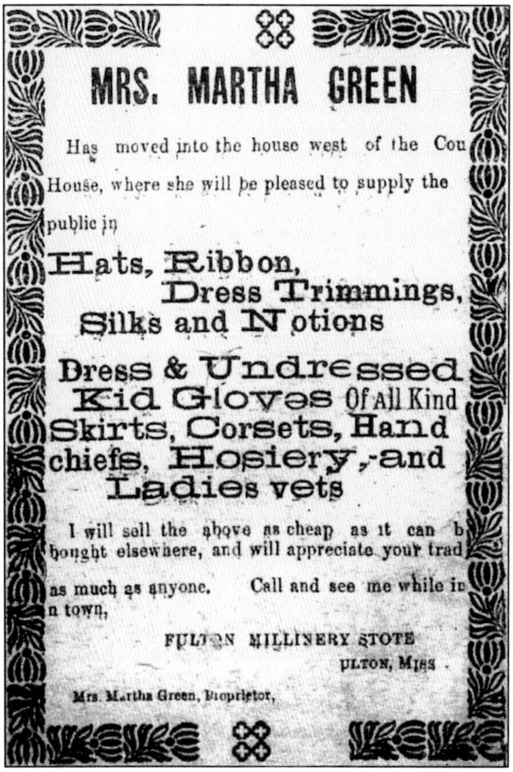

Sisters Martha and Willie Ward were among the first female entrepreneurs in Fulton when they opened a millinery shop in 1895. Martha married James Greene, and later, in 1901, she reopened the millinery store on the Fulton square. Martha's daughter, Zereda Greene, wrote that her mother's millinery store "was once in a wooden building later used for a number of years for the Fulton Bank." The advertisement shown here was published in the *Fulton Herald* in 1903. In 1928, an advertisement boasted the "latest style millinery" with trimmings, hosiery, stationery, and toilet articles. The store closed in 1934.

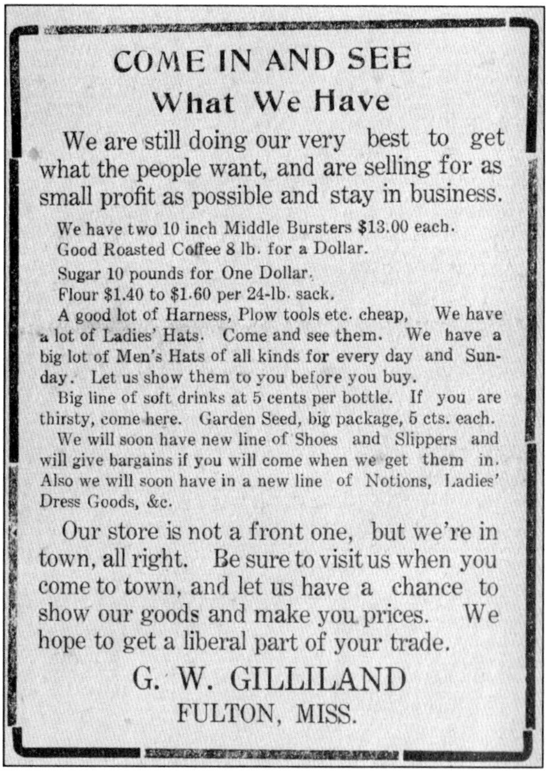

Gilliland's Store, owned by George W. and Mary Frances Gilliland, ran this advertisement in the March 24, 1921, issue of the *Itawamba County News*. The Gilliland family moved to Fulton in 1919, when George was elected chancery clerk. Their son Jim served as town marshal, alderman, city clerk, and mayor.

Busy Bee Café was on the west side of the court square, an area known as the Sheffield Block. The building was said to have been built in 1839 by Dr. Andrew J. McWilliams and sold to Fulton lawyer Newnan Cayce in 1874. It was later used by attorney Isaac Lewis Sheffield. Dr. Hatch Cummings, nephew of Malachi C. Cummings, took this picture of the popular eatery on July 29, 1925.

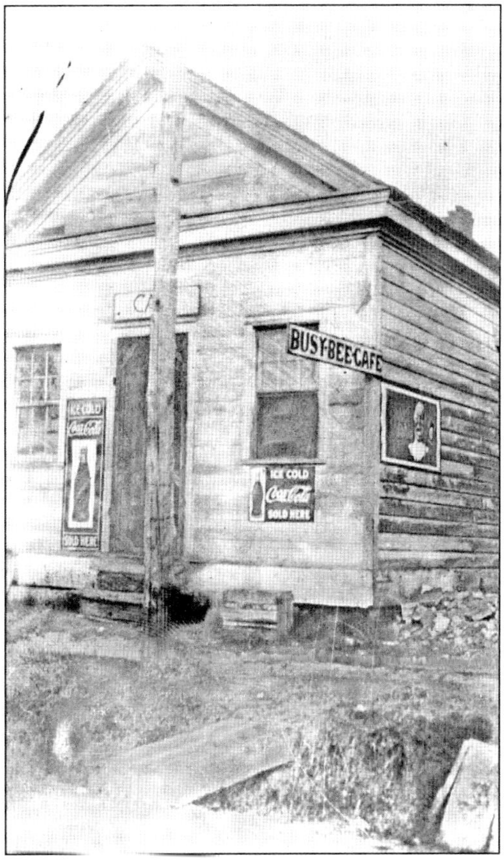

Holcomb and Guin was a grocery and general merchandise store on the north side of the Fulton square in the 1920s. Jonathan Harris Holcomb and his wife, Aurilla Guin Holcomb, moved to Fulton in 1924 from Marion County, Alabama. Pictured inside the store are Jonathan Holcomb (left) and his son Cecil. (Courtesy of Nan Holcomb Comer.)

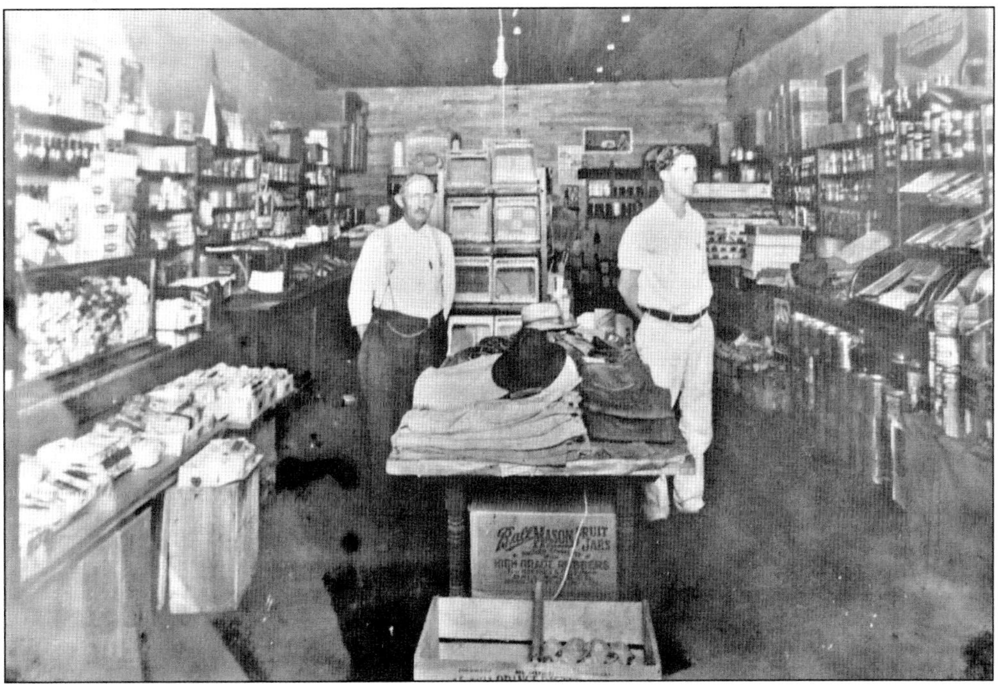

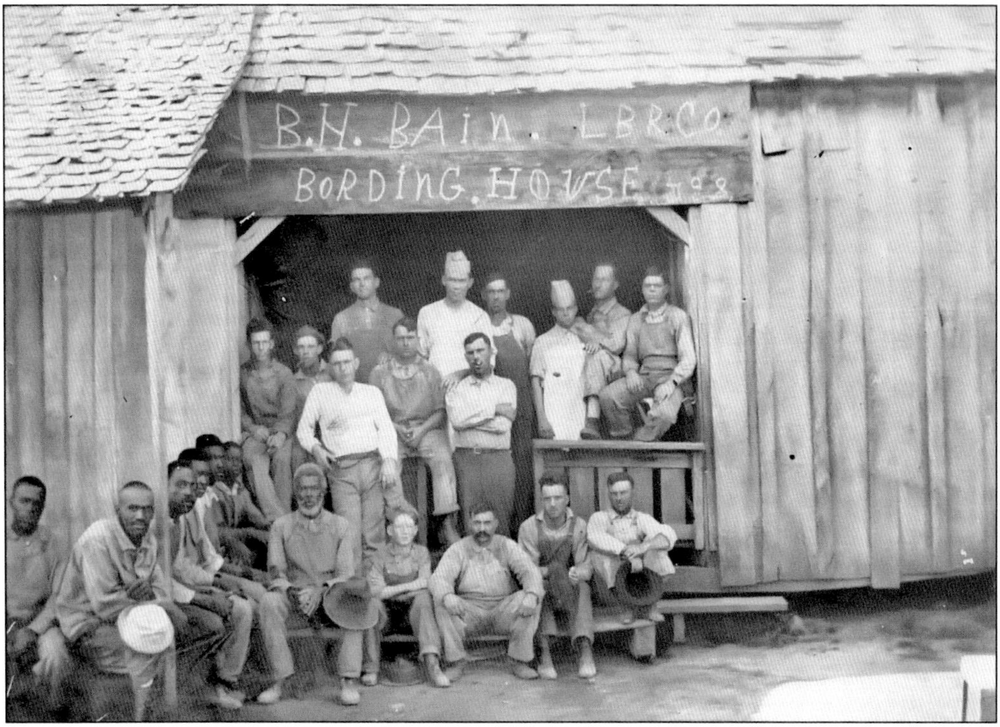

B.H. Baine built a successful lumber business in Houston, Mississippi, before opening a mill and lumber yard in Fulton in 1924 with J.M. Gibbs. Mill workers were often housed in boardinghouses such as this one. The 1920s lumber boom that followed World War I was the second such economic boom for Itawamba County, the first taking place in the 1890s and into the 1900s. (Courtesy of Itawamba Historical Society, T.C. Gibbs Collection.)

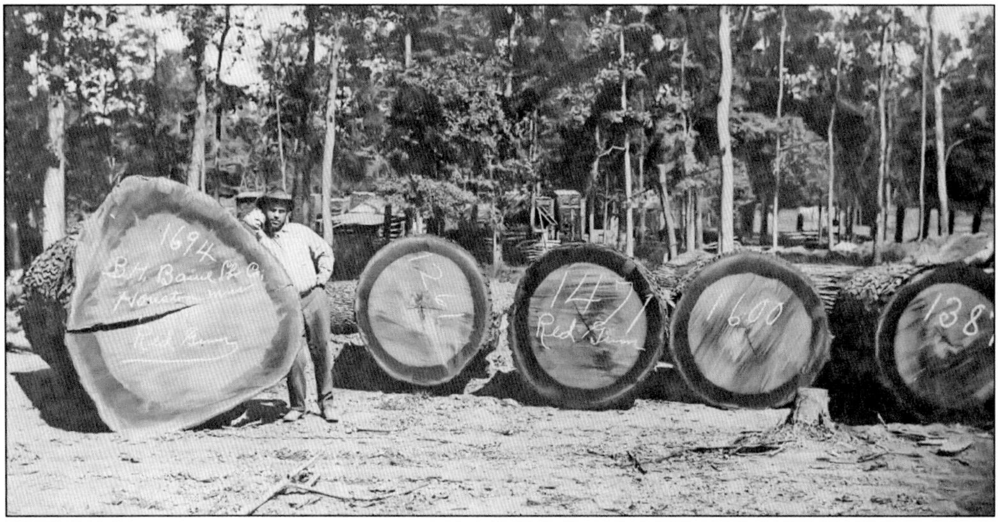

James Miles Gibbs, a Tennessee native, relocated his family to Fulton from Chickasaw County in the 1920s during the lumber boom. In 1924, Gibbs and B.H. Baine established Fulton Band Mill west of Fulton on property that is now the site of Itawamba Community College. Gibbs was a civic leader and owner of several businesses in Fulton. Here, Gibbs poses with red gum logs bound for the Fulton mill. (Courtesy of Itawamba Historical Society, T.C. Gibbs Collection.)

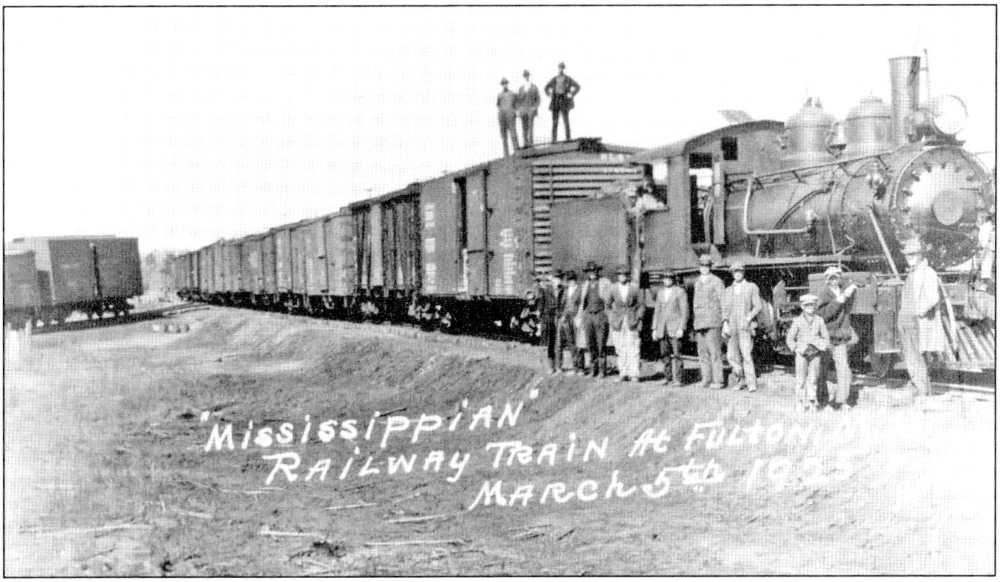

Completed in 1924, the Mississippian Railway provided a direct link to the Frisco Railroad from Fulton to Amory for Fulton's lumber yards and mills, thus bypassing the need to truck lumber to Tupelo. In the cab of engine No. 10 is Jake Carlisle, a longtime engineer. Carl Carlisle stands on the gangway, while Olen Dozier stands on top of the boxcar with his hands on his hips. The fifth man standing from right is J.T. Cochrane Jr. At its peak, the railroad carried 20 cars of lumber per day. (Courtesy of Jerry Stubblefield.)

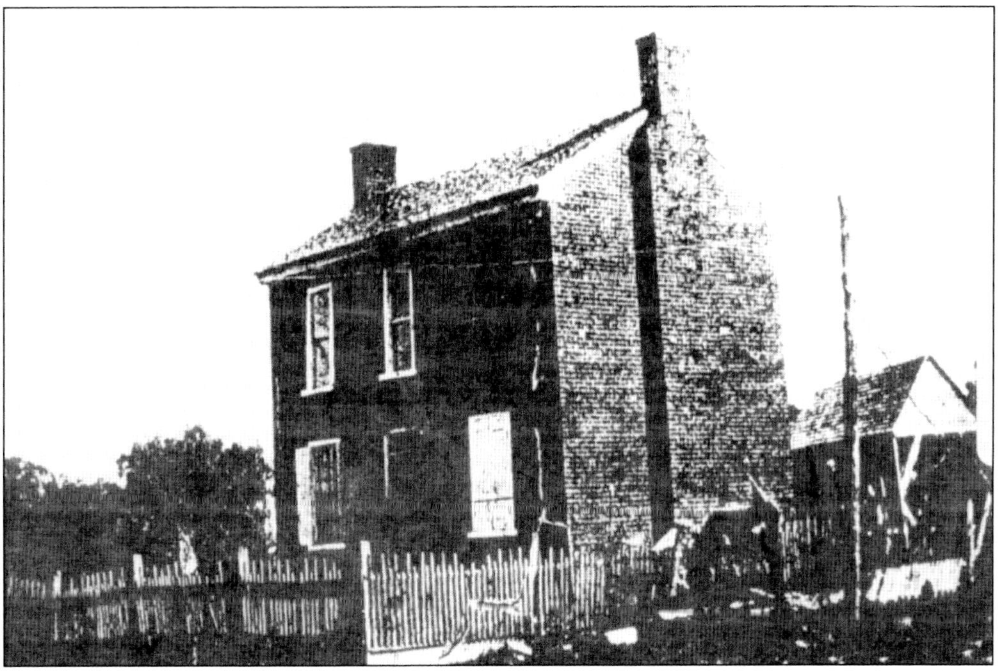

The county jail, built in 1854, was originally located at the corner of Cummings and Wiygul Streets, where Fulton City Hall sits today. Before the jail burned down in 1942, its prisoners were fed by John R. and Armanda Webb, who ran a boardinghouse (later known as Bennett Hotel) across from the jail. (Courtesy of Paulette O'Rear.)

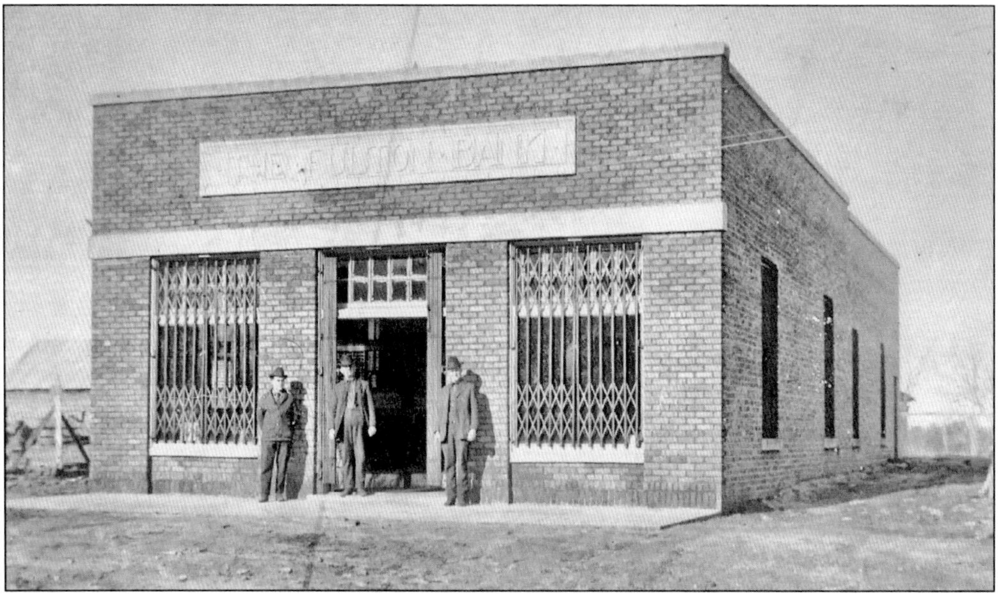

Fulton Bank was the only bank in Itawamba County when it opened in 1905 as a branch of the Bank of Guntown. In 1906, the bank merged with Bank of Tupelo. Originally a wood-frame building, the bank was located on Cummings Street across from the courthouse. Above, Jaudon C. Whitehead Sr., Prentiss Howard, and Richard Senter stand in front of a new brick building in 1921. Below, in 1947, the interior of the Fulton Bank was completely renovated with wood-paneled tellers' windows and coffered ceilings. Notice the spittoons on the tiled floor. Jaudon C. Whitehead Sr. became the bank manager in 1923 and served for many years. In 1931, Fulton native J.P. Nanney was elected president of the Bank of Tupelo, and at Nanney's death, J.C. Whitehead Jr. took over the bank's highest office, serving until his retirement in 1983. For 54 years, the Bank of Tupelo (later, Bank of Mississippi and Bancorpsouth) was led by Fulton natives. (Both, courtesy of Itawamba Historical Society.)

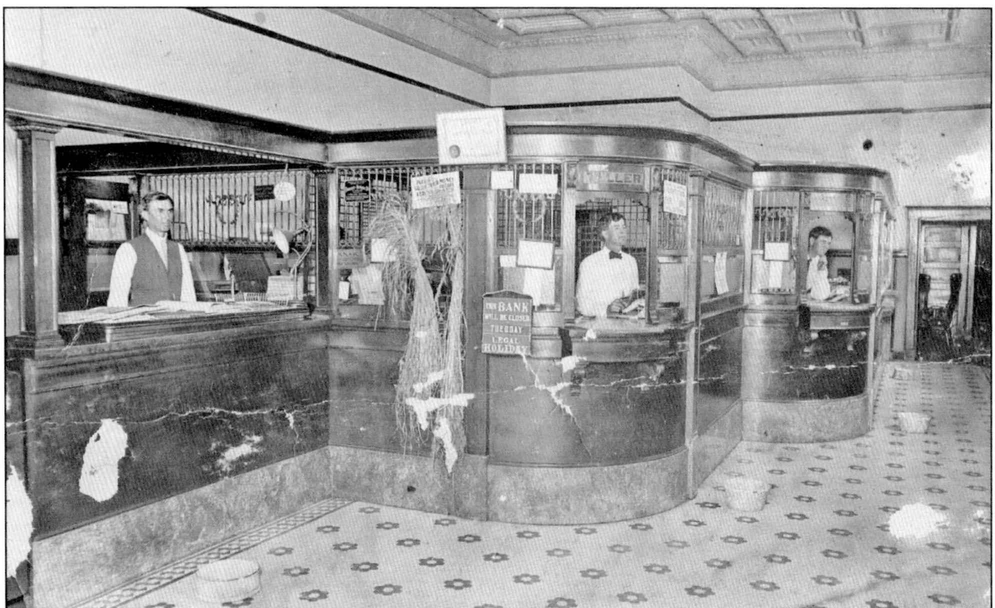

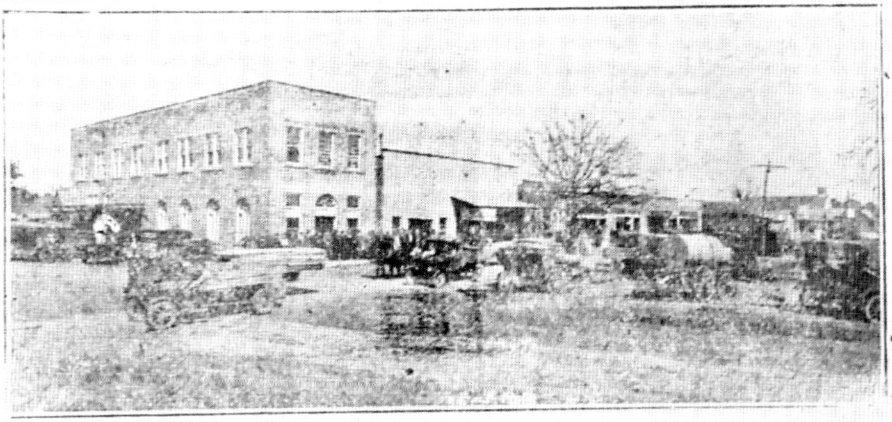

Main Street in FULTON Showing Itawamba County Bank

Whose Stockholders and Directors are Itawamba County people and whose Deposits are rapidly growing. Other business houses are seen in the picture. Lumber is a principal industry while cotton throngs our streets in fall months.

The Itawamba County Bank, Fulton's second bank, was located in a two-story brick building on the northeast corner of Main and Cummings Streets until it closed in 1930. By 1937, the two-story building shown here was occupied by Tombigbee Electric Power Association, which remained at this location until 1957, when it moved around the corner from C&P Auto Parts.

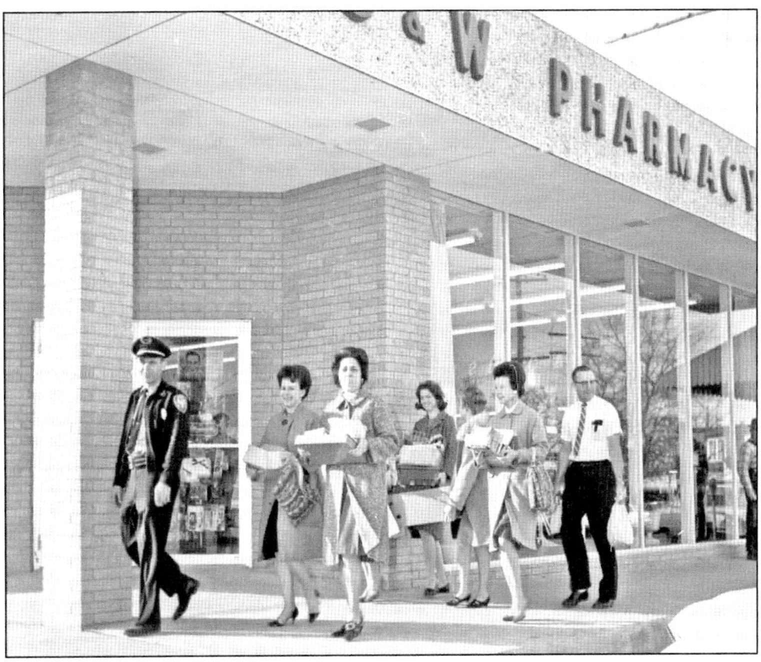

In 1967, employees of the Bank of Mississippi (formerly Fulton Bank) are escorted by Fulton policeman Joe Turner as they move down the street to their new location at the southwestern corner of Wiygul and Cummings Streets. Following Turner are, from left to right, Clytee Prestage, Martha Yawn, Catherine Maxcy, Libby Jones, Odelle Wood, and Luzerne Wheeler.

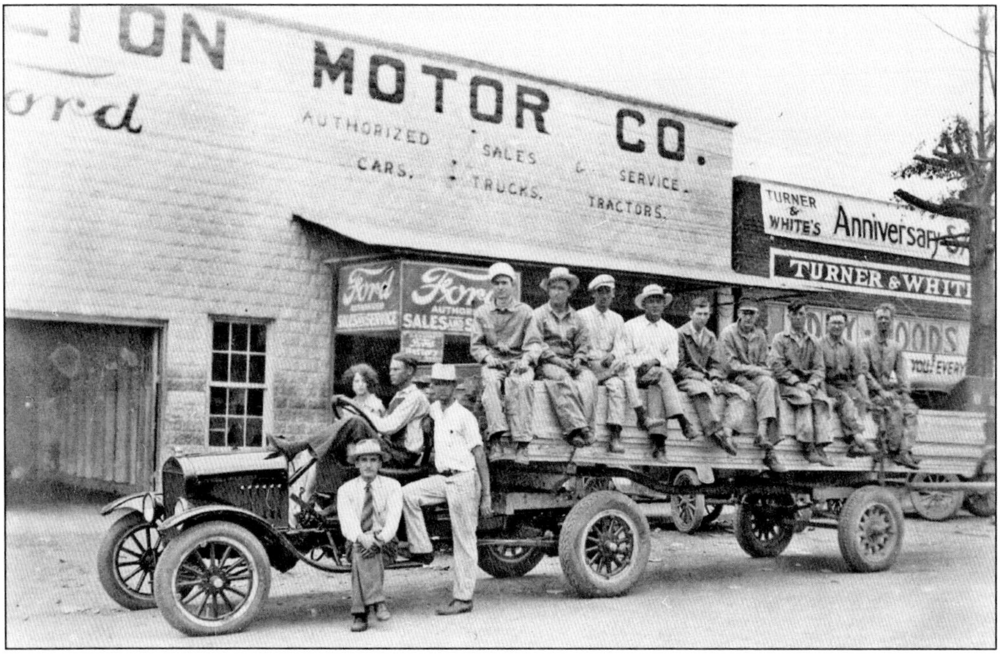

In 1927, salesman Bonner Murff sits on the fender of a truck parked in front of Fulton Motor Company, the town's first automobile dealership. Opened in 1921 by James M. Brown and L.A. Alsworth and initially located on the northeast corner of Cummings and Main Streets, the company was an authorized dealer for Ford vehicles and Fordson tractors. With his foot on the fender is Bill Burch; Walter Wilemon is the driver, while office worker Mamie Gates sits next to him. On the load of lumber are, from left to right, Leonard Clark, Grady Wood, Bruce Smith, Curtis Thornberry, Bascum Brunson, Sidney Summers, Paul Smith, Orvil Dozier, and Jess Smith.

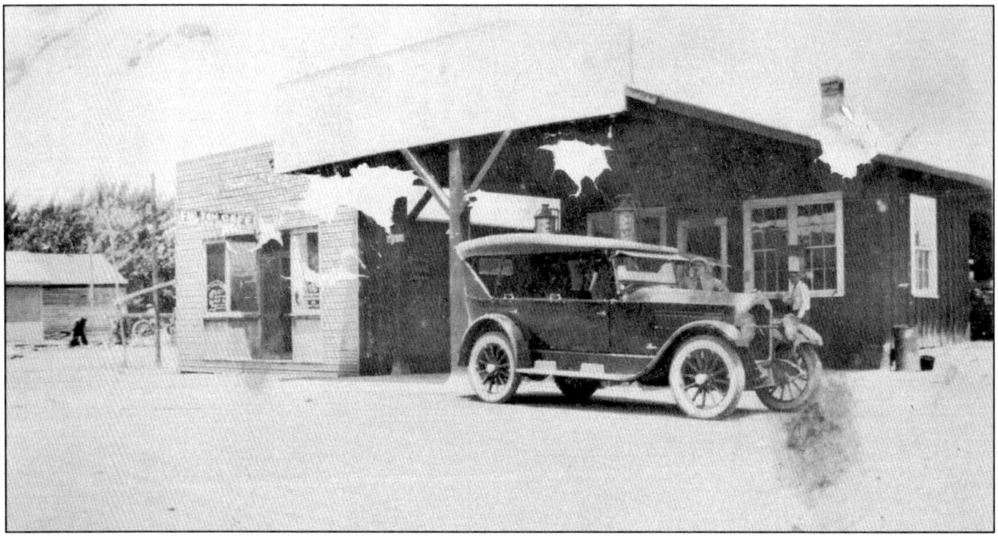

One of Fulton's first service stations, shown here about 1923, was owned by Escar Mattox and sold Sinclair brand gasoline. The station was on the northwest corner of Main and Clifton Streets, where the Mills Law Office is now. Fulton Café was located next door, and together with the adjacent vacant lot, this location later became home to Cowden Chevrolet until 1965, when Western Auto remodeled the building for its use.

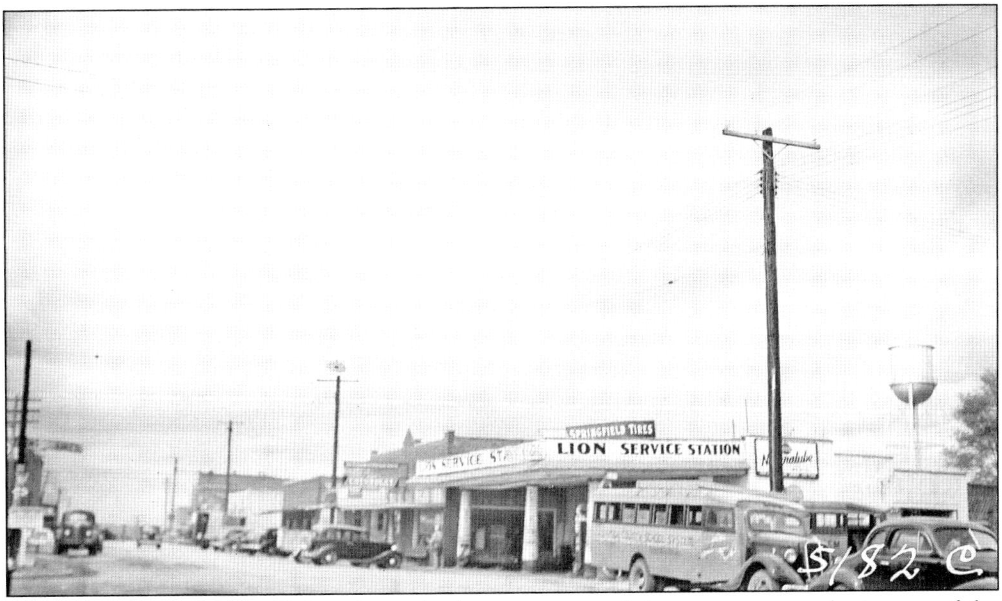

In this 1938 photograph of Main Street looking west toward the court square, the impact of the automobile on Fulton in just 10 years' time can be easily seen. Lion Service Station occupies a busy corner, and Cowden Chevrolet sits adjacent to the station in a fairly new brick building. Notice the old school bus. (Courtesy of Itawamba Historical Society.)

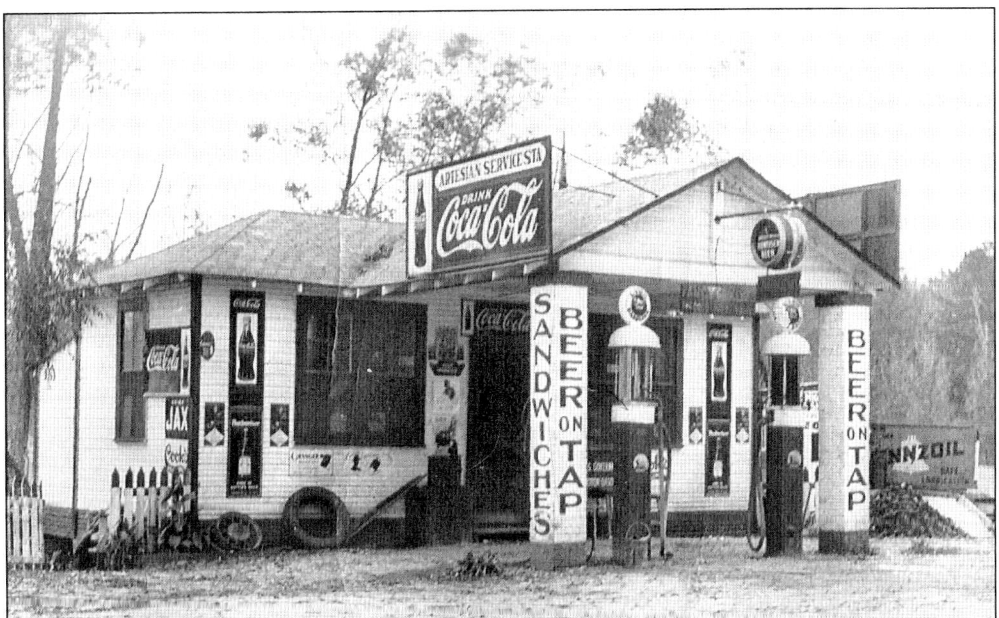

The Artesian Service Station was on the western edge of town near the old artesian well, selling beer, sandwiches, and gasoline. National Prohibition laws passed in 1920 ended the sale of alcoholic beverages, but "near beer" was allowed, and in 1933, all beer sales became legal. This convenience store likely operated in the 1930s. (Courtesy of Itawamba Historical Society.)

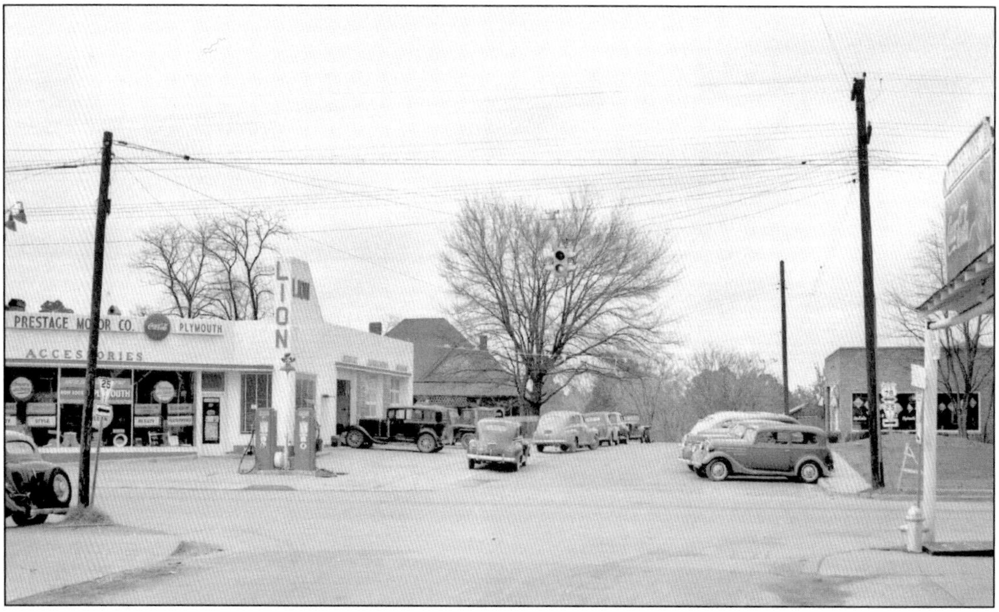

Prestage Motor Company, owned by brothers Hollis and Gaddis Prestage, opened in 1935 at the northwest corner of Main and Clifton Streets, site of one of the first service stations in Fulton. In addition to gasoline and repair services, their company featured Plymouth and Desoto vehicles. This 1949 photograph shows the newly renovated business and an additional building on the right that later housed C&P Automotive Parts. The hipped roof of attorney A.T. Cleveland's house can be seen to the rear.

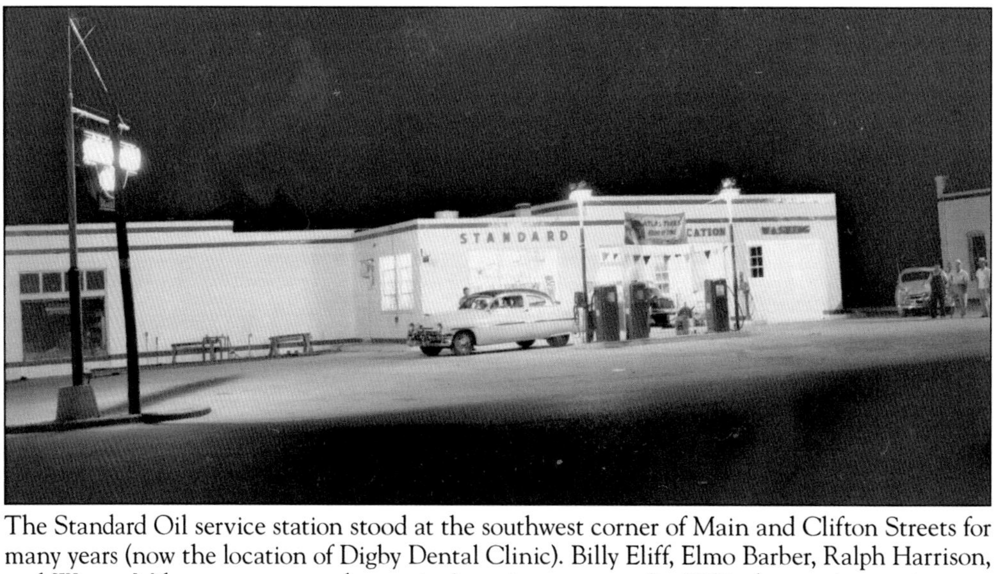

The Standard Oil service station stood at the southwest corner of Main and Clifton Streets for many years (now the location of Digby Dental Clinic). Billy Eliff, Elmo Barber, Ralph Harrison, and Wayne Miles were among the station's various owners. In 1950, the service station was modernized with neon lighting for nighttime use, encouraging travelers along Highway 78 to stop for gasoline.

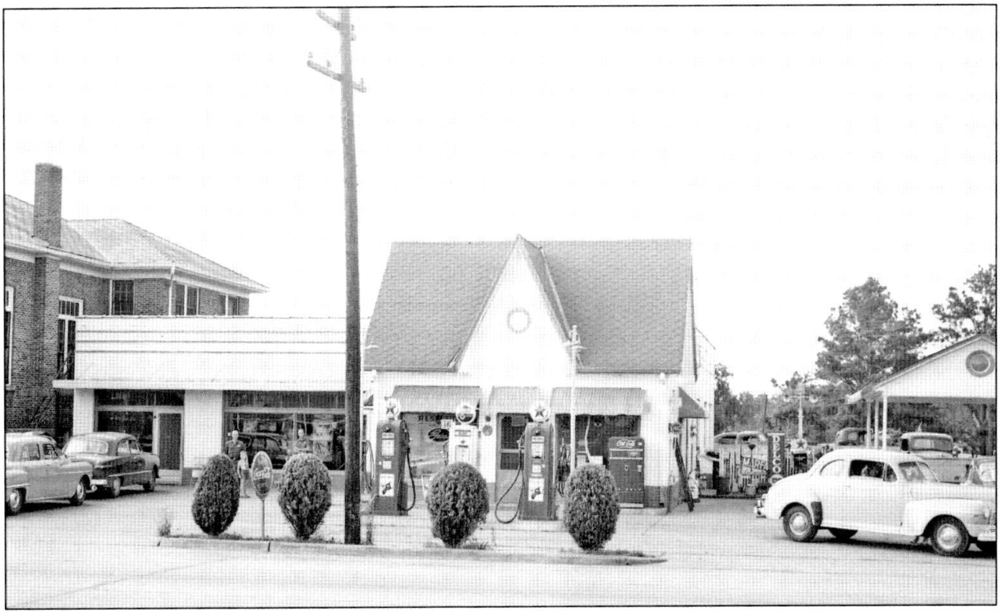

When Hilton Holcomb opened Holcomb Auto Parts and Texaco station on Main Street in 1952 in the former Conoco Oil building, the town of Fulton, like the rest of the country, was enjoying a postwar economic boom. Widespread use and affordability of automobiles created a demand for auto parts and supplies. Standing in front of the new business are, from left to right, Hilton Holcomb, his son Barry, and Gordon Pierce.

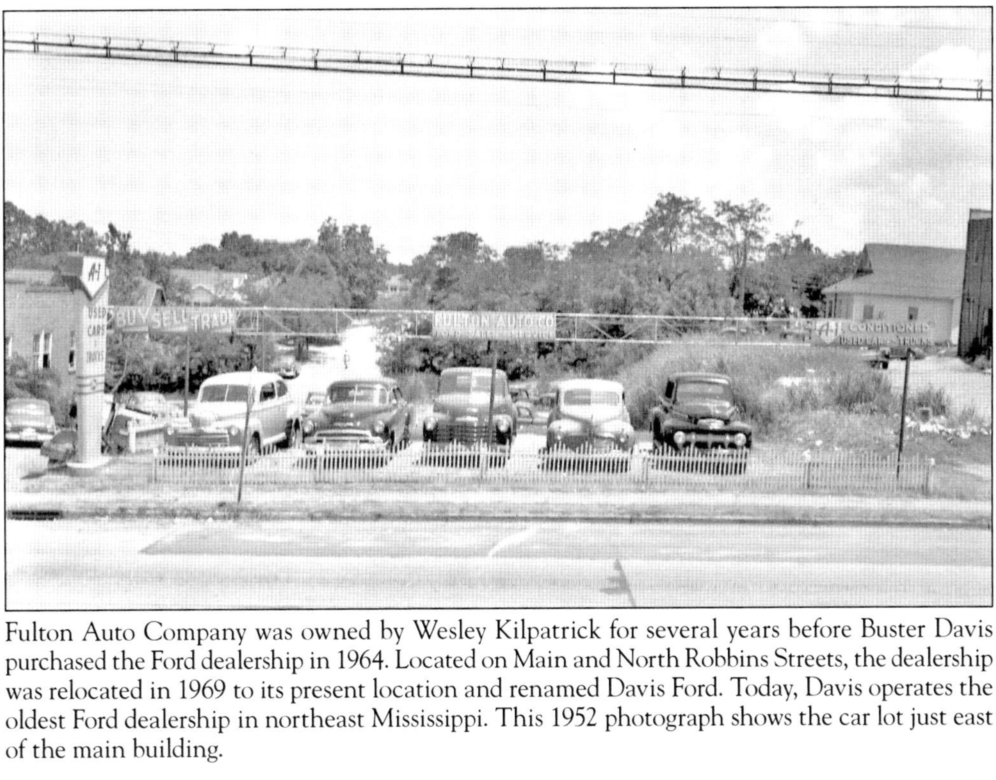

Fulton Auto Company was owned by Wesley Kilpatrick for several years before Buster Davis purchased the Ford dealership in 1964. Located on Main and North Robbins Streets, the dealership was relocated in 1969 to its present location and renamed Davis Ford. Today, Davis operates the oldest Ford dealership in northeast Mississippi. This 1952 photograph shows the car lot just east of the main building.

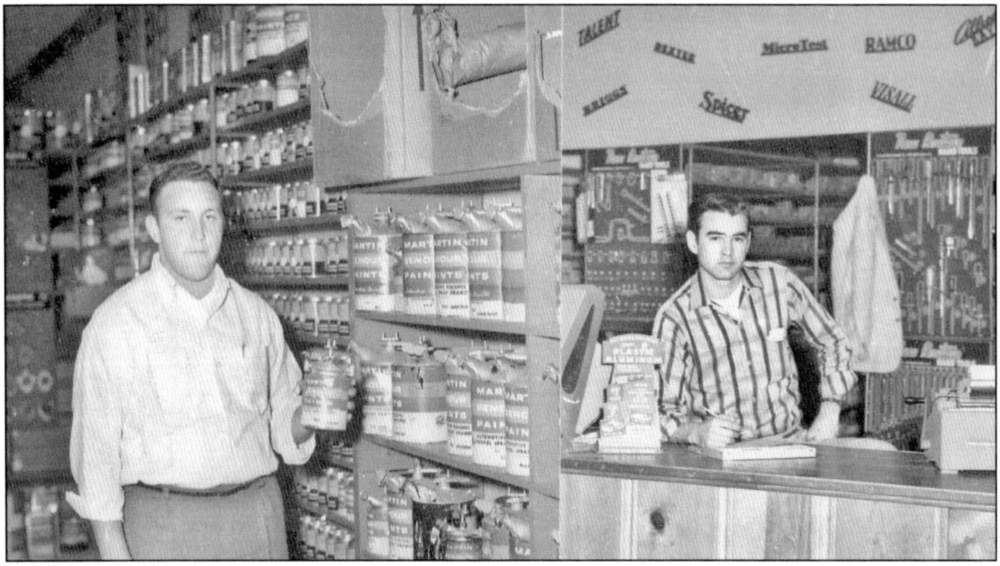

Fulton, like the rest of the country, enjoyed a postwar boom in the 1950s. Brothers-in-law and business partners Kelly Wade Prestage (left) and James Chatham opened C&P Automotive Supply in 1958 to serve the needs of a growing town. Nearly 60 years later, the company continues to operate in the same location on Clifton Street and is one of the town's oldest businesses.

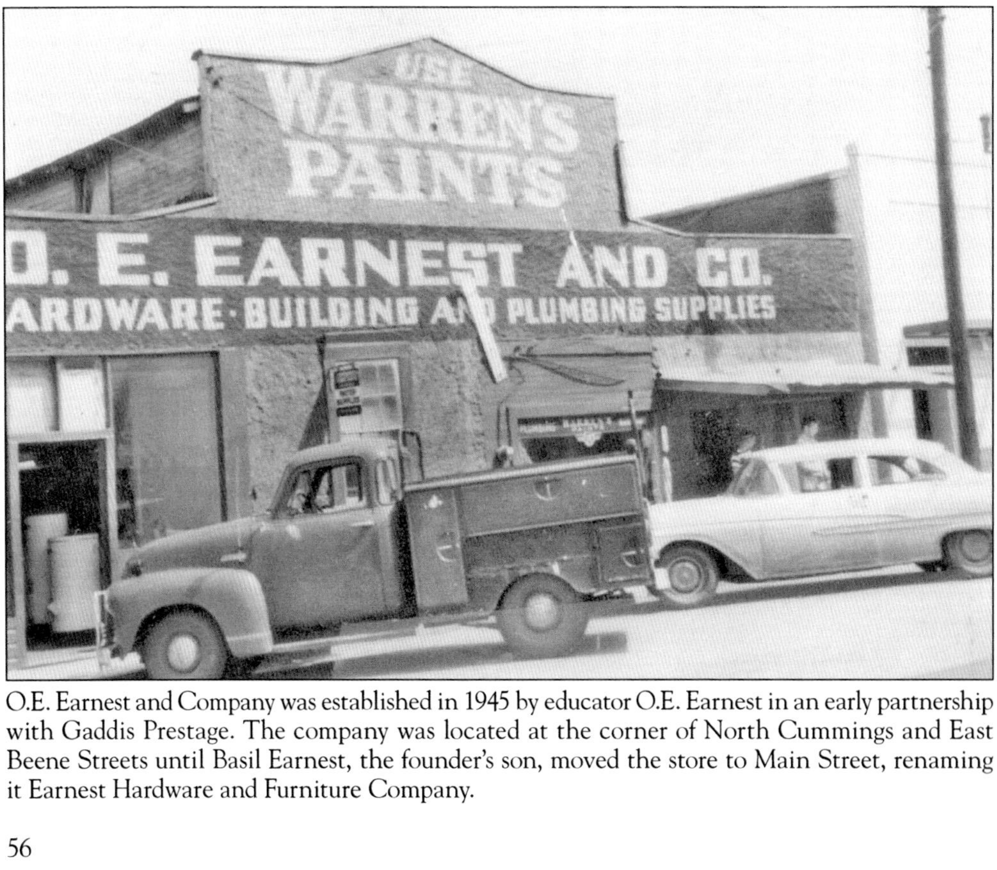

O.E. Earnest and Company was established in 1945 by educator O.E. Earnest in an early partnership with Gaddis Prestage. The company was located at the corner of North Cummings and East Beene Streets until Basil Earnest, the founder's son, moved the store to Main Street, renaming it Earnest Hardware and Furniture Company.

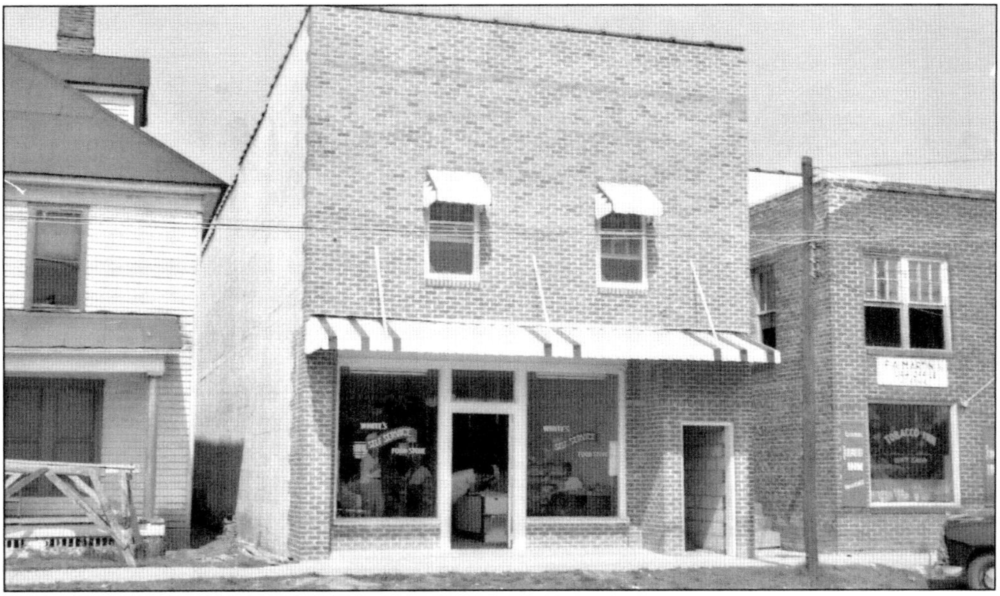

White's Self-Service Food Store opened in 1949 with a novel concept: self-service grocery shopping. The store was next to Bennett Hotel, now S&W Pharmacy, on the west side of the court square and was operated by Chester Kearney White. Adjacent to the store was P.A. Martin Law Office and Tobacco Inn, a tobacco and gift shop opened in 1946 by Frank and Frances Redfield.

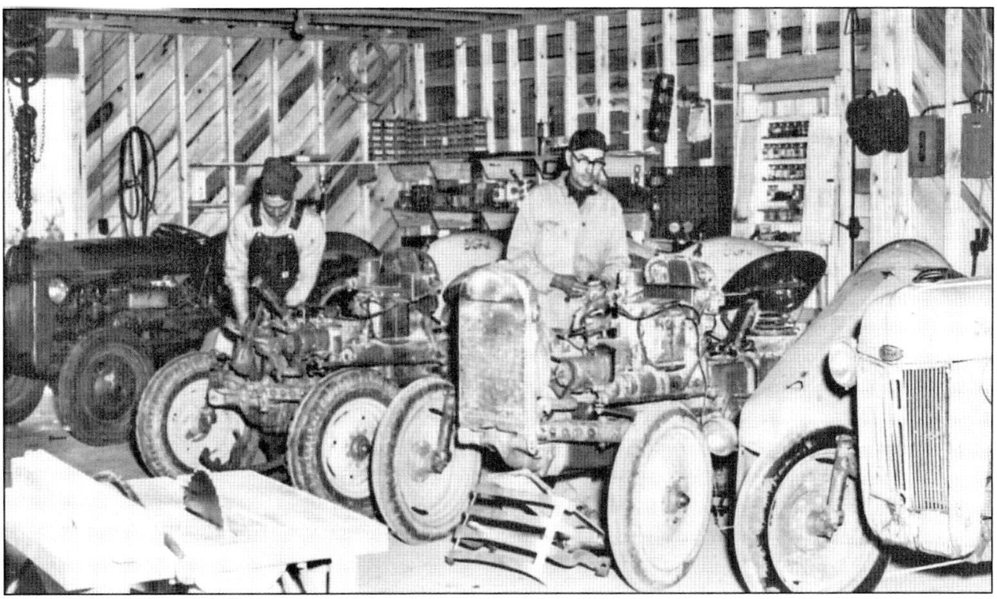

Jessie Riggs was known throughout the county as one of the best tractor repairmen, and his shop east of Fulton stayed busy. Riggs was a co-owner with Gene Spencer of Spencer & Riggs Repair Shop on Highway 78. In addition to farm equipment, the shop also did furniture repairs and cabinet work.

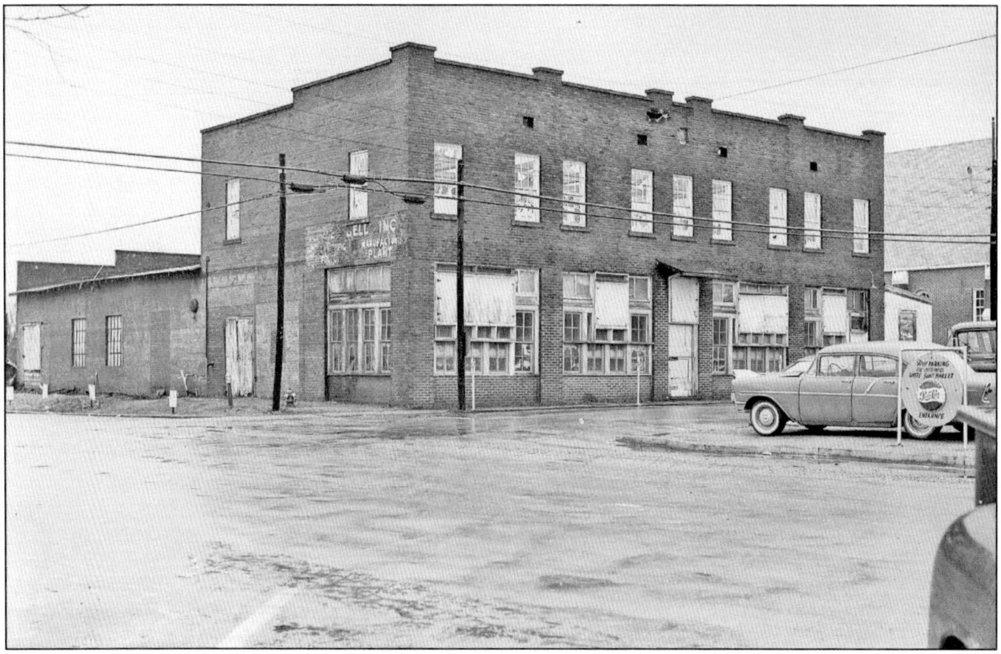

Fulton Garment Company was the first large employer of women in Itawamba County. Opened in 1932 by Rex Reed and W.B. Fields of Tupelo, the company made men's work shirts that were carried to Tupelo for shipping to other locations. In the 1930s, approximately 150 workers were employed at the company, which was on the southwest corner of Cummings and Wiygul Streets. Blue Bell Inc. purchased the company in 1947, and in 1952 moved the plant northeast of town.

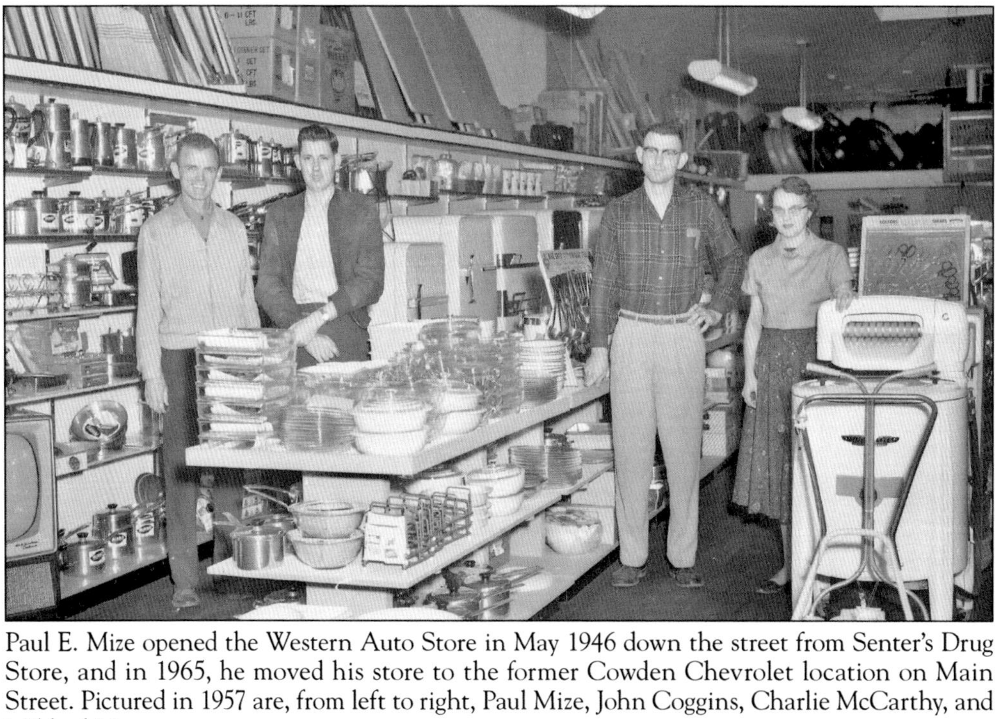

Paul E. Mize opened the Western Auto Store in May 1946 down the street from Senter's Drug Store, and in 1965, he moved his store to the former Cowden Chevrolet location on Main Street. Pictured in 1957 are, from left to right, Paul Mize, John Coggins, Charlie McCarthy, and Mildred Moore.

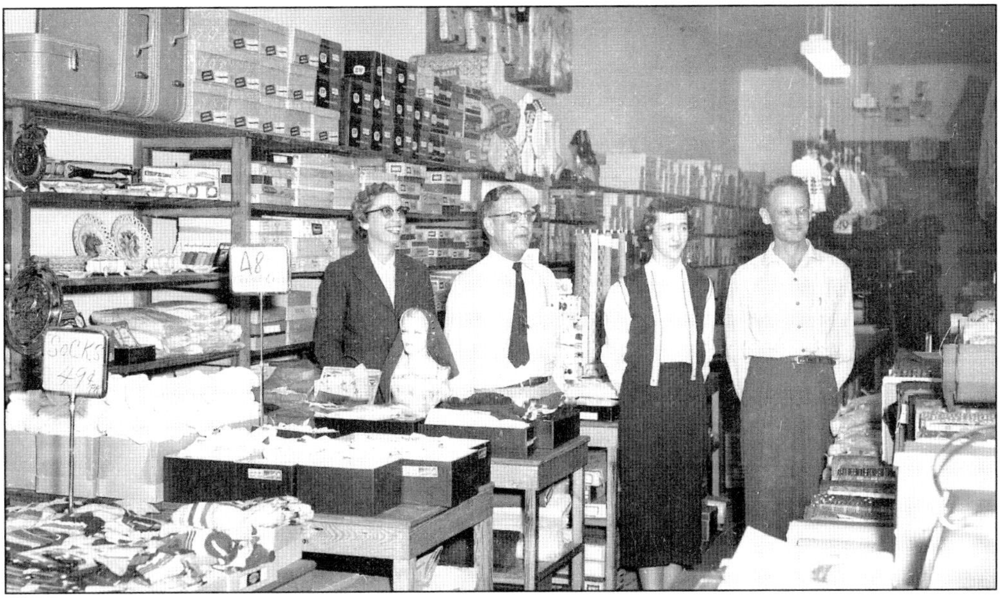

Many Fultonians have fond memories of shopping at Grady Gaither General Merchandise, known simply as Grady Gaither's to distinguish it from Gaither Brothers Store. The store was operated for many years by Grady and Opal Gaither. In this 1958 photograph, the Gaithers (left) are standing with employees Billie Turner and Clyde Comer. The store sold clothing and household items.

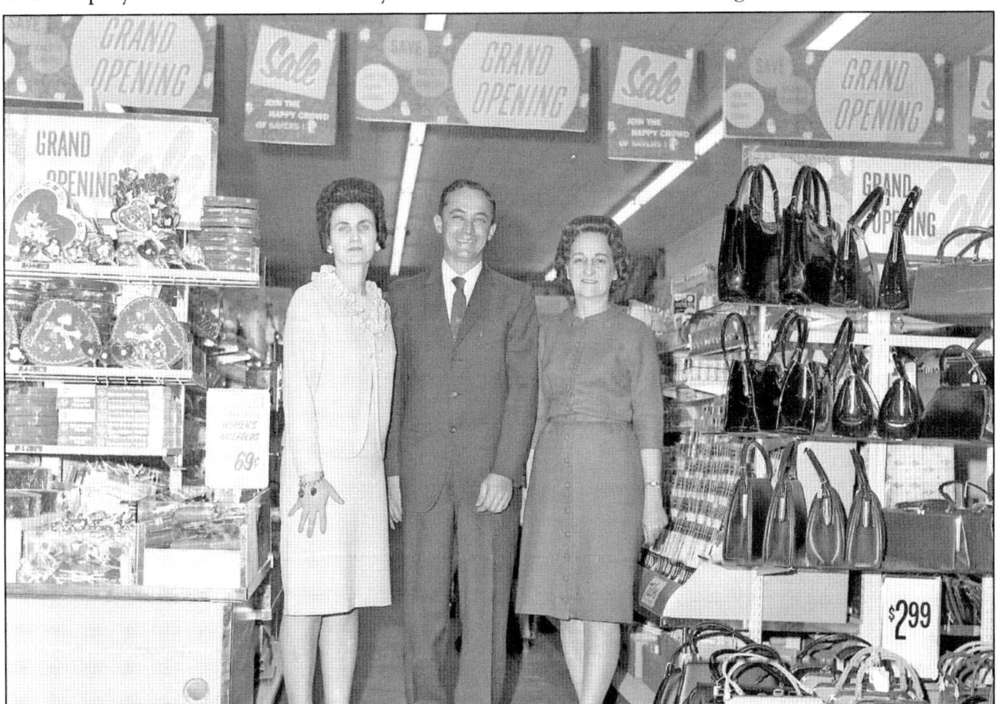

Ben Franklin, a five-and-dime chain store, opened in Fulton halfway between the stores of Cecil Whiteside and Grady Gaither on Main Street in 1966, offering a modern shopping environment. Ben Franklin was one of the first chain stores to locate in Fulton. From left to right, Christine Dulaney, Reese Dulaney, and Marie Spencer welcome customers to the newly opened store.

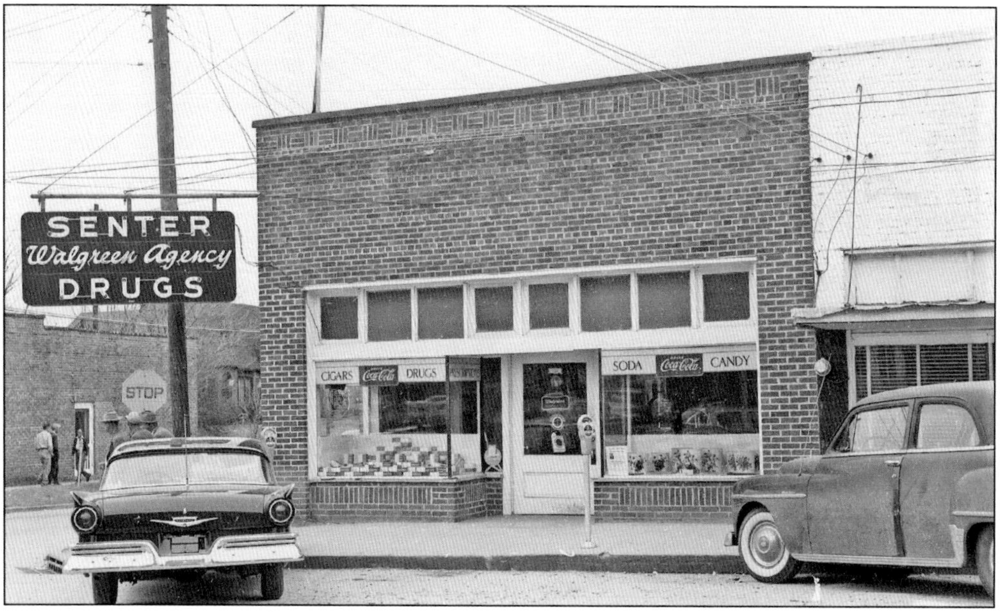

Senter Drug Store opened in February 1921 as J.T. Senter & Son, located at the northwest corner of Cummings and Main Streets, and was in business for over 60 years. In 1921, the store advertised in the *Itawamba County News* of a new preparation of its "Anti Malarial Tonic for the cure of Chills and Malaria," for 60¢ a bottle. In Fulton's earlier years, this corner was the location of a mule barn.

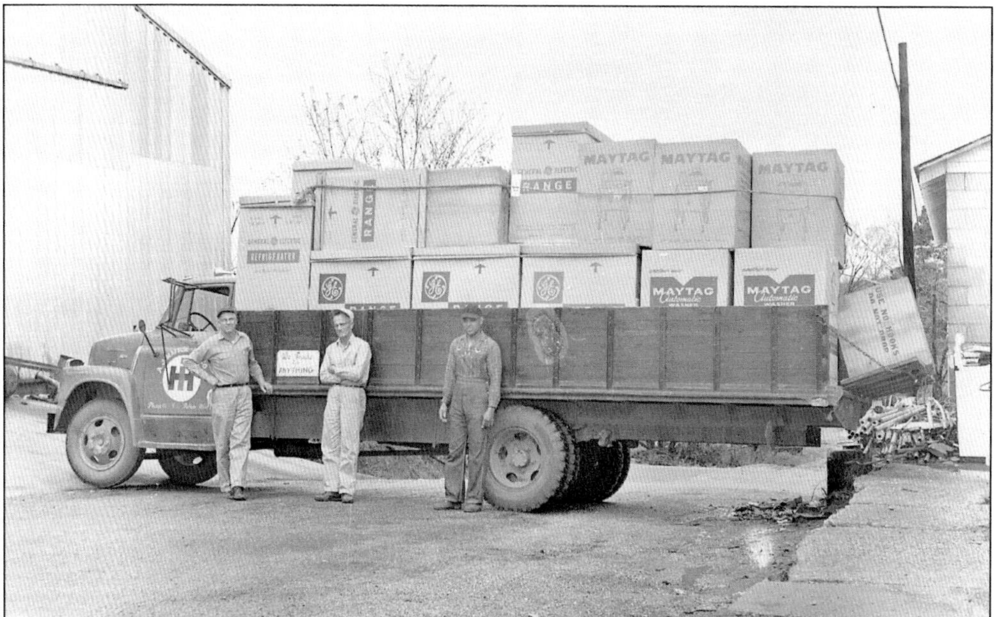

A.J. Mattox started Mattox Implement Company about 1926, selling farm implements and household appliances. Mattox was the first electric appliance dealer in Fulton and sold General Electric and Maytag products. His store's motto was "We service what we sell—We trade for anything—3% interest." Mattox also served as mayor of Fulton. Pictured from left to right are Fred Grimes, Avis Senter, and James Vasser.

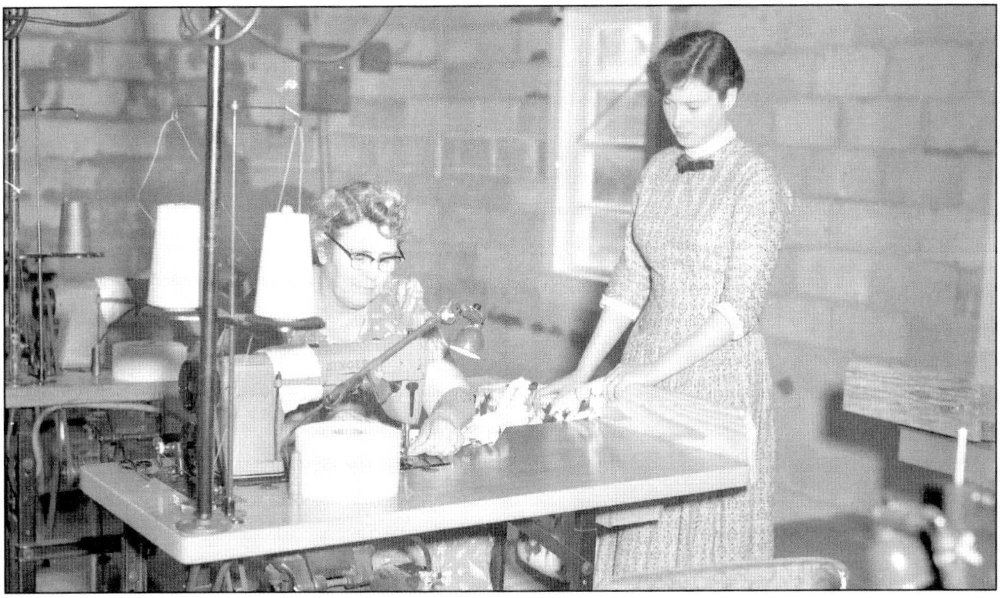

In 1958, Gilliland's Drapery and Curtain Shop opened to provide Fulton with a source for locally made curtains and drapes. Owner Retha Summerford Gilliland is shown here with her daughter Betty Gilliland Pearson. Pearson served Fulton as city clerk for 38 years and was a fixture at city hall for many more.

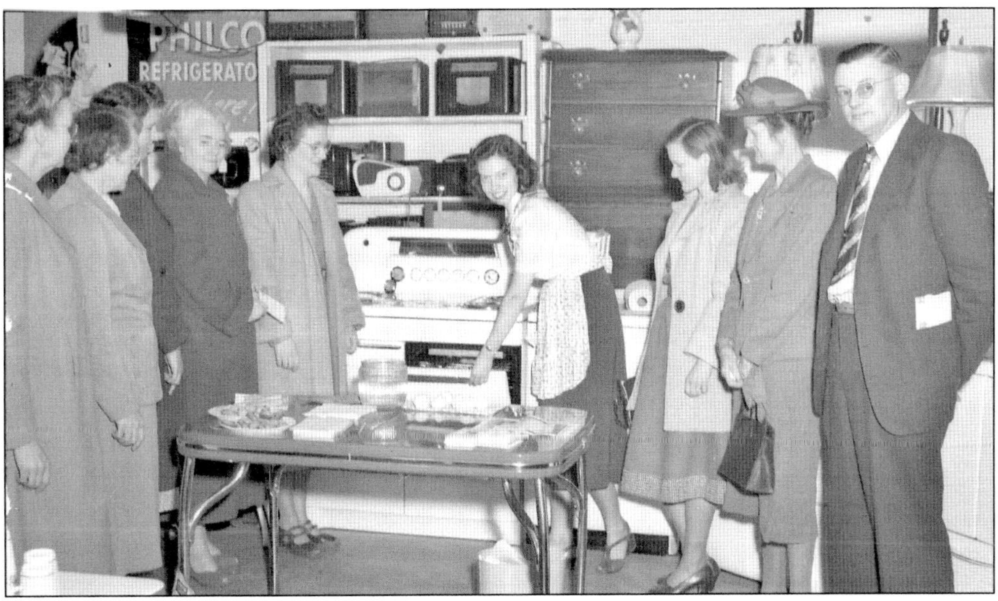

Mitchell McNeece, far right, manager of the F.K. Willis Furniture Company on the square in Fulton, watches as Betty Tillman, working at the stove range, shows the modern appliance's features to the visitors who attended a demonstration at the store in 1950. The furniture and appliance store opened in 1927.

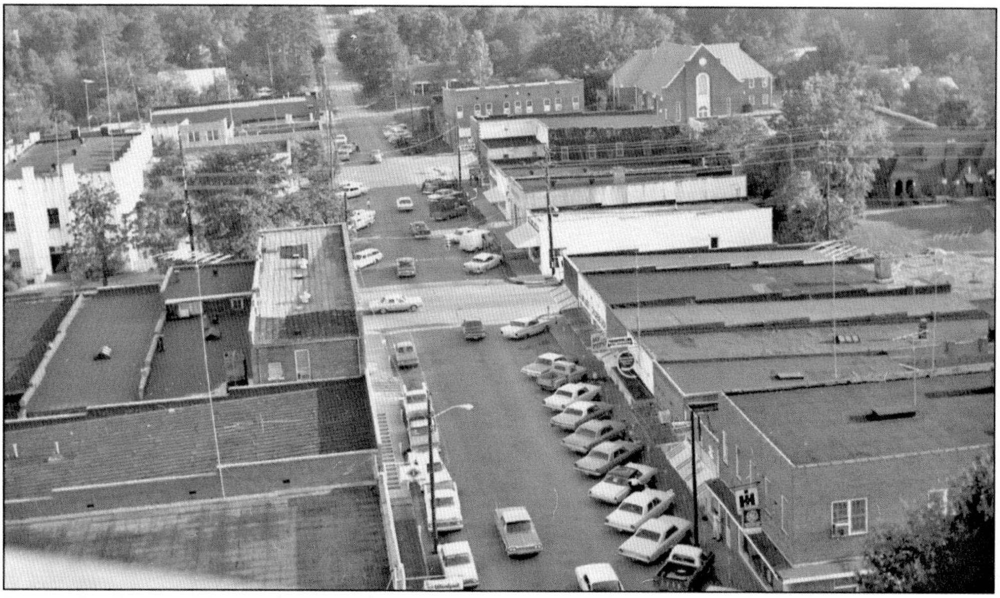

Itawamba County Times photographer Jimmy Comer took this picture of Cummings Street in 1965 from a downtown water tank. Beside First Baptist Church at upper right is the old Blue Bell building. Behind Blue Bell is the former home of early Fultonian W.H. Keys; the house would later be torn down for Dr. Billy Collum's clinic. Traveling down Cummings Street, the block included White's Grocery, the Fulton Bank, W.H. Wilson, and other businesses. Crossing Main Street, the businesses were Senter Drug Company, Lee Ann's Children's Shop, Western Auto, Fulton Hotel, and Mattox Implement Company.

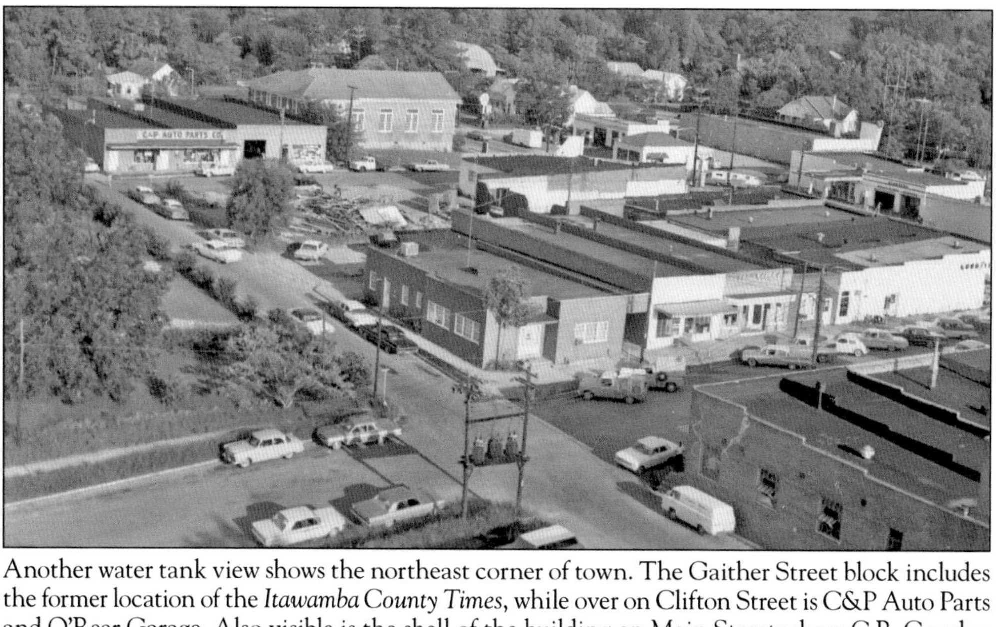

Another water tank view shows the northeast corner of town. The Gaither Street block includes the former location of the *Itawamba County Times*, while over on Clifton Street is C&P Auto Parts and O'Rear Garage. Also visible is the shell of the building on Main Street where C.B. Cowden Chevrolet used to be—the future home of a Western Auto store owned by Paul Mize.

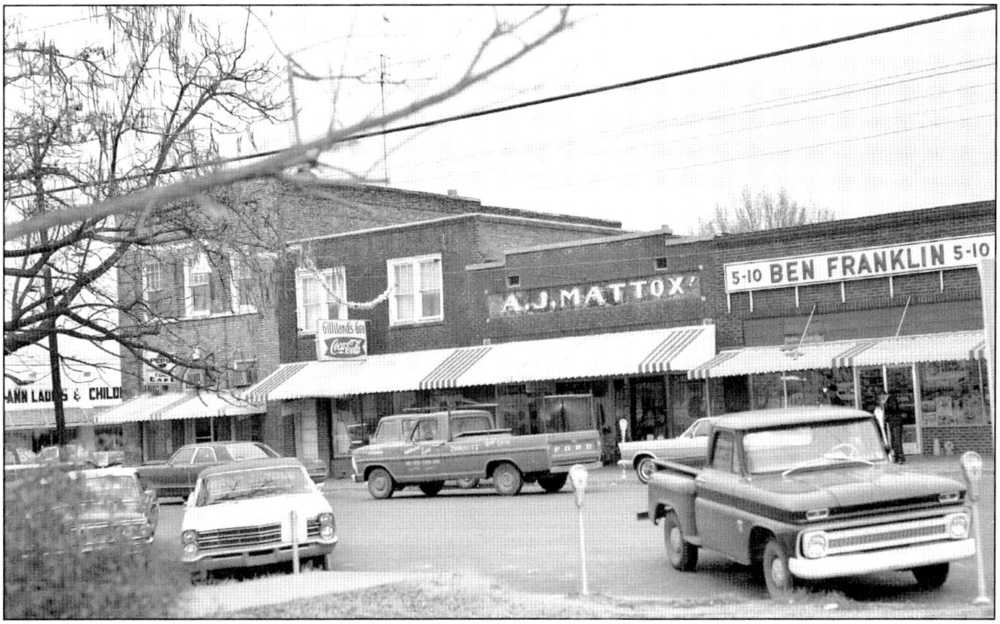

The tradition of closing for business on Wednesday afternoons in downtown Fulton was started in 1946. The business closures gave employees an afternoon during the middle of each week for gardening to address a national food-shortage crisis following World War II, and the tradition continued for many years. Here is a street scene from November 1967.

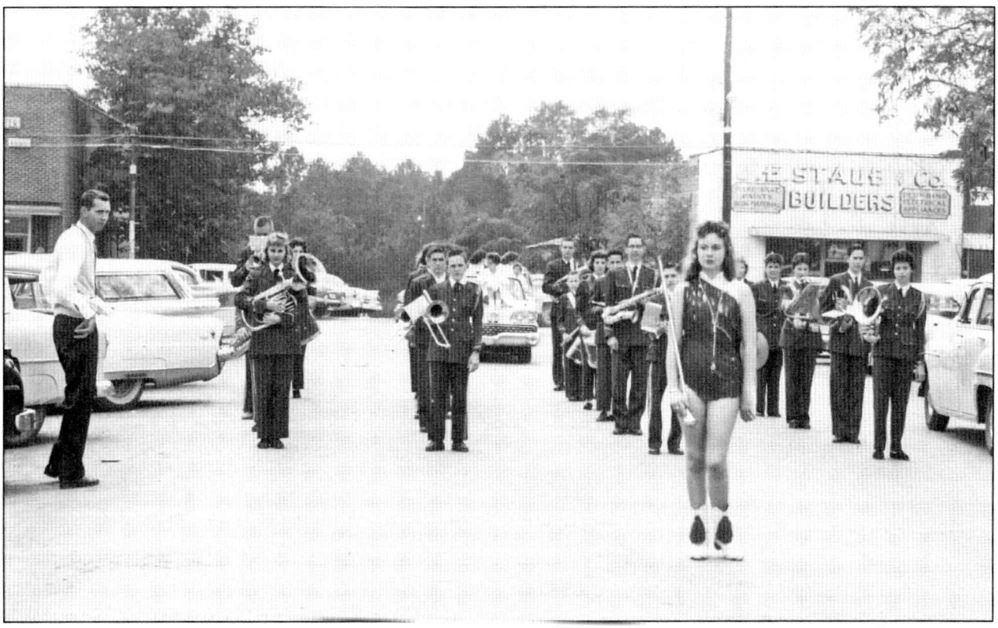

Looking south down Gaither Street in this 1950 scene, the future site of Fulton's Play Garden Park can be seen. On the right corner is the early home of J.E. Staub & Company, Builders, later known as JESCO, an outgrowth of the Staub-Stewart Hardware Company, which was opened in 1927 by A.J. Staub Jr. and W.G. Stewart. On the left corner is the familiar building that formerly housed Senter Funeral Home, opened by Wayne Senter and Hillman Senter. The south side of the Fulton square was merely a field until the 1920s.

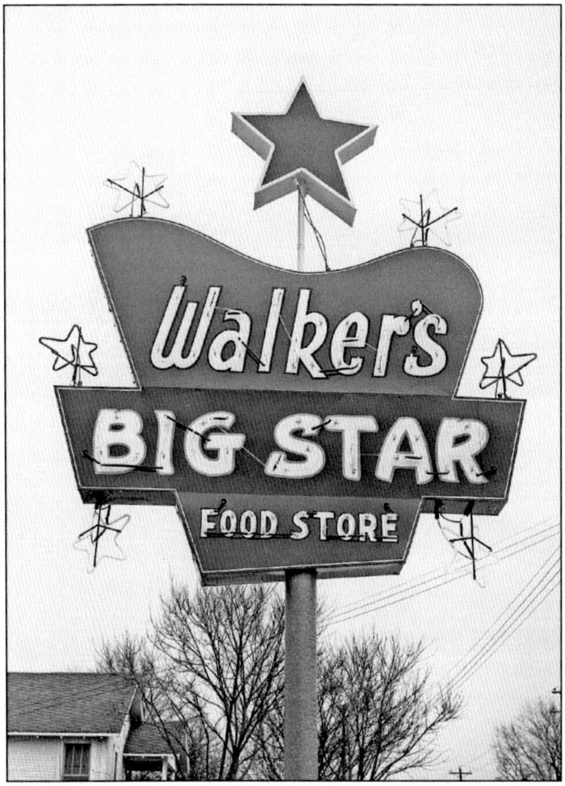

Walker's Big Star opened in 1965 as Fulton's first large-scale grocery store, and this familiar sign greeted customers for many years on Main Street. Roy Murl Walker entered the grocery business in 1959 when he bought Scott's Grocery and Market from Burnell W. Scott. Scott's Grocery was located on the square in downtown Fulton in the former location of Jim's Sandwich Shop.

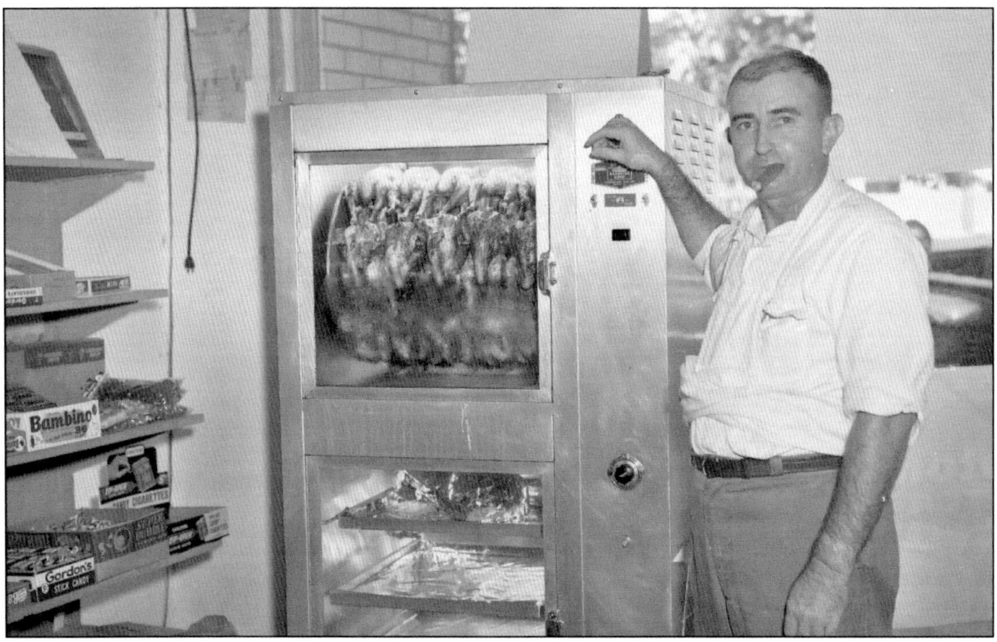

Burnell W. Scott, nephew of Angelo Scott, the founder and owner of A. Scott Grocery & Feed, stands by a newfangled chicken-roasting machine in his store in 1957. Burnell served as an alderman for the town of Fulton and later as a county supervisor. Today, "A. Scott 1953" can still be seen at the top of the building on the east side of the court square.

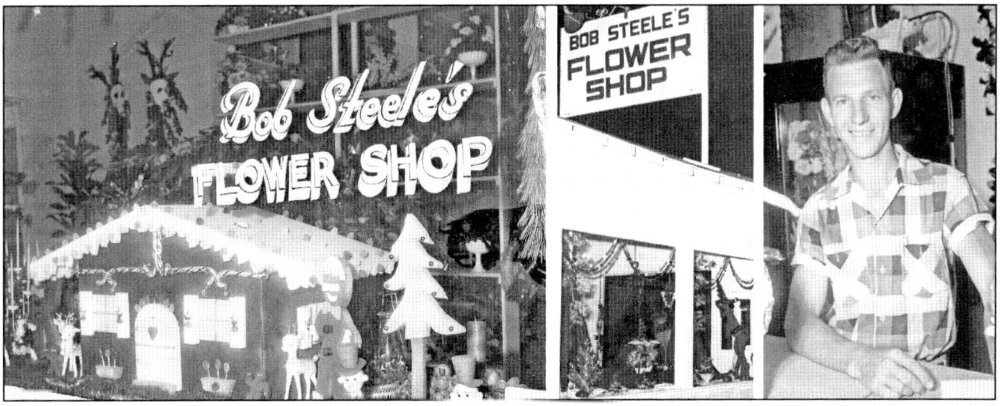

Bob Steele was hired in 1949 as manager of Debow's Florist and Gift Shop but later opened his own store, Bob Steele's Flower Shop. For many years, the shop was on the southeast corner of Clifton and Main Streets, but later moved to the former Western Auto location on Main Street. Several generations bought gifts and flowers at Bob Steele's before the family closed the store in 2016.

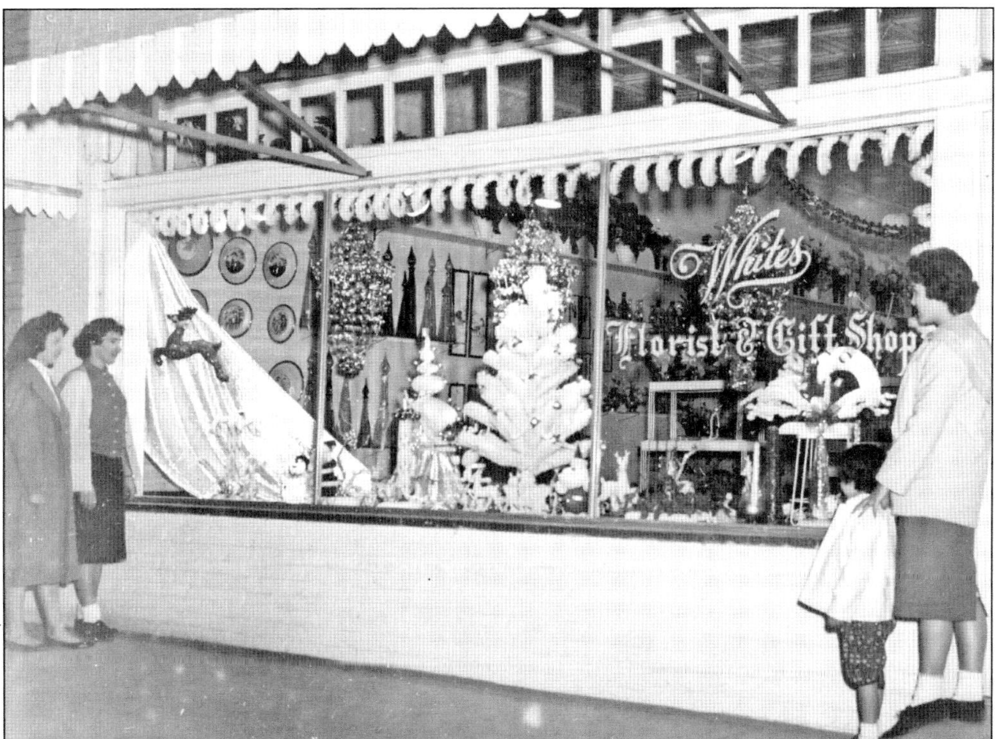

White's Florist and Gift Shop was owned by Bill and Kathleen White and was located on the west side of the court square, next to Fulton Bank. The Whites later closed the store to focus on the wholesale floral business. This storefront scene is from 1959.

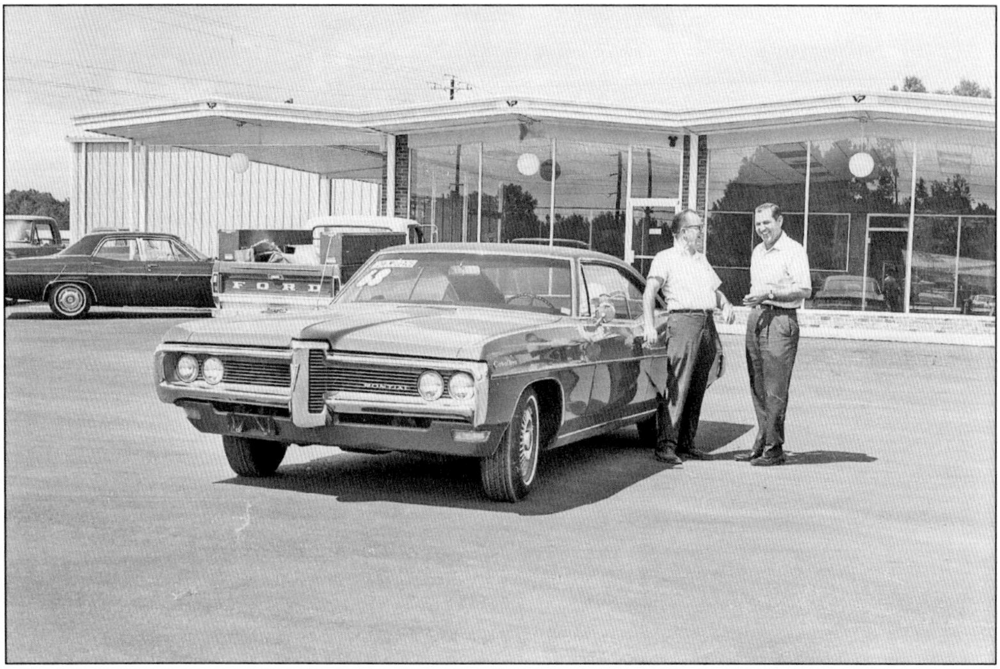

The last remaining automobile dealership in Fulton is also its oldest, having been established in 1921. Buster Davis bought the Ford dealership in 1964, when he was a successful basketball coach at Itawamba Junior College, and moved the business in 1969 to its present location, the site of the former McKee Tourist Courts. Davis (right), pictured with customer Cleveland Franks, still runs the business today.

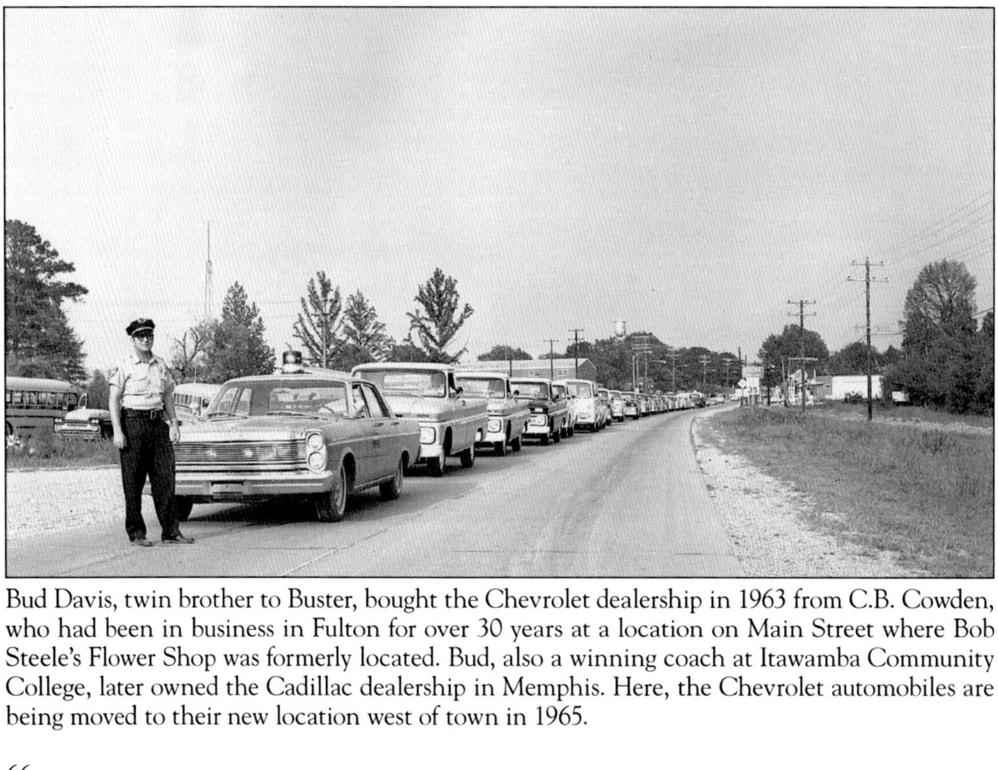

Bud Davis, twin brother to Buster, bought the Chevrolet dealership in 1963 from C.B. Cowden, who had been in business in Fulton for over 30 years at a location on Main Street where Bob Steele's Flower Shop was formerly located. Bud, also a winning coach at Itawamba Community College, later owned the Cadillac dealership in Memphis. Here, the Chevrolet automobiles are being moved to their new location west of town in 1965.

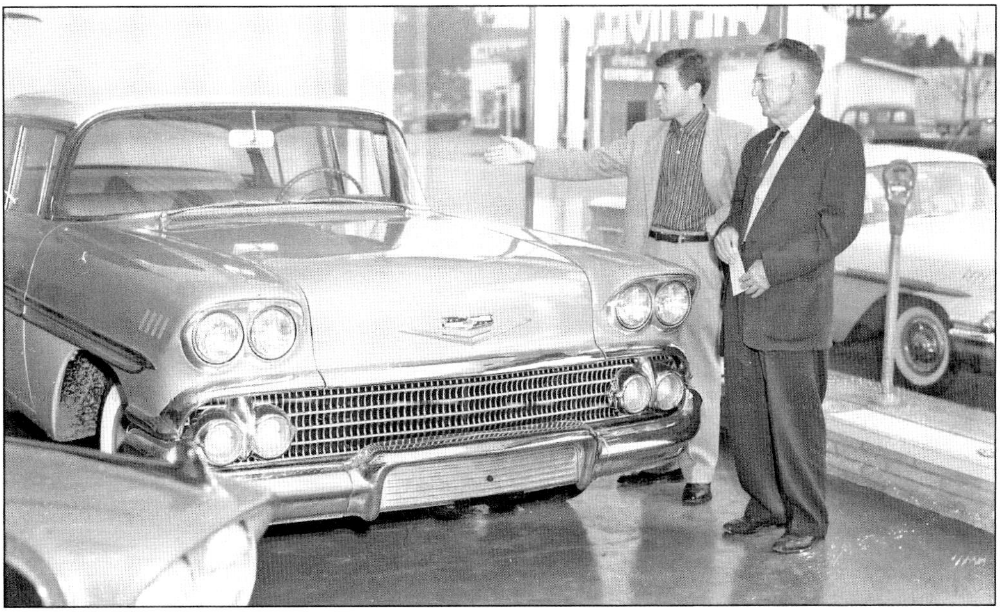

Cowden Chevrolet Company was a longtime automobile dealership in downtown Fulton that opened about 1930. In 1957, manager E.R. Garofalo (left) and owner C.B. Cowden look over the recently arrived new-model Chevrolet. Through the window, the Texaco service station located where the post office is today can be seen.

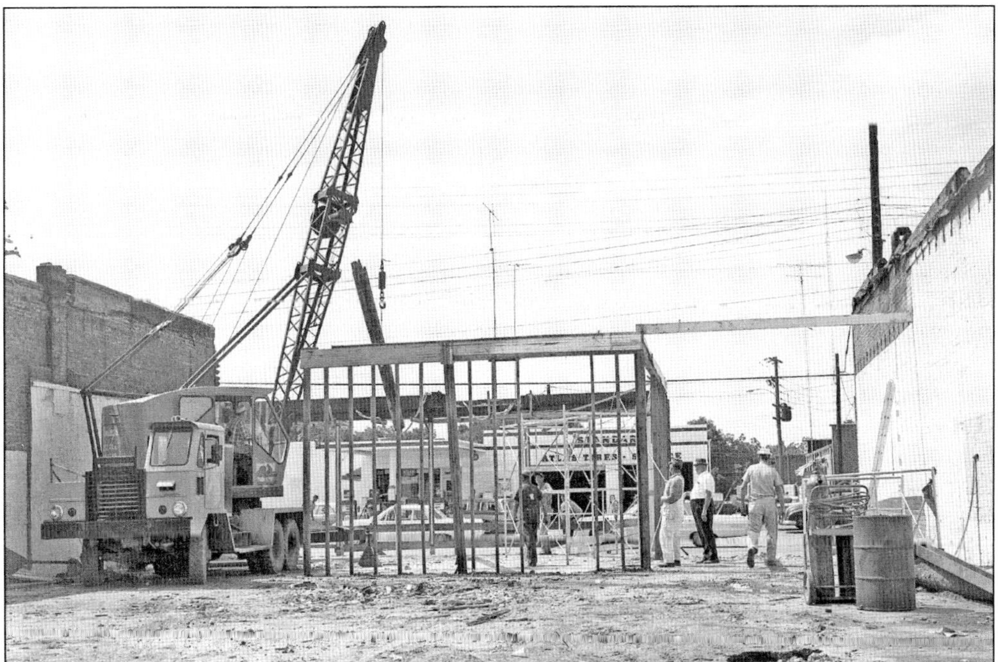

After the Chevrolet dealership was moved west of Fulton in 1965 to a new location (now home to Tombigbee Electric Power Association), the old building was torn down to make room for the new Western Auto Store. In later years, Bob Steele's flower shop occupied the building, its third and final location. Here is the scene from 1965 when the old dealership building was torn down.

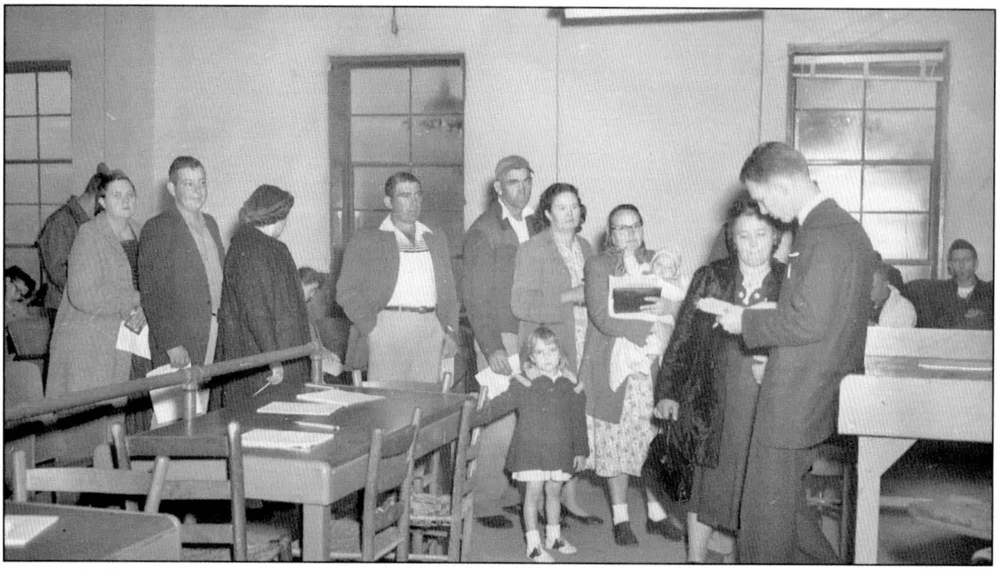

General Shoe Company, or GENESCO, later known locally as Charm Step, opened its doors in a newly built, modern manufacturing plant in 1958, hiring about 200 employees to produce women's shoes. In this photograph from November 1957, potential employees line up with their applications at the county's courtroom.

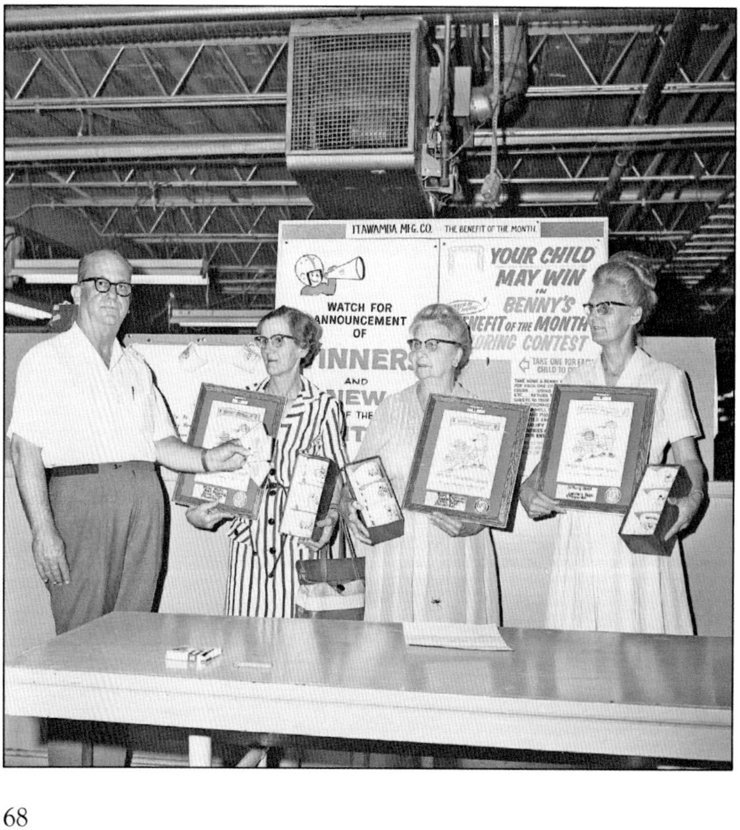

Rex Brown of Itawamba Manufacturing Company awards prizes to employees (from left to right) Pearl Dulaney, Capitola Bowman, and Lila McCarley in 1968. The homegrown company started in 1948 in a building uptown on West Wiygul Street across from the former Baptist church and later moved to a new plant location south of town, where it became a leading employer in Fulton for many years.

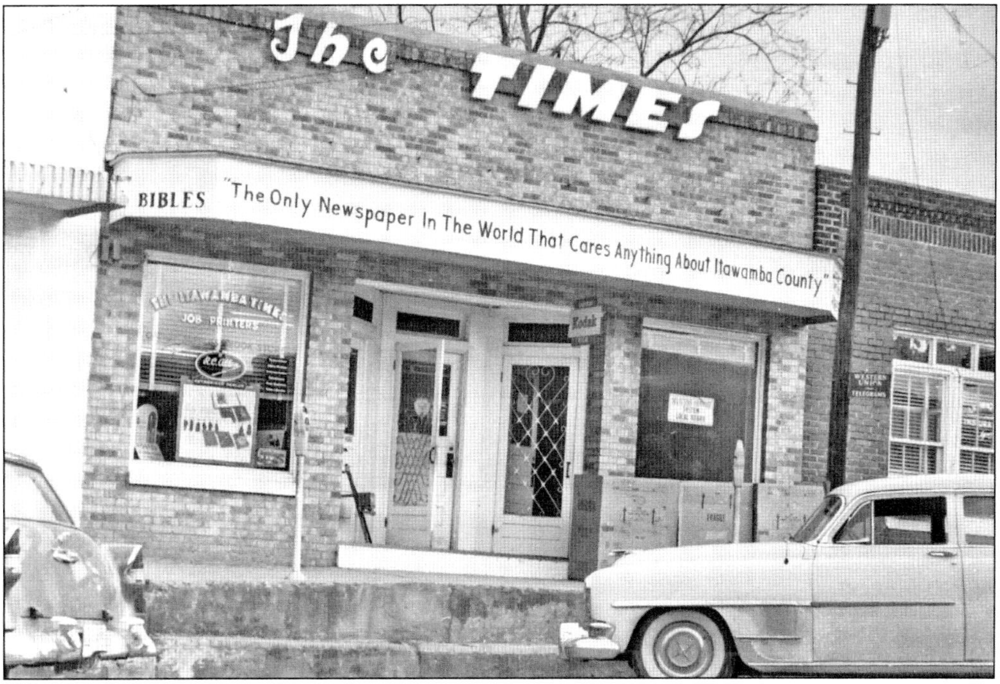

Delmus Harden took over as owner and publisher of the *Itawamba County Times* in 1945 and adopted the slogan "The Only Newspaper in the World That Cares Anything about Itawamba County." After his death in 1977, the newspaper was published at varying times by his daughters, Rubye Del and Rosa Lee. The newspaper plant was originally located on North Gaither Street, as shown here about 1959.

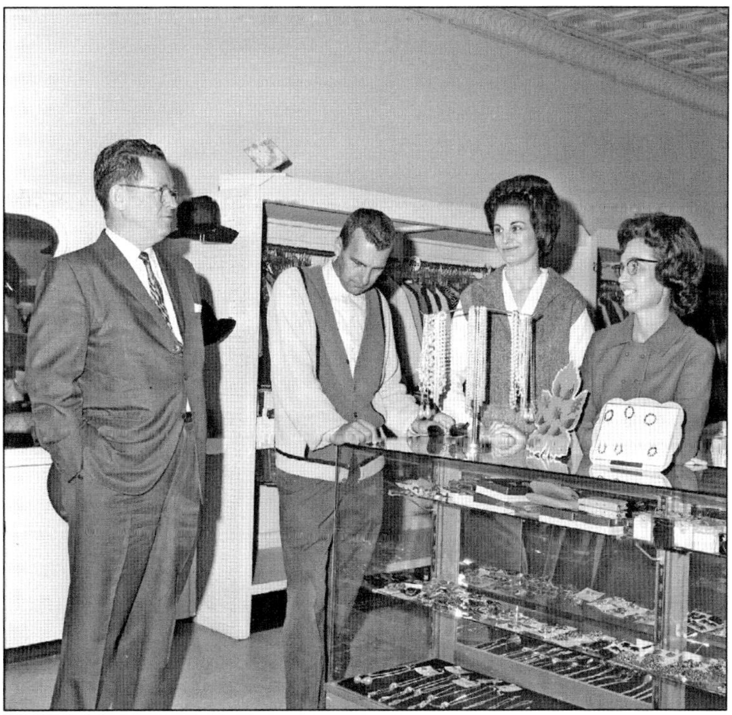

The Children's Shop held its grand opening on February 23, 1946, and operated for just over 70 years in the same location, closing its doors following the death of owner Margueritte Senter Critz. Generations of children wore clothes purchased from "Mrs. Margueritte," and many fond memories remain of her and her store. In 1966, Critz (far right) visits with Congressman Jamie Whitten (left).

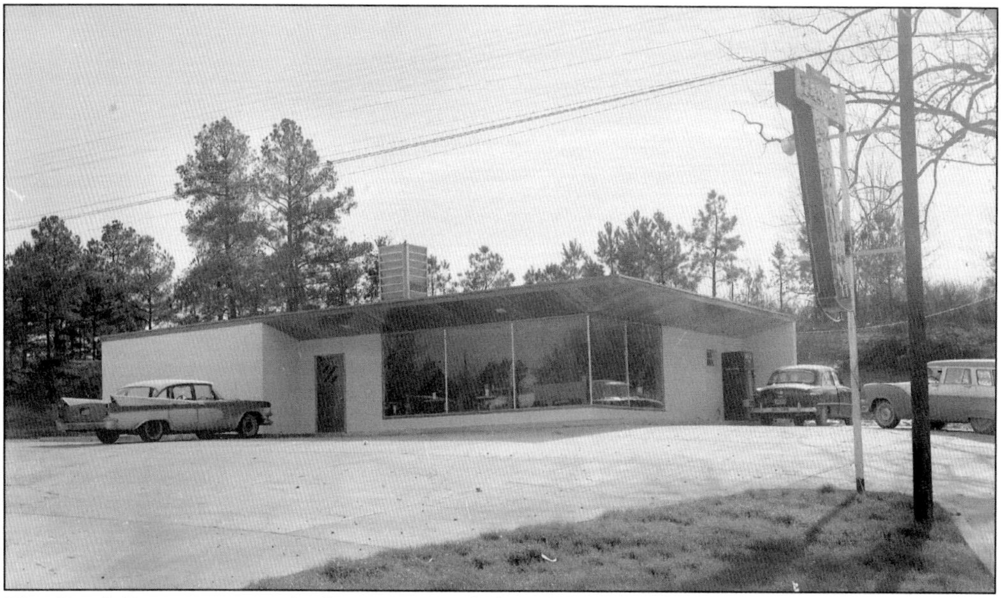

The Sands Restaurant was built in 1957, and the adjoining motel was built the following year by Mr. and Mrs. Tommy Strawhorn. The motel and restaurant served locals as well as travelers along Highway 78 between Birmingham and Memphis. For many years, the Sands Motel was the only lodging available in Fulton, but the new four-lane highway bypassed town and greatly affected business.

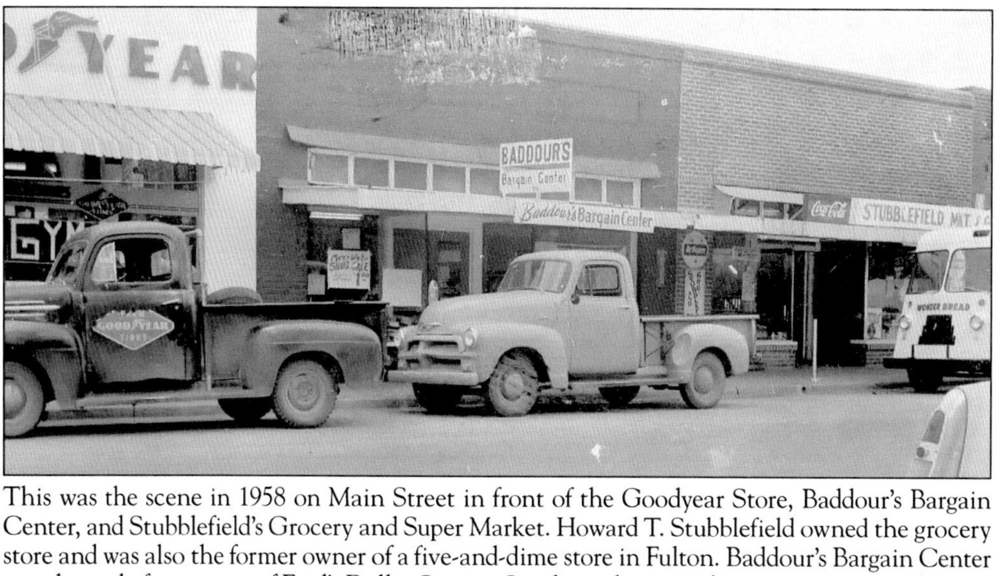

This was the scene in 1958 on Main Street in front of the Goodyear Store, Baddour's Bargain Center, and Stubblefield's Grocery and Super Market. Howard T. Stubblefield owned the grocery store and was also the former owner of a five-and-dime store in Fulton. Baddour's Bargain Center was the early forerunner of Fred's Dollar Store, a Southern discount department store with roots in Mississippi.

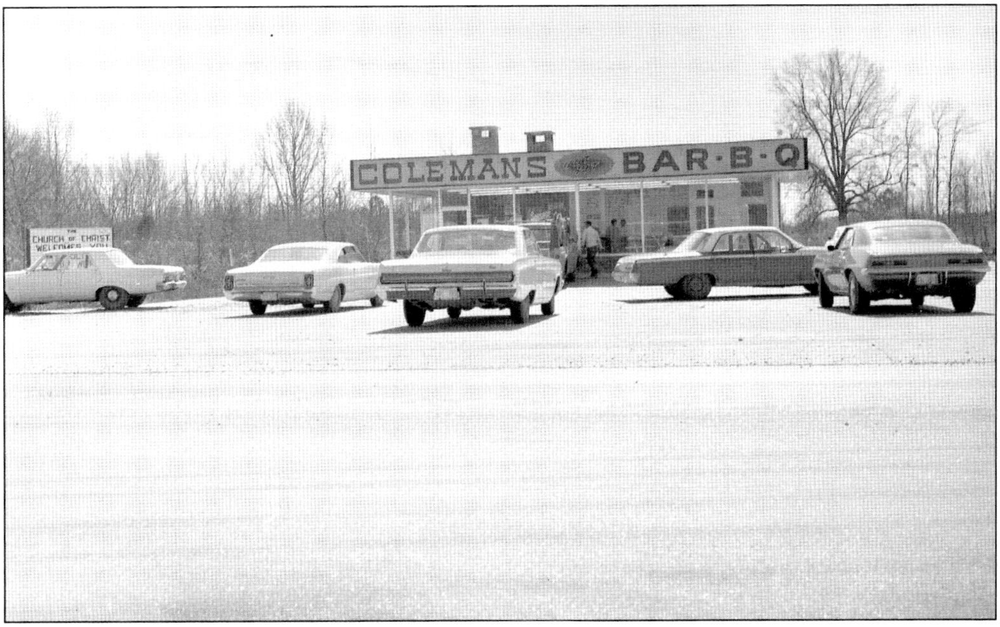

Coleman's Bar-B-Que started in Tupelo and became one of the largest barbecue chain restaurants in the Mid-South. About 1970, a restaurant franchise opened just west of Fulton along busy Highway 78 serving locals, travelers, and college students. After the highway was rerouted, business declined, and the restaurant closed.

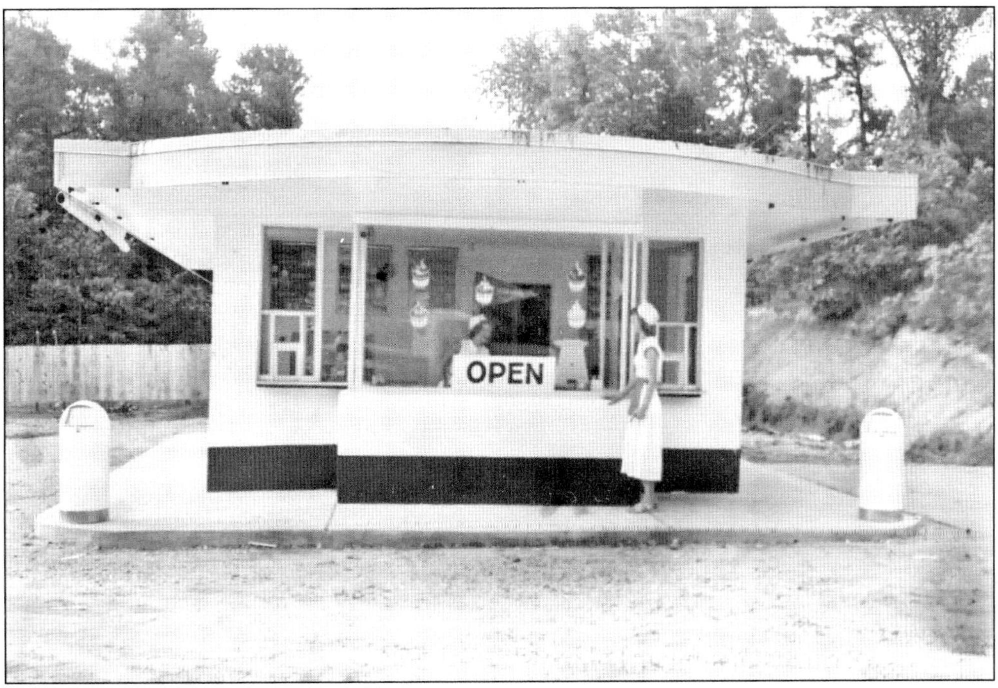

Tastee-Freeze was Fulton's first modern-day dairy cream bar. Located east of town on Highway 78, about where Kwik Sak is now, the ice cream and sandwich shop was opened by John Paul Harrison in 1953. Later owners were William and Charlie Mae Kilpatrick, Marvin and Jeffie Haynes, and Shorty Hughes.

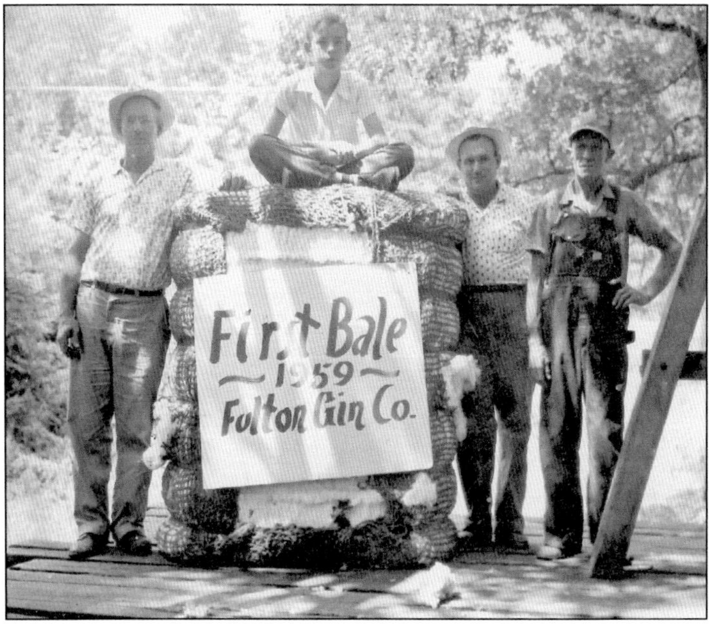

In 1959, the first bale of cotton was ginned at Fulton Gin Company. Grown by Leland Pierce, left, and his son Jerry, seated atop the bale, it weighed 493 pounds. Also pictured are manager C. Dulaney (second from right) and ginner Ott Gann (far right). Old-timers will remember the gin at the intersection of Highways 78 and 25 just east of downtown Fulton. Cotton played a big role in the county before the economy switched more to industry during the 1950s and 1960s.

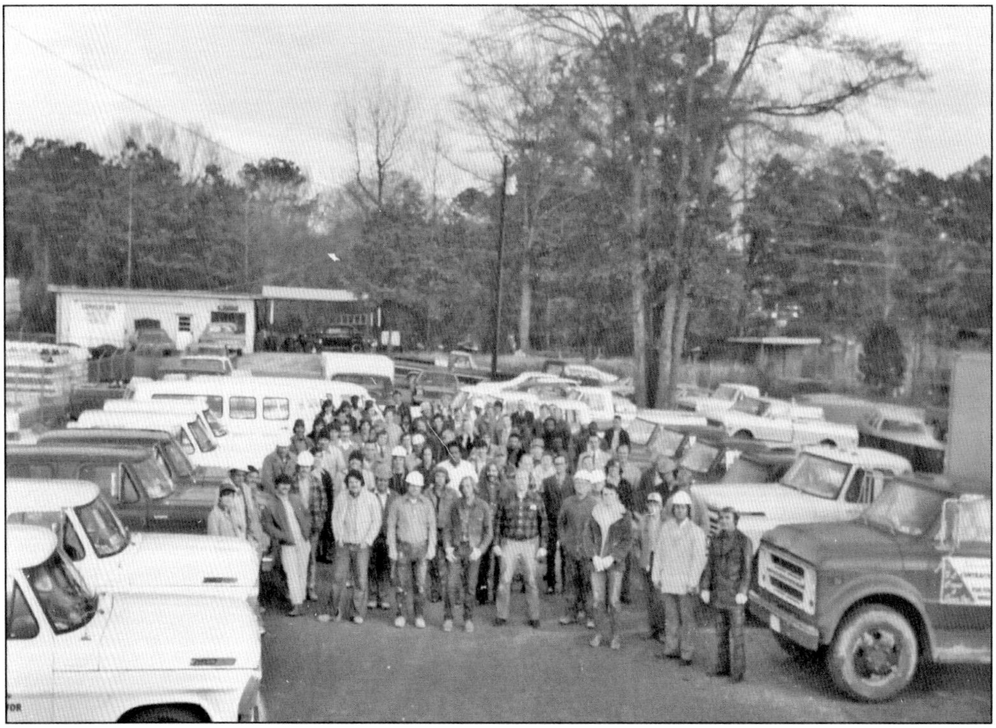

F.L. Crane & Sons was founded by Floy Lee Crane in 1947 as a drywall business, and under the leadership of his sons, Jimmie and Johnny, the company grew to be one of the leading finishing contractors in the country, headquartered in Fulton. Today it employs over 500 workers. The company continues to be locally owned.

Four

School Time

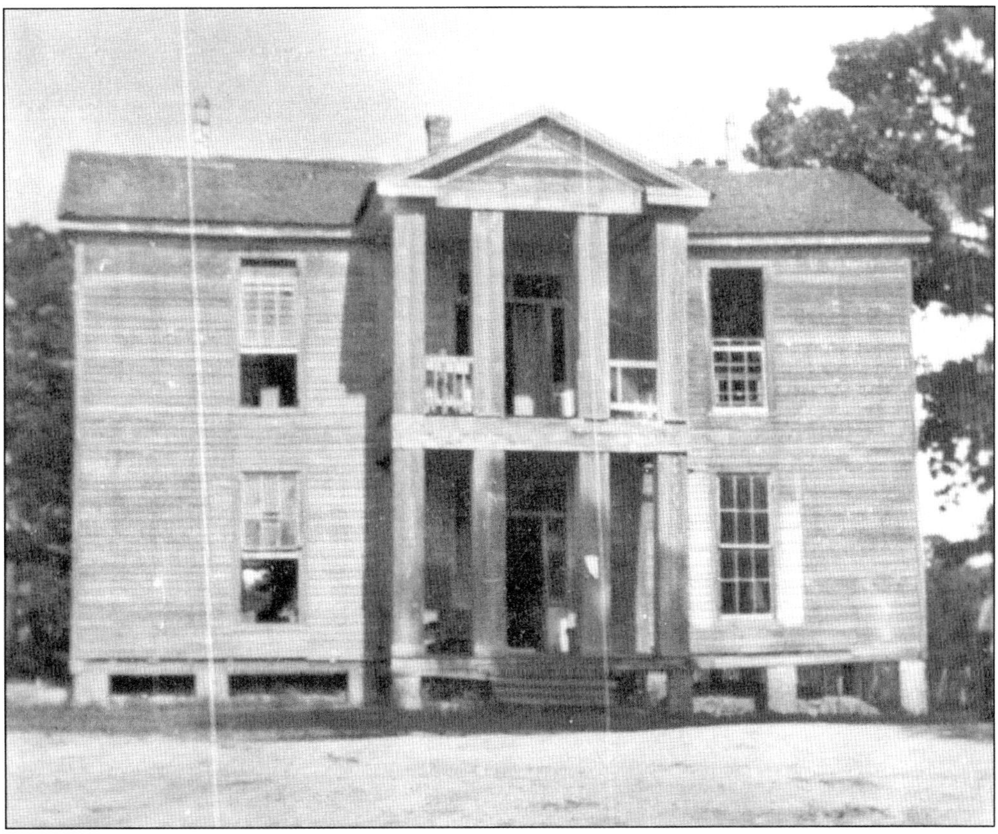

According to local historian Zereda Greene, who attended school in this building starting in 1903, this two-story Fulton School was in use at least by 1883 and served the community until 1922, when it was dismantled and replaced by a more modern structure. The school was located on lots later occupied by the Stubblefield and Alexander homes on Clifton Street.

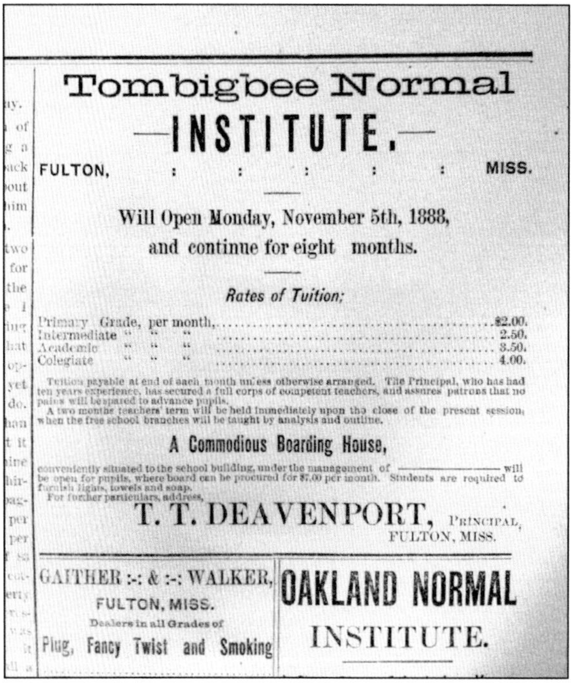

Tombigbee Normal

—INSTITUTE.—

FULTON, : : : : : MISS.

Will Open Monday, November 5th, 1888,

and continue for eight months.

Rates of Tuition;

Primary Grade, per month,	$2.00.
Intermediate " " "	2.50.
Academic " " "	3.50.
Colegiate " " "	4.00.

Tuition payable at end of each month unless otherwise arranged. The Principal, who has had ten years experience, has secured a full corps of competent teachers, and assures patrons that no pains will be spared to advance pupils.

A two months teachers' term will be held immediately upon the close of the present session, when the free school branches will be taught by analysis and outline.

A Commodious Boarding House,

conveniently situated to the school building, under the management of ———— will be open for pupils, where board can be procured for $7.00 per month. Students are required to furnish lights, towels and soap.

For further particulars, address,

T. T. DEAVENPORT, Principal,
FULTON, MISS.

GAITHER :-: & :-: WALKER,
FULTON, MISS.
Dealers in all Grades of
Plug, Fancy Twist and Smoking

OAKLAND NORMAL
INSTITUTE.

Early schools were subscription schools or private academies, such as the Fulton Male Academy, located near the present Fulton Cemetery in 1850. The Civil War disrupted the educational process, and for some time following the war, there were no schools operating in Itawamba County. Tombigbee Normal Institute, advertised in this 1888 issue of the *Fulton Reporter* newspaper, served the town of Fulton for several years.

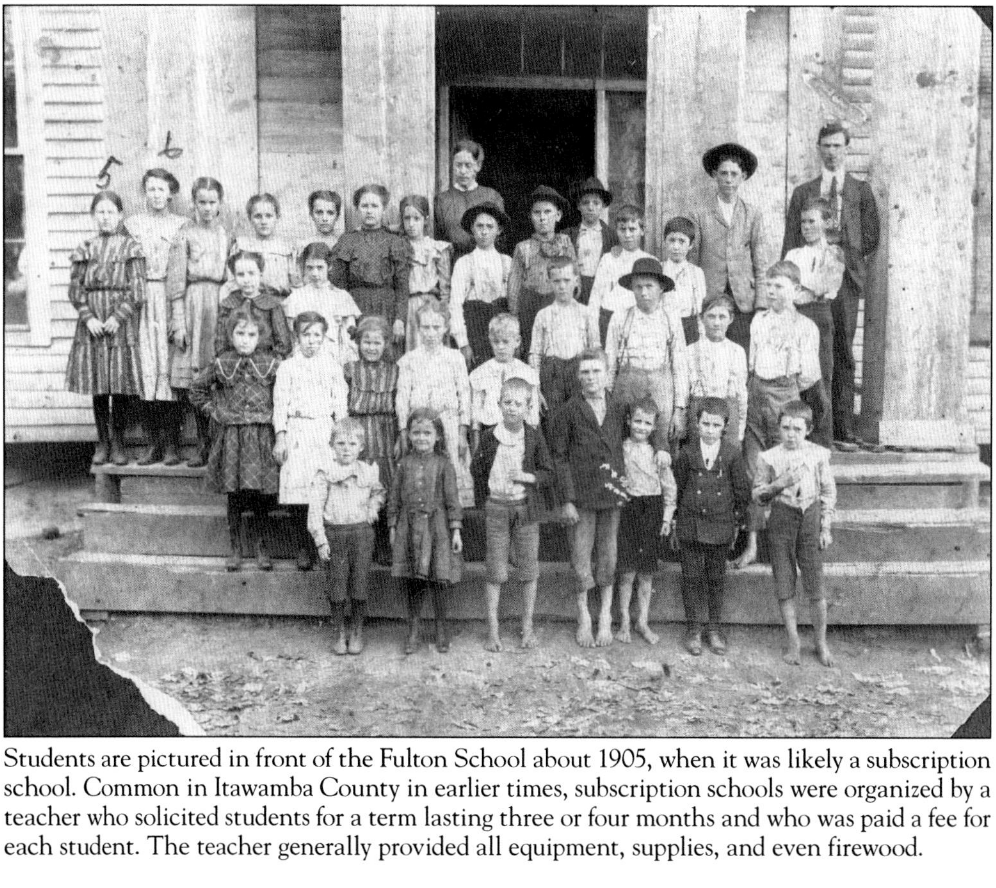

Students are pictured in front of the Fulton School about 1905, when it was likely a subscription school. Common in Itawamba County in earlier times, subscription schools were organized by a teacher who solicited students for a term lasting three or four months and who was paid a fee for each student. The teacher generally provided all equipment, supplies, and even firewood.

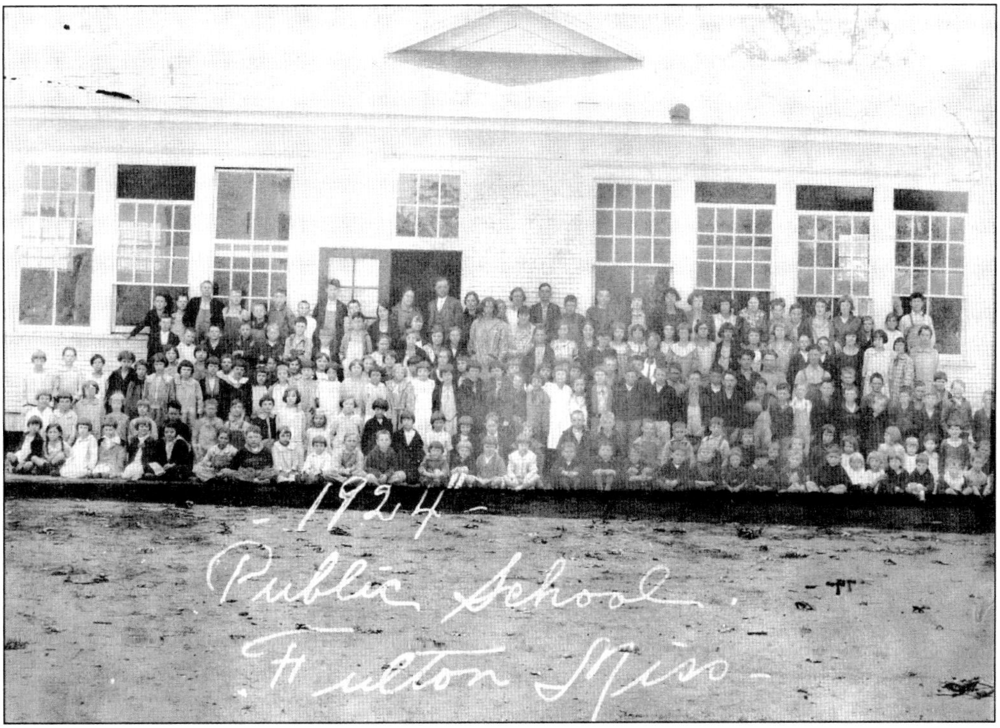

Fulton built a new school in 1921 for its younger students in grades one through eight. Located on Clifton Street near the earlier school, this new wood-frame building was used until destroyed by fire during the 1939–1940 school year. As evidenced in this 1924 picture, a large number of students enrolled in the Fulton Public School. During this period, Fulton was undergoing an economic and population boom due to the flourishing timber industry.

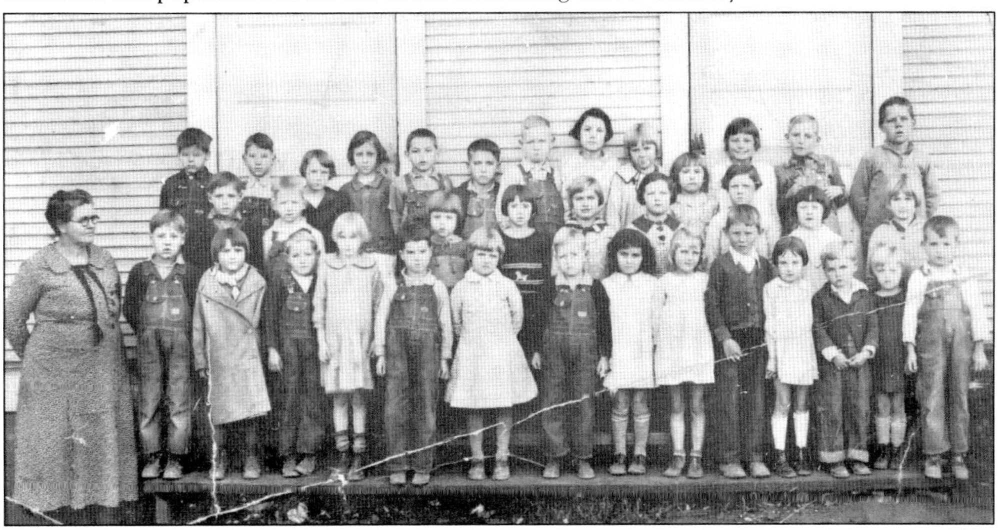

Josie Sims was the teacher for this class of 36 students at Fulton Public School about 1933. Other teachers during the early 1930s were Euple Thornberry, Reda Brown, Marie Prestage, T. Moore, Gertie Kilpatrick, W.G. Rutledge, Irene Burch, Corrinne Ballard, Verdie Reed, Thelma Spencer, and Bessie Gregory. The school had 12 classrooms, with music, expression, and dancing taught as special courses.

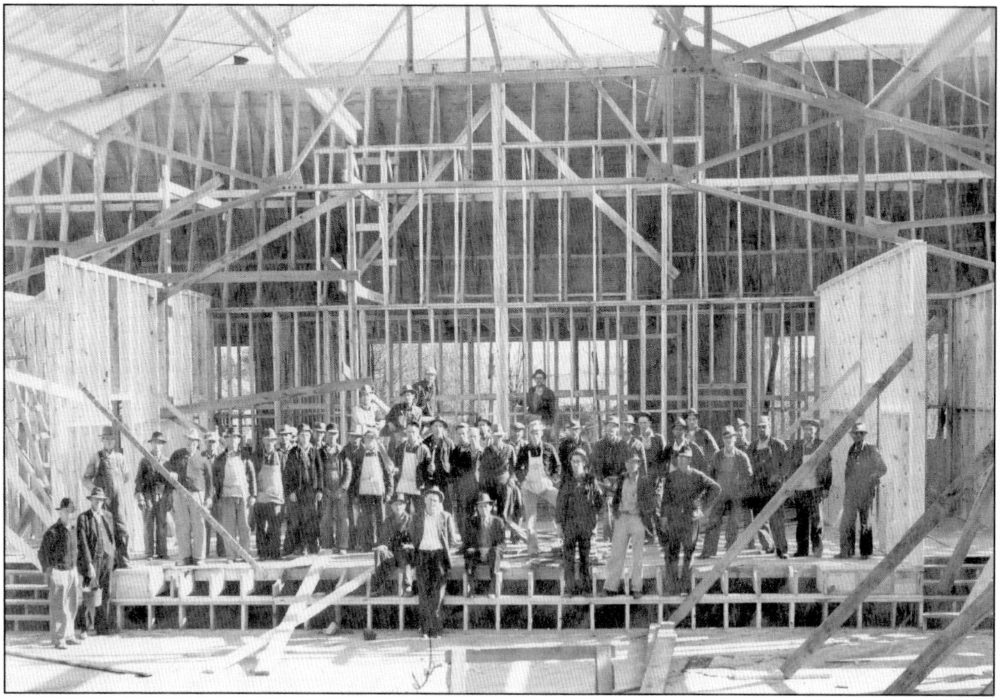

Construction workers pause for a photograph in 1941 while building Fulton's new grammar school. The school was built as a project of the Works Project Administration at a cost of about $80,000; the federal government paid $34,000, and the local government contributed the rest through the issuance of school bonds. During the interim period when the new school was being constructed, students attended class in temporary barracks.

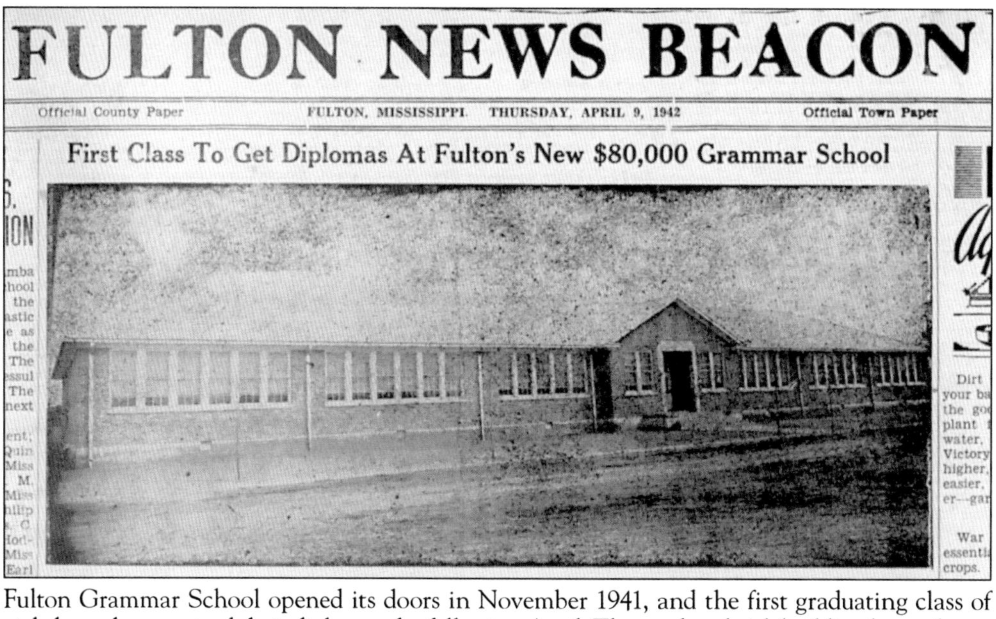

FULTON NEWS BEACON

Official County Paper FULTON, MISSISSIPPI THURSDAY, APRIL 9, 1942 Official Town Paper

First Class To Get Diplomas At Fulton's New $80,000 Grammar School

Fulton Grammar School opened its doors in November 1941, and the first graduating class of eighth-graders received their diplomas the following April. The modern brick building housed over 600 students, led by Principal R.L. McDonald. Two of the features of the new school were a modern steam heating plant and a large auditorium that is still being used today for community events.

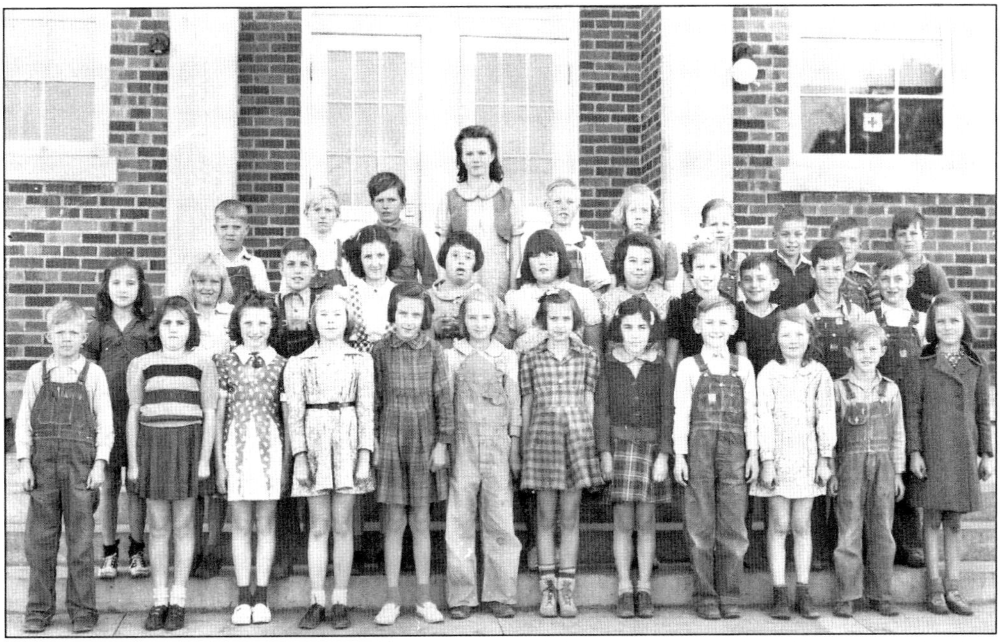

Halivee Dulaney's third-grade class poses in front of the newly built Fulton Grammar School in 1941. From left to right are (first row) Edward Holiday, Ann Roberts, Jean Betts, Elween Pearce, Wilma Comer, Millie Steele, unidentified, Armentha Bourland, David Mattox, Lovie Moore, Peewee Robinson, and Raomi Pearce; (second row) Galaine Reeves, unidentified, Noel Morris, Elizabeth Miller, Dot Gaither, unidentified, Louise Coker, Betty Jo Tucker, Travis Staub, Pete Miller, and Jo Pierce; (third row) Frank Pearce, two unidentified, Halivee Dulaney, unidentified, Maureen Franks, Romie Wilemon, unidentified, Frank Davis, and Otis Ray Wilson.

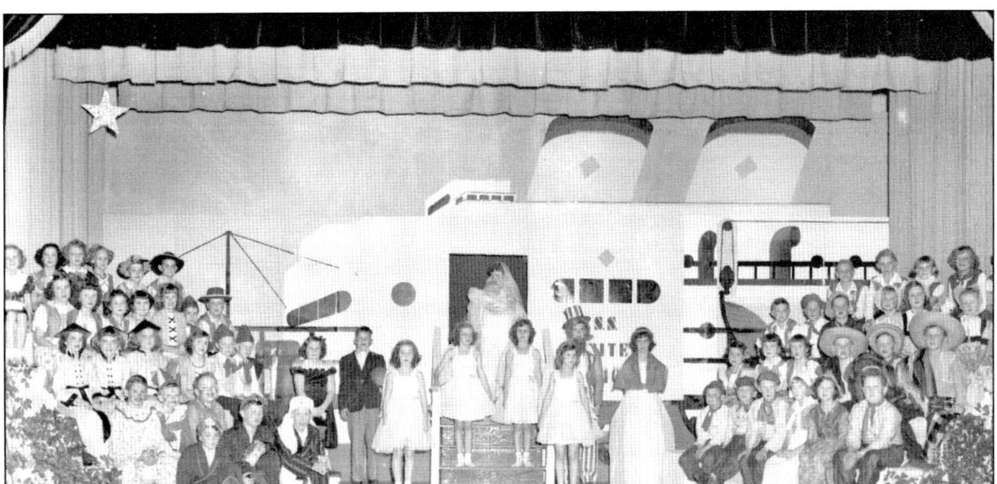

The new auditorium at Fulton Grammar School was quickly put to good use. Prior to the school auditorium being completed, Fultonians used the Dixie Theatre or the courtroom on the second floor of the courthouse for community gatherings, since the high school auditorium was more of a study hall, having desks instead of seats. Above, students from the fourth and fifth grades perform "Merry Christmas to the World" during the 1951 Christmas season.

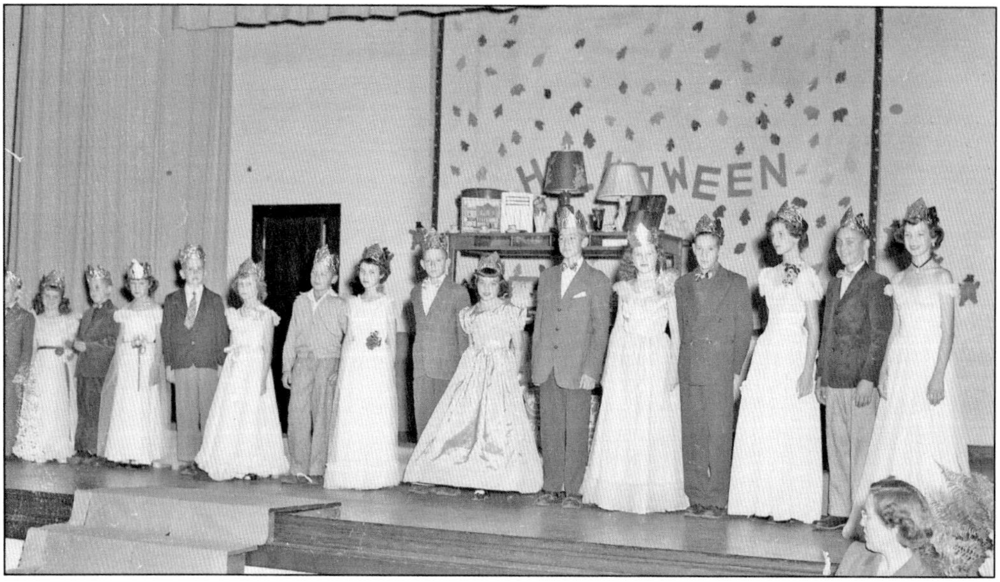

Above, competing for the Halloween King and Queen titles at Fulton Grammar School (FGS) in 1951 are, from left to right, Jerry Stubblefield and Glenda Gregory, Richard Prestage and Martha Ann Wood, Tommy Randle and Janice Overton, Neal Brown and Jan McKee, Phil Izard and Patsy Wiygul, Edward Christian and Rebecca Moore, Bernard Shaw and Edna Mae Shaw, and Tommy Bullard and Sarah McKinney. Contestants not pictured are Frankie Nanney and Sandra Roberts and Mitchie McNeece and Laura Crane. Below, FGS faculty entertain the crowd at the Halloween Carnival that same year. The performers are, from left to right, Principal Oren Wren, second-grade teacher Shelby Gilmore, and custodian Roy Maske. The Halloween Carnival was a tradition for many years at the grammar school.

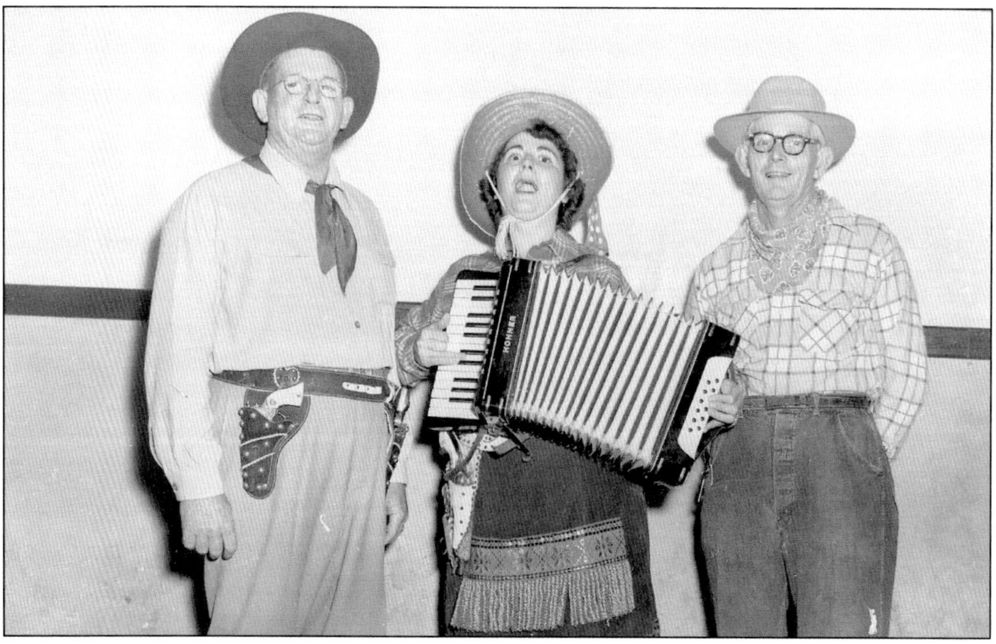

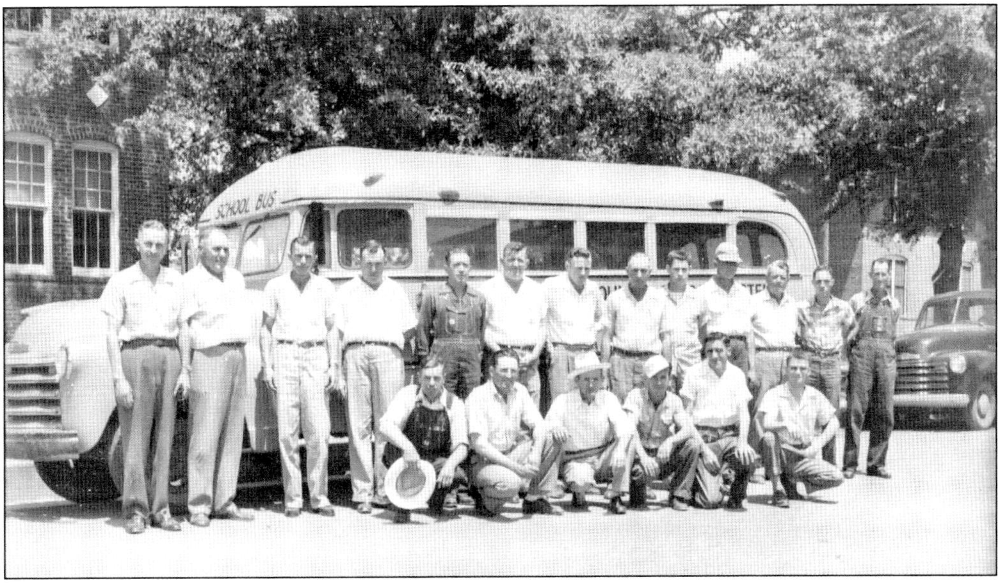

School bus drivers, like this group from 1954, attended yearly safety courses to remain up to date on state traffic regulations. In the early days, drivers bid on routes at their local schools and were paid by the families to transport their children. School consolidation eliminated many routes, and eventually the county bought buses and hired drivers. From left to right are (kneeling) W.L. Grissom, T.E. Ray, C.E. Russell, H.C. Tennison, Windle Walton, and Hulon Gray; (standing) instructor John Shelton, Coy Wilson, N.E. Swindle, C. Dulaney, M.C. Rushing, R.S. Jamerson, L.M. Kennedy, H.J. Guntharp, James Ballard, Dillard Murphy, W.J. Kennedy, Ted Johnson, and W.C. Young.

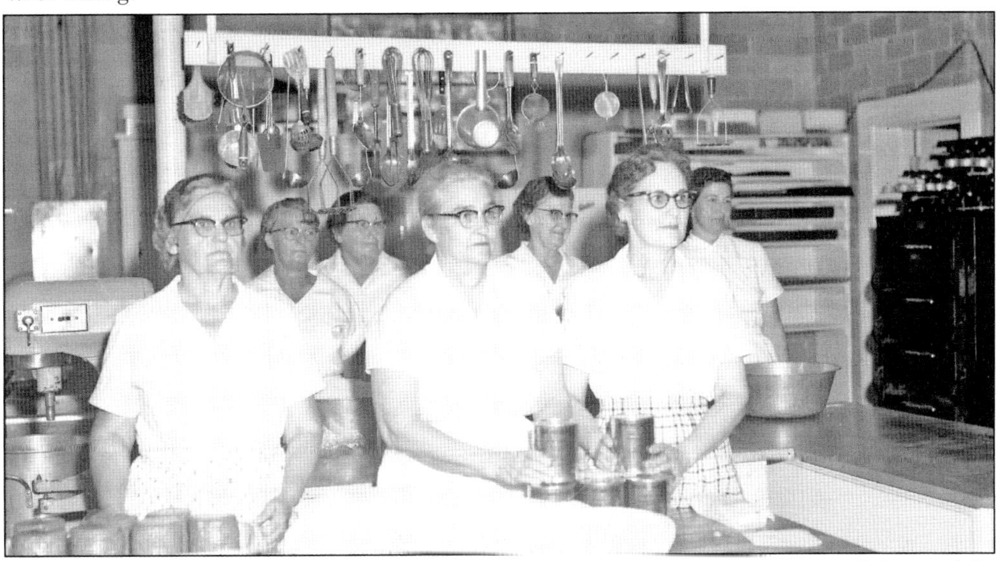

The principal at Fulton Grammar School, longtime educator D.R. Raper, promoted the need for a school lunchroom in 1952 and, with the assistance of editorials by Delmus Harden, secured approval for bond issuances to build the lunchroom. These cafeteria workers are pictured at the grammar school in 1962. From left to right are Mrs. Trenton Bennett, Mrs. Dorsey Green, Mrs. P.W. Montgomery, manager Mrs. Dexter McKee, Mrs. Ellis Bowen, Mrs. Nolan McKee, and Mrs. Dolan Moore.

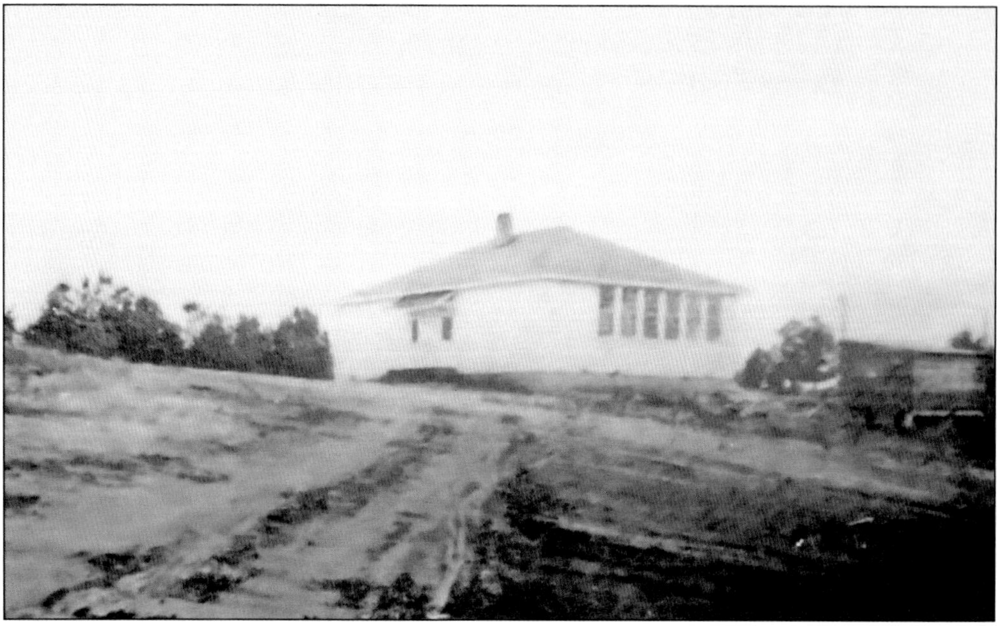

The two-room Shiloh School building was built in 1947 and served Fulton's African American students from grades one through eight during segregation. J.M. Gibbs purchased and donated an acre of land for the school building. O.C. Cullins, Nez Stone, Cleveland Clifton, and Tom Billups served on the building committee. Shiloh first shows up in the records in 1923 with Ozelle White as teacher, but a school for African Americans existed in Fulton before then. During the 1950s, two teachers taught an average of 50 students.

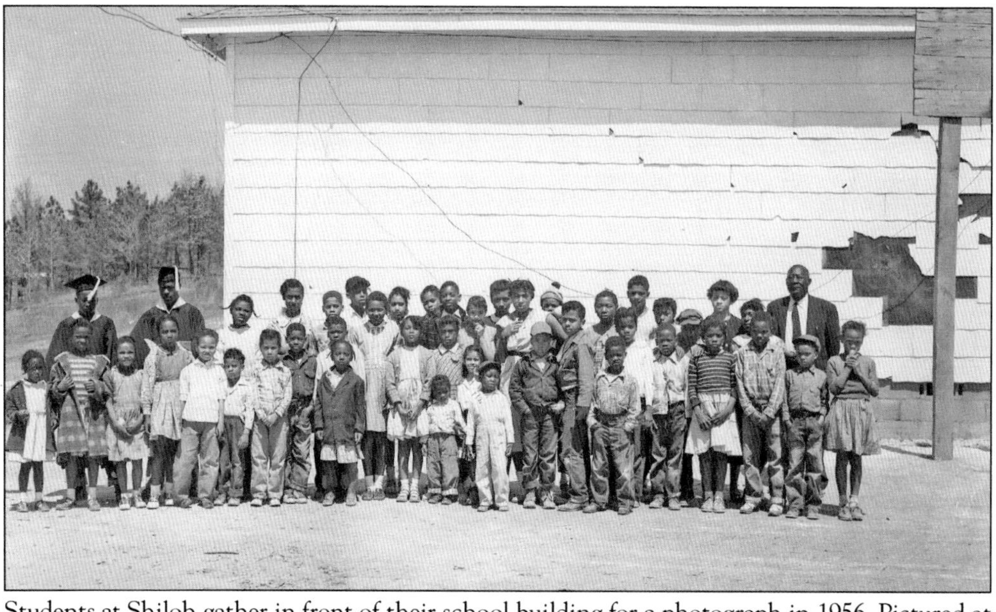

Students at Shiloh gather in front of their school building for a photograph in 1956. Pictured at far left are the two graduates of the eighth grade, Hayward Wilson and Charles Crayton. O.C. Cullins, far right, was the principal.

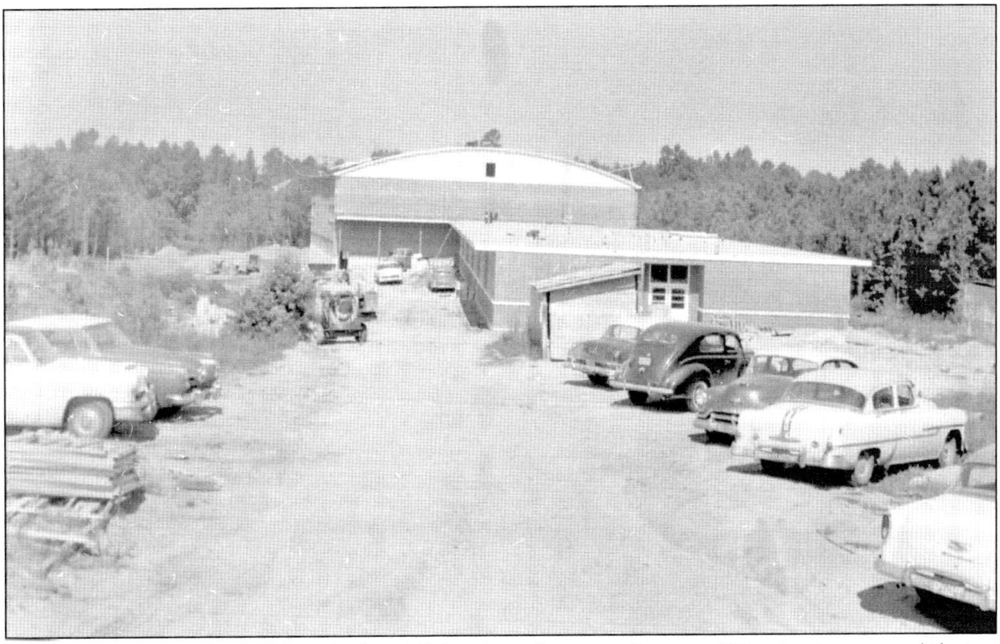

In 1958, the county built Fulton Colored School as a "separate but equal" institution, consolidating and closing all other schools for African American students. The school opened in September with 250 students. Edward Horton was principal with the following instructors: Lennell Luckett, Susie Mae Tucker, Mary Ruff, O.C. Cullins, Annie Lou Cummings, Comora Horton, Jewell Mae Turner, C.C. Cummings, and Dozie Lee Kilgore.

In 1962, Fulton Colored School's name was changed to East High School, although the school was also an elementary school. High school graduates in 1960 were, from left to right, Joe Casey, Monzell Dabbs, Hayward Wilson, Carol Pruitt, Willie Randolph, and Annie B. Stegall. Prior to 1958, the only option available to African American students in Fulton who wished to attend high school was to travel to Pleasant Grove, a school near Evergreen.

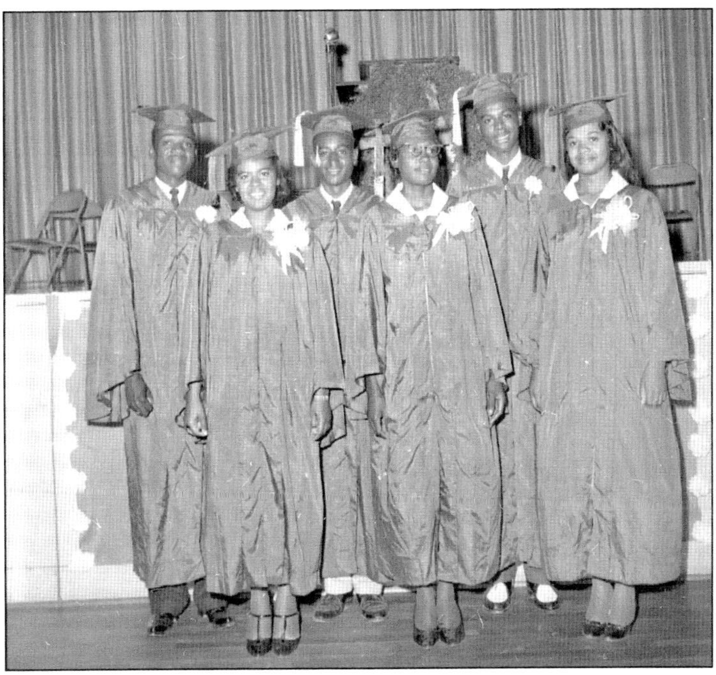

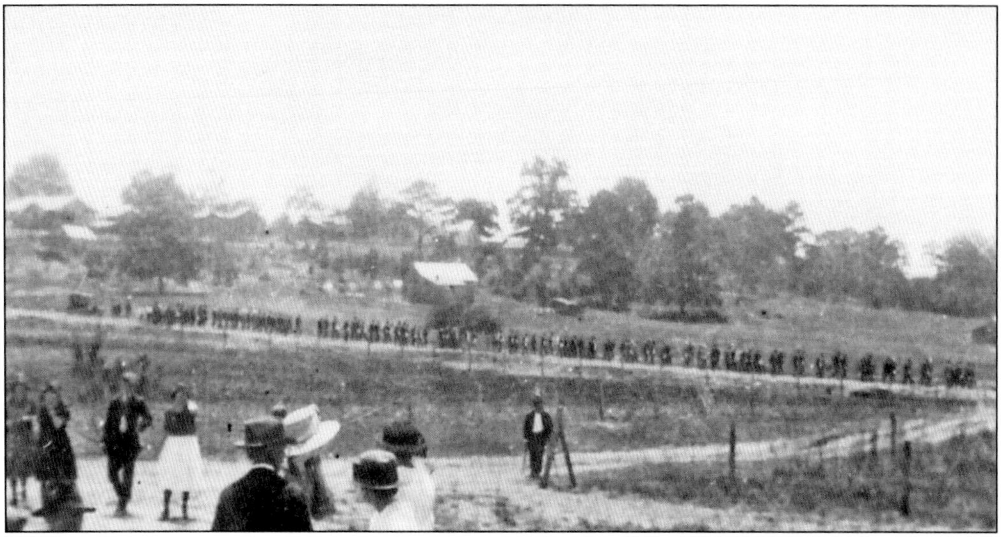

The laying of the cornerstone for Itawamba Agricultural High School (IAHS) took place at 11:00 a.m. on Thursday, May 19, 1921. The ceremony to dedicate the building was conducted by members of the Grand Masonic Lodge of Mississippi in conjunction with members of the local county lodges. A huge crowd gathered as citizens and dignitaries paraded on Bankhead Highway down the hill from the court square in Fulton. The entrance road shown here later became the main artery of the campus; today, it is a pedestrian-only thoroughfare.

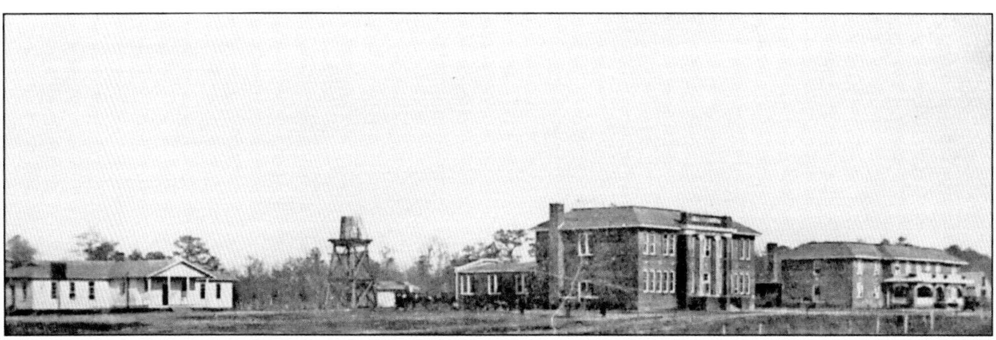

This 1922 photograph shows only part of the early grounds of IAHS; the campus comprised in total about 100 acres. From left to right are the wood-frame building that was the boys' first dormitory (it burned down in 1927); the Administration Building, which housed the classrooms and auditorium; and the girls' dormitory. Brick for the first buildings on the IAHS campus were made on site, using a boiler and engine that belonged to Sam Summers. A one-acre vegetable garden was planted just north of the first buildings.

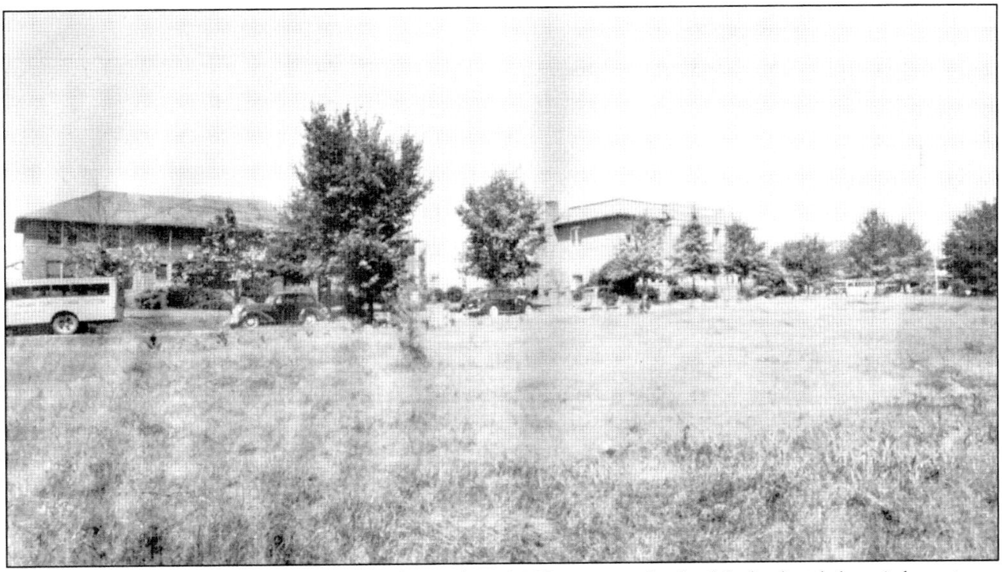

By 1939, when this photograph was taken, the IAHS campus had added a brick boys' dormitory (left, south of the Administration Building). The trees shown here were likely among the 50 that had been donated in 1921 by Congressman John E. Rankin, an Itawambian. Today, the photographer would be standing in the southeastern corner of the campus, in the general location of the parking lot of today's Student Services building at Itawamba Community College.

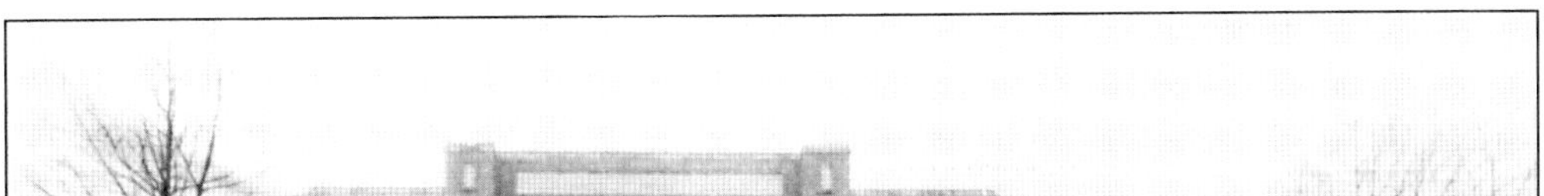

The two-story Administration Building originally housed male students on the top floor until a wooden dormitory was built for them the following year. About 150 students were enrolled the first year, many living on campus or boarding in homes of Fulton residents. As roads improved and bus transportation was initiated, fewer students lived on campus, and eventually the dormitories were turned into classrooms.

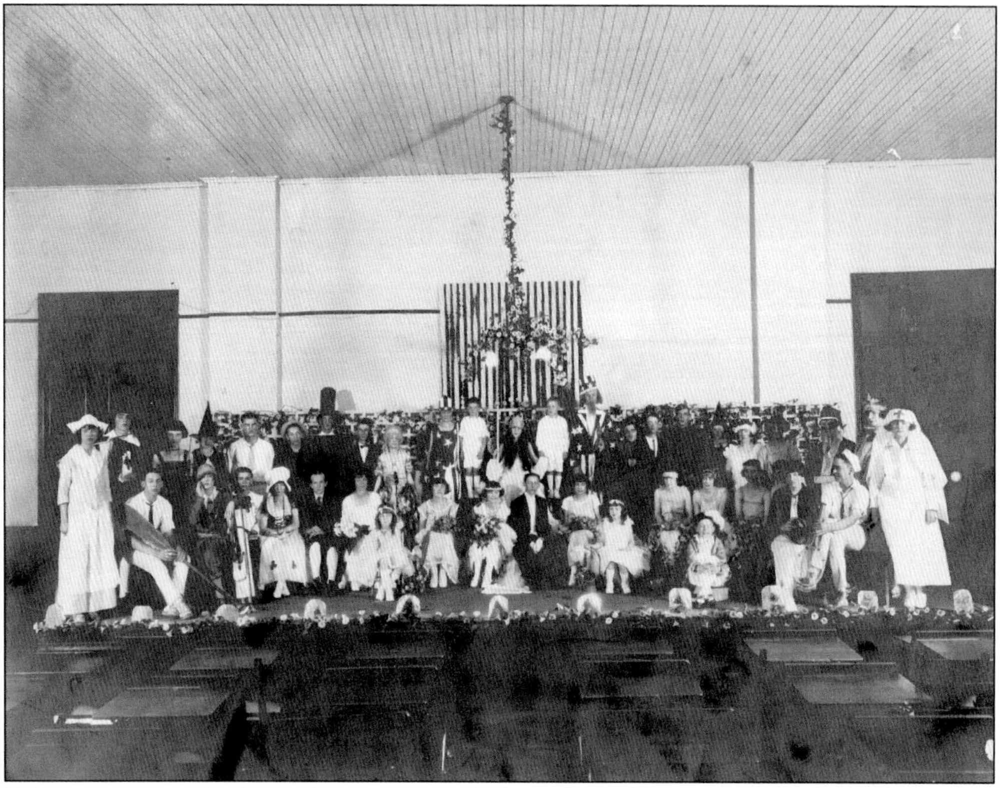

Tableaux were popular forms of entertainment before radio and "moving picture shows." According to Ruth Boren Sheffield, tableaux were frequently held at the new IAHS auditorium in the 1920s in which participants dressed as characters from literature or specific events in American history, often patriotic in nature. This scene is believed to date from about 1923. (Courtesy of Itawamba Historical Society, Benson Collection.)

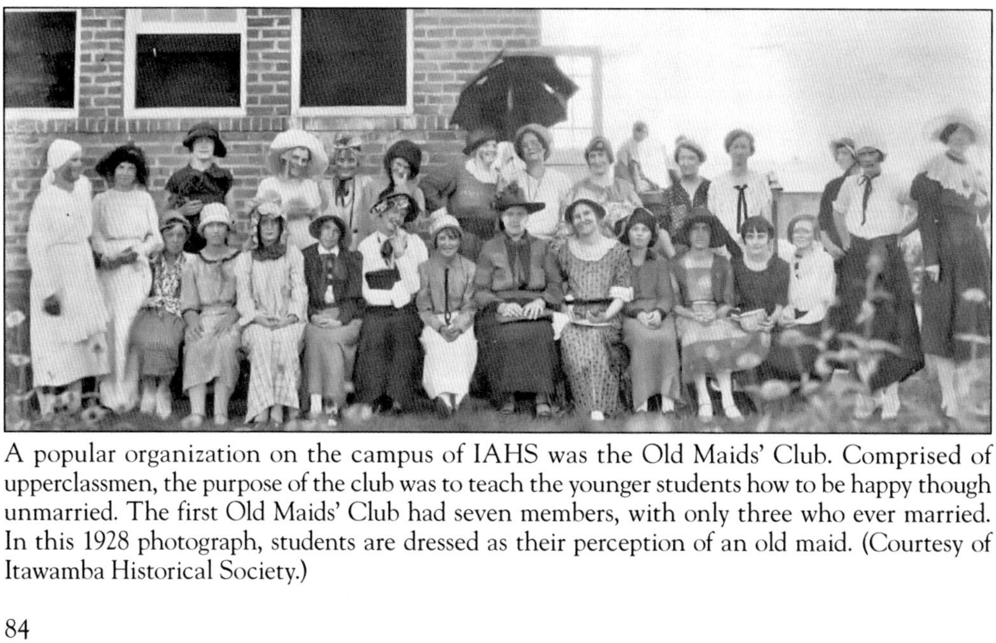

A popular organization on the campus of IAHS was the Old Maids' Club. Comprised of upperclassmen, the purpose of the club was to teach the younger students how to be happy though unmarried. The first Old Maids' Club had seven members, with only three who ever married. In this 1928 photograph, students are dressed as their perception of an old maid. (Courtesy of Itawamba Historical Society.)

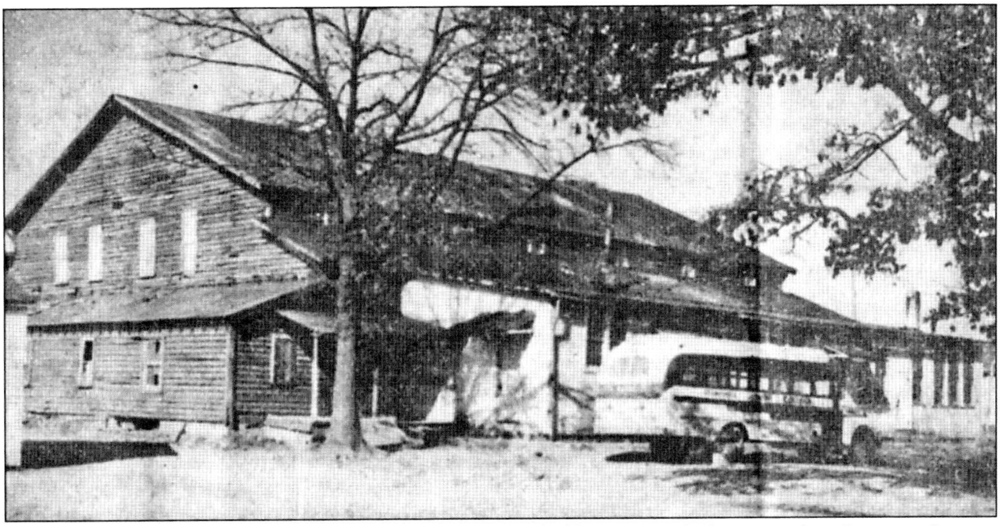

This gymnasium was home to the high school basketball teams and also served as the site of many tournaments played by county schools. Shortly after Itawamba Junior College started classes on the campus of the high school, this old wood-frame building was torn down and replaced in 1950 with a new brick structure that no longer stands, having been replaced by the Davis Event Center.

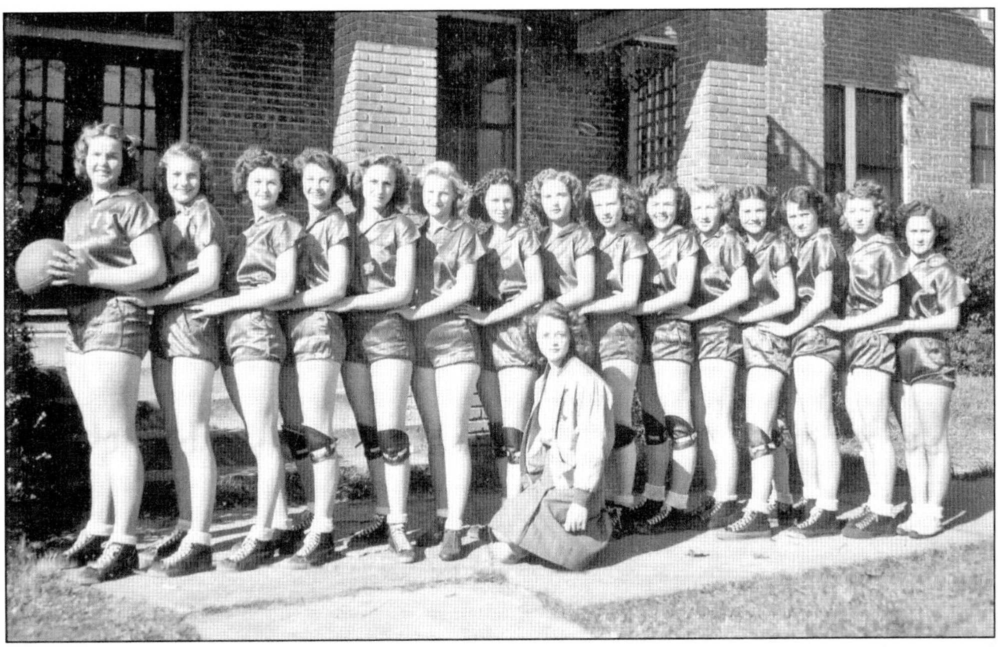

The 1947 girls' basketball team at IAHS continued the strong tradition of success at the regional and state levels, winning the state championship that year by defeating Cleveland. Members of the squad were, from left to right, Bertha Mae Reich, Dorothy Ford, Opal Pierce, Jane Williams, Lillian Sanderson, Zereda Grissom, Eva Mae Clayton, Esther Foster, Betty Jean Cole, Marlene Graham Huey, Wilma Joyce Stovall, Bennie Merle Spradling, Mildred Bullard, Medford McFerrin, and Sue Moore. Kneeling is manager Robbie Jean Nichols. The team was coached by Mary Nell Senter, who was on a state championship team herself a few years earlier.

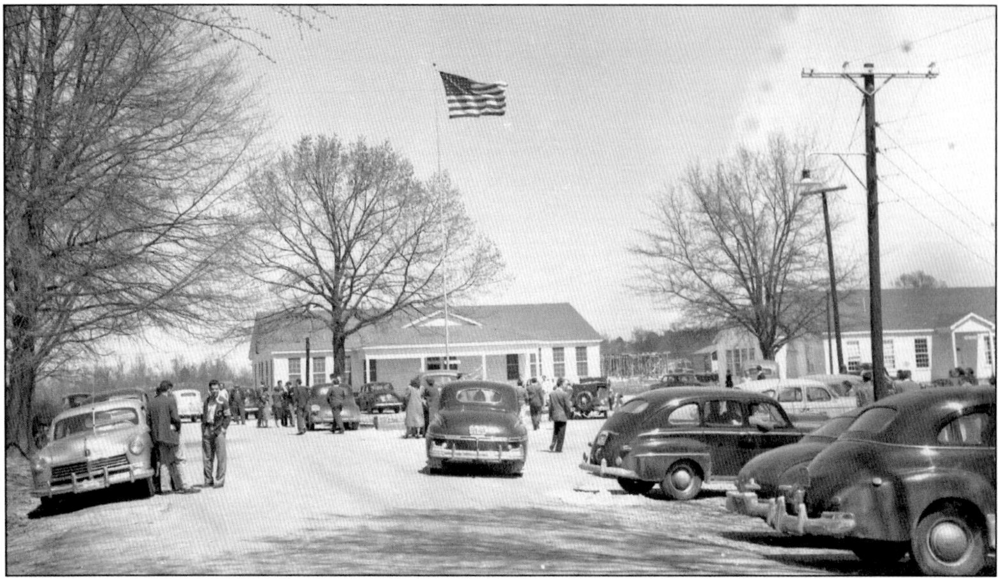

In 1948, Itawamba Junior College (IJC) began classes, coexisting on the same campus with the high school and sharing administration, instructors, school annuals, band, athletics, and more until 1993, when IAHS moved south of Fulton. To accommodate the additional students, the original high school campus underwent tremendous growth in the 1950s. In this busy scene in 1950, a new recreation hall stands on the left, and the home economics building is on the right.

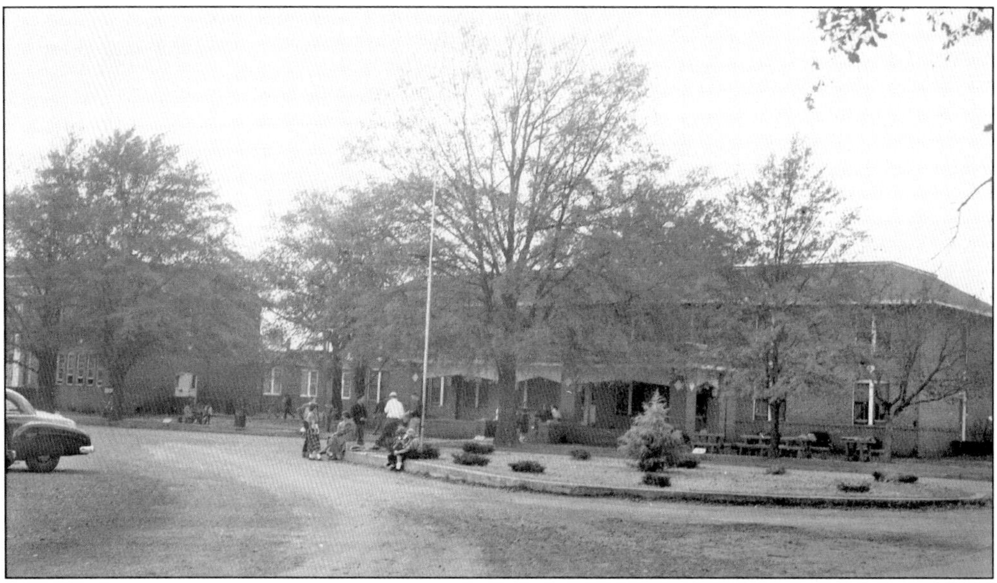

This circular area was known as "the horseshoe" to students at the high school and community college. Built in 1950, it was a turnabout for traffic on campus as well as a popular gathering spot. The building to the right was originally the girls' dormitory but was converted to classrooms to accommodate a growing student population on campus. On the left is the Administration Building, which was torn down in 1964 to make room for a liberal arts building.

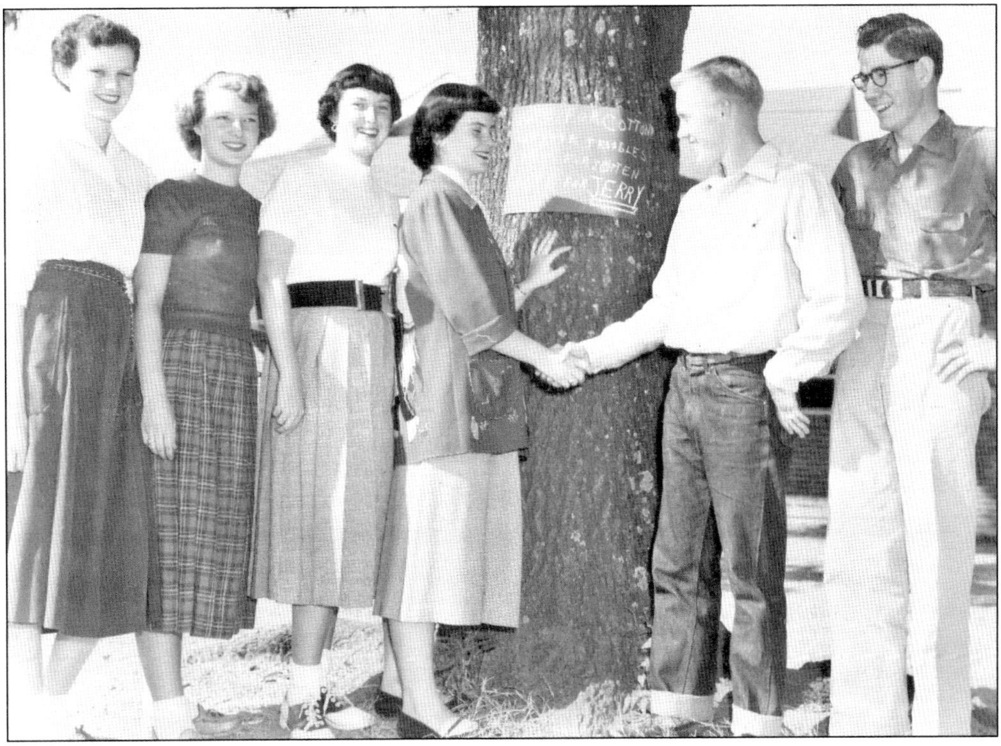

Jerry "Cotton" Wallace receives a congratulatory handshake from his opponent Betty Jean Pennington following his election as president of the IAHS Student Council in 1953. Pennington would serve as the council's vice president; her campaign manager, Betty Gilliland, stands next to her. At far left is Ruvene Beard, manager for Sue Franks, who would serve as secretary, and at far right is Mariel Mitchell, who managed Wallace's campaign.

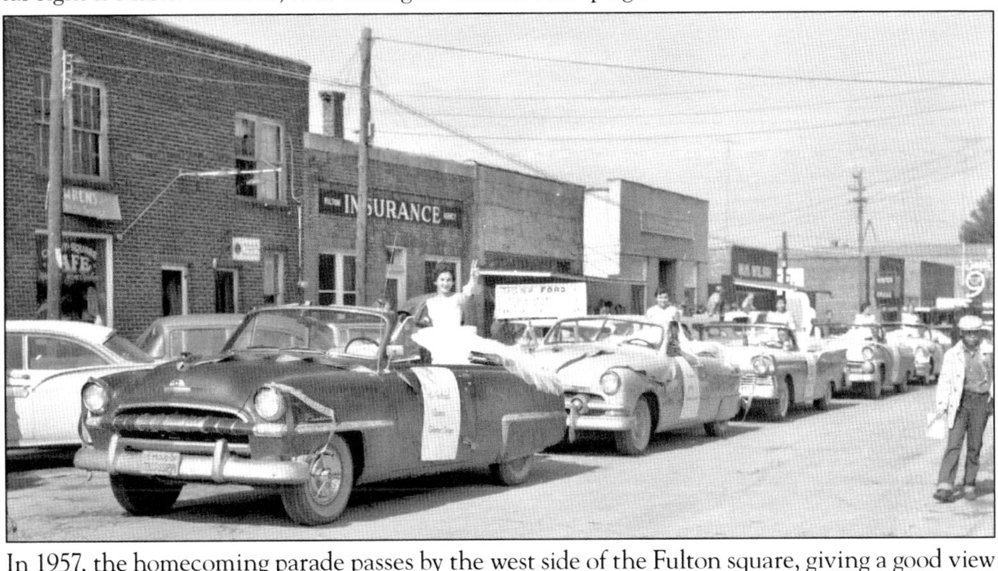

In 1957, the homecoming parade passes by the west side of the Fulton square, giving a good view of the two-story Sheffield building flanked by Fulton Insurance Agency. Fulton Bank and W.H. Wilson Store anchor the far corner. Dianne Googe rides in the front convertible as the high school football queen.

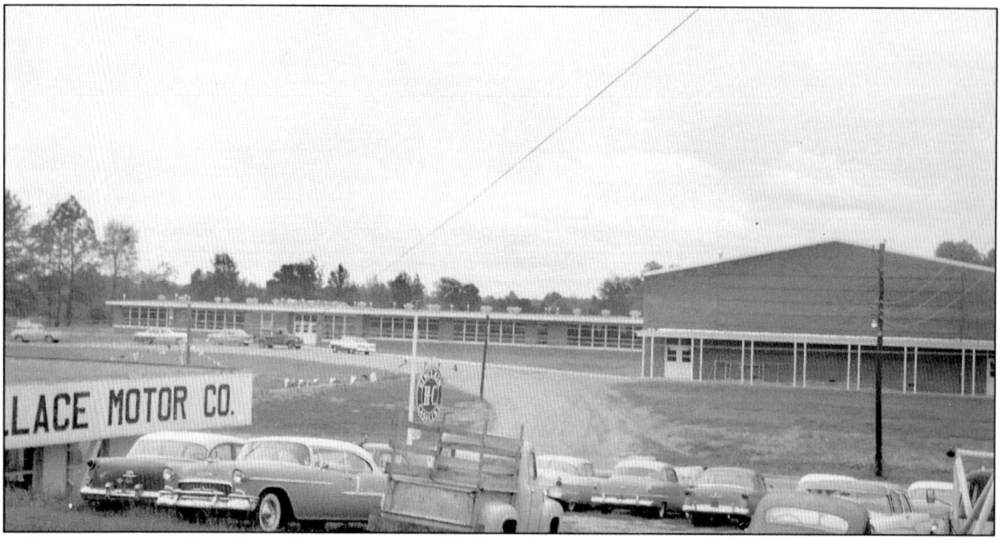

Fulton Junior High School (FJHS) opened during September 1959 to accommodate the town's white seventh-, eighth-, and ninth-graders. Prior to that time, students attended Fulton Grammar School through the eighth grade, then Itawamba Agricultural High School. When Itawamba Attendance Center opened south of Fulton in 1999, the junior high school building was closed, and was eventually torn down. Dexter Digby served as principal of FJHS from 1959 until 1970.

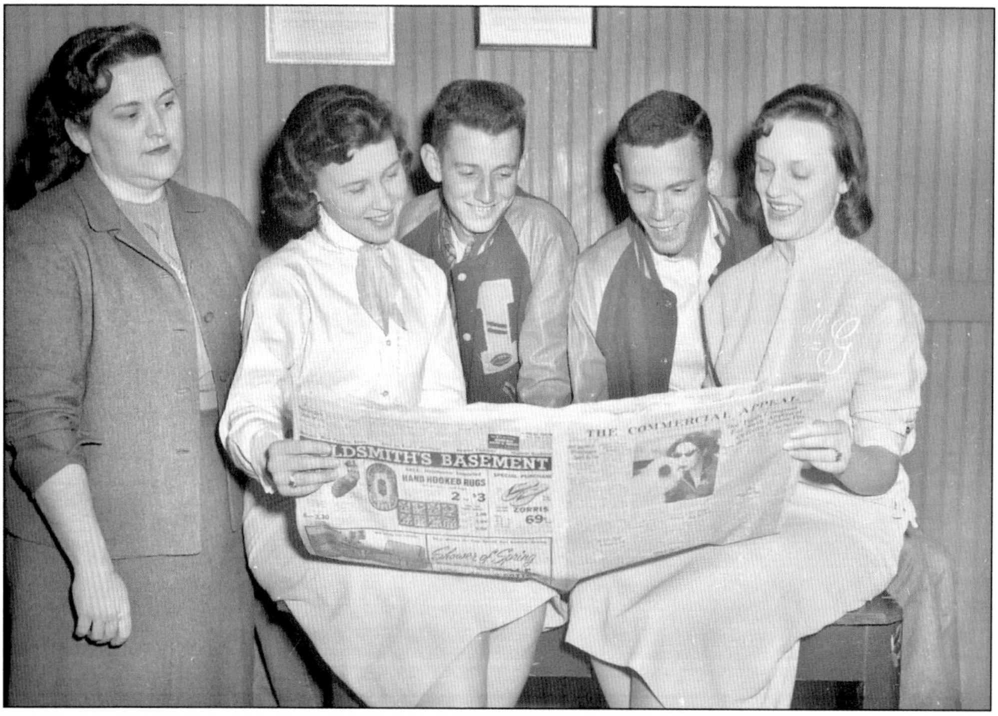

For three straight years, a team from IAHS defeated other Mid-South high school teams to win the popular "Quiz 'Em on the Air" competition, sponsored by a Memphis television station. Bonnie Ruth Owings (far left) was the team's sponsor, and in 1958, the winning team was, from left to right, Nannette Holcomb, Phil Izard, Bobby Moore, and Martha Ellen Gibbs. Here, the team reads of its success in the *Commercial Appeal*.

In 1963, school patrol members receive their training certificates from East High principal J.Y. Trice. From left to right are Herman Standifer, Roger McKinney, James Pounds, Larry Nichols, Larry Marshall, Johnnie Crayton, Samuel Martin, L.C. Clemons, Mereace Warren, and Principal Trice. Members were assigned to buses with the purpose of overseeing the safety of students.

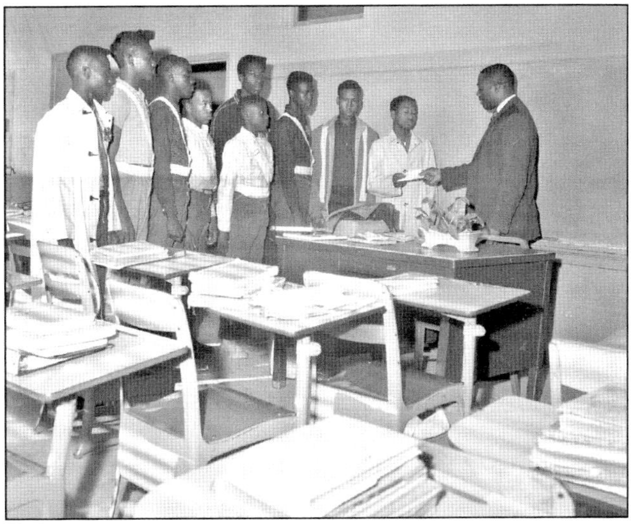

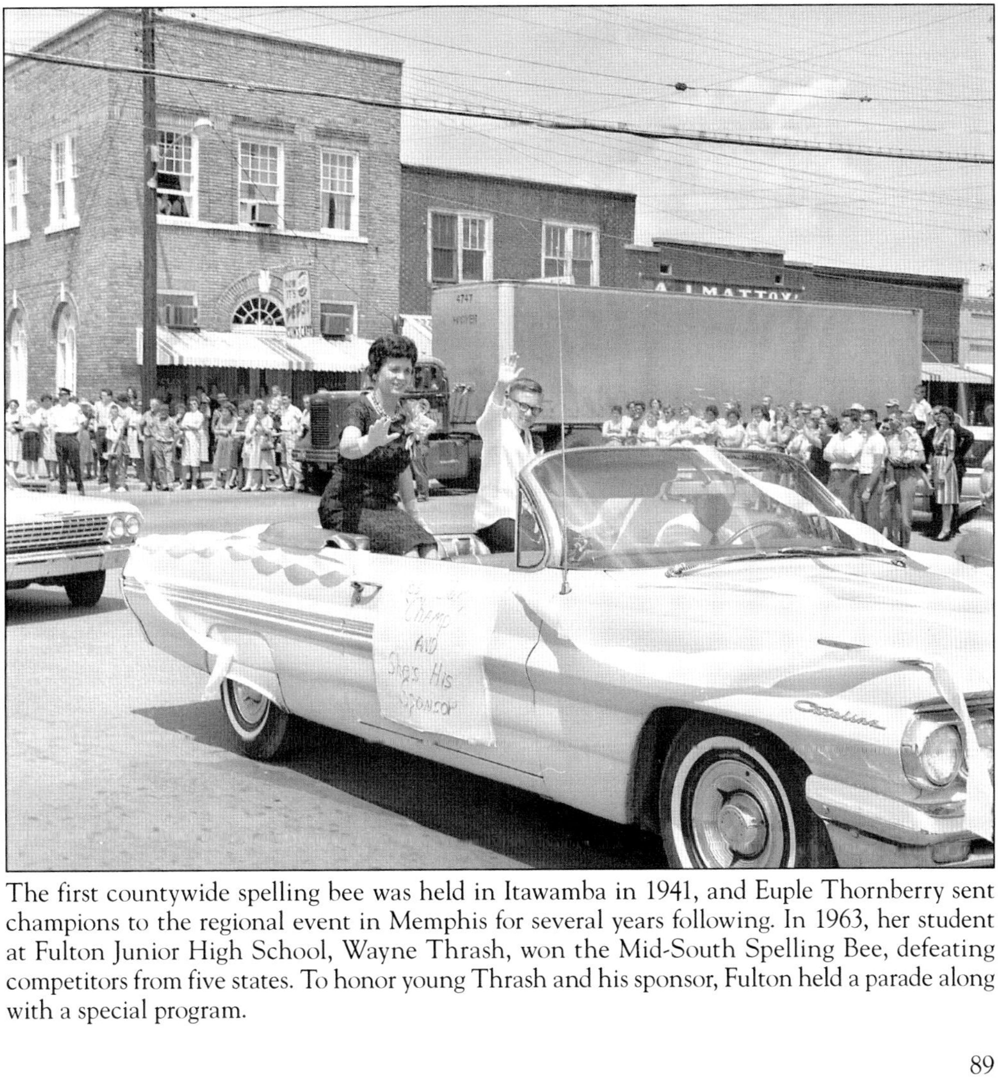

The first countywide spelling bee was held in Itawamba in 1941, and Euple Thornberry sent champions to the regional event in Memphis for several years following. In 1963, her student at Fulton Junior High School, Wayne Thrash, won the Mid-South Spelling Bee, defeating competitors from five states. To honor young Thrash and his sponsor, Fulton held a parade along with a special program.

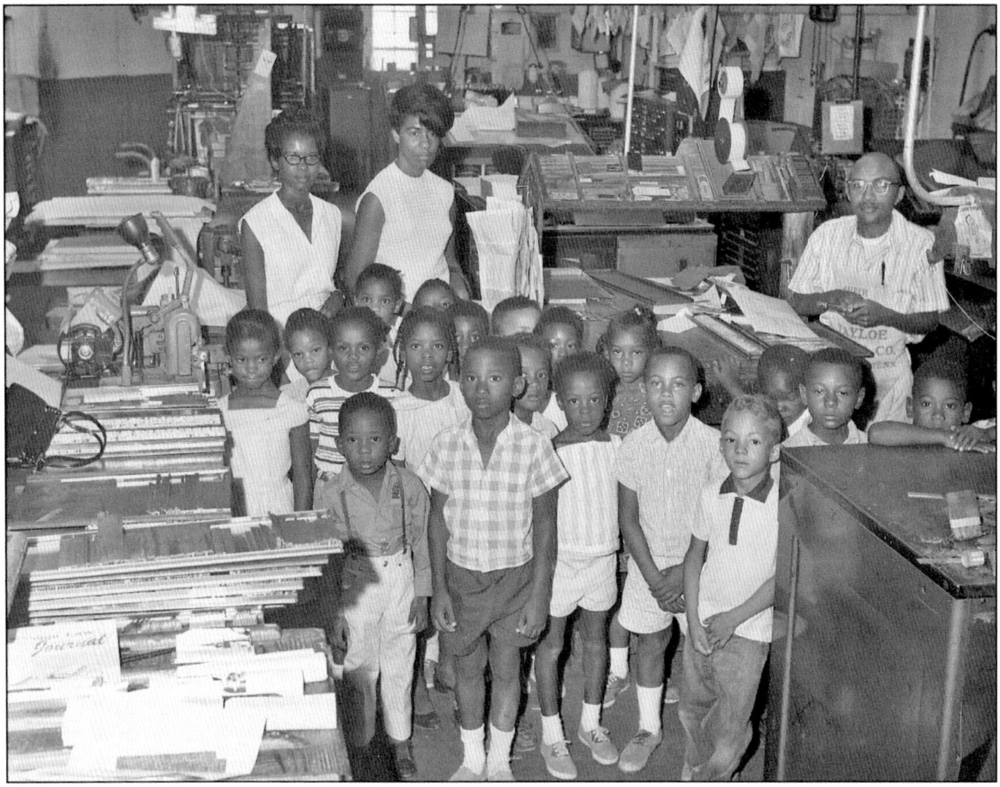

Members of the East High School head-start group visit the *Itawamba County Times* newspaper office in 1965. Fred Stone, longtime *Times* employee, gives a tour of the newspaper plant to the group.

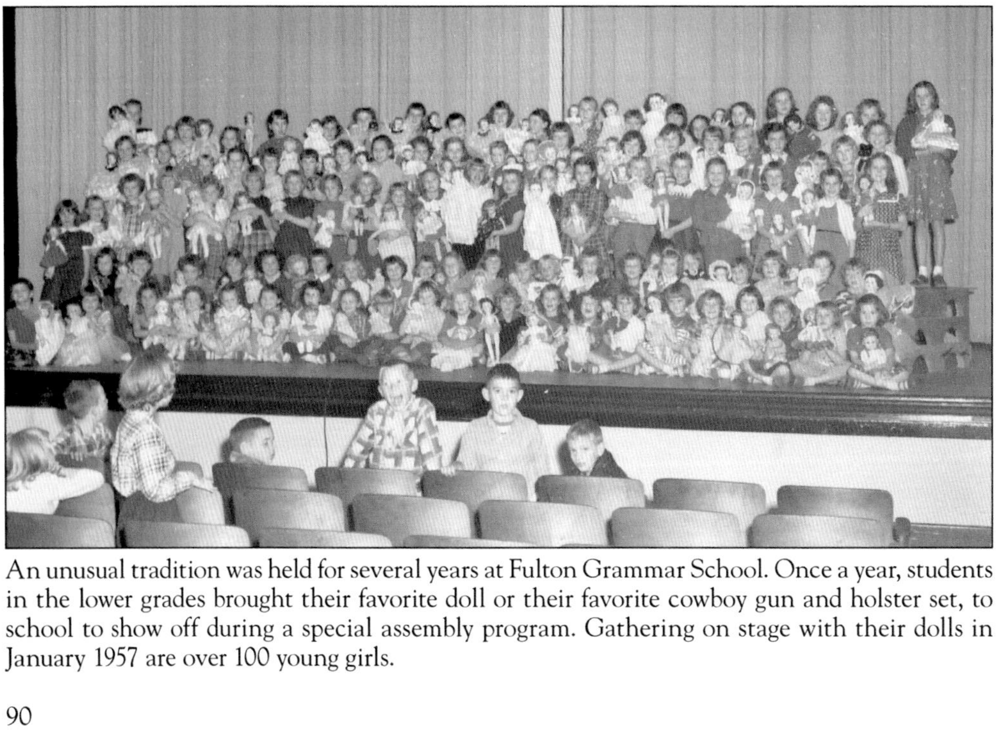

An unusual tradition was held for several years at Fulton Grammar School. Once a year, students in the lower grades brought their favorite doll or their favorite cowboy gun and holster set, to school to show off during a special assembly program. Gathering on stage with their dolls in January 1957 are over 100 young girls.

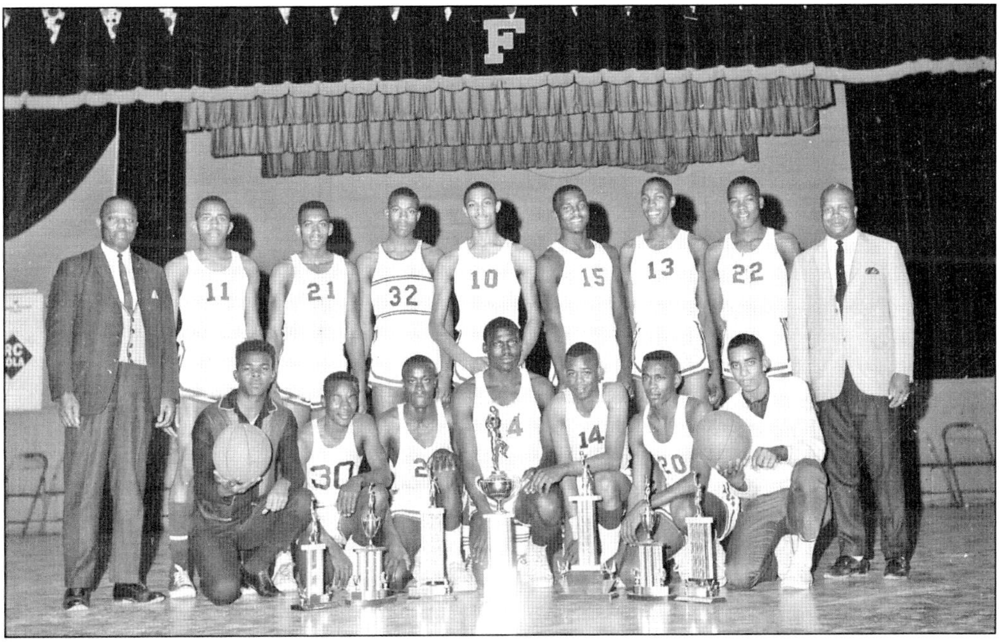

In February 1967, East High School captured the conference basketball championship, winning 14 games without a single loss. From left to right are (first row) R. Kinney, H. Standifer, R. Colburn, J. Shumpert, S. Martin, O. Riley, and R. Clemons; (second row) Principal J.Y. Trice, W. Blackmon, M. Dabbs, C. Cowley, H. Trice, J.T. Strode, J. Ferguson, L. Martin, and coach Robert Pruitt. Integration occurred the following year.

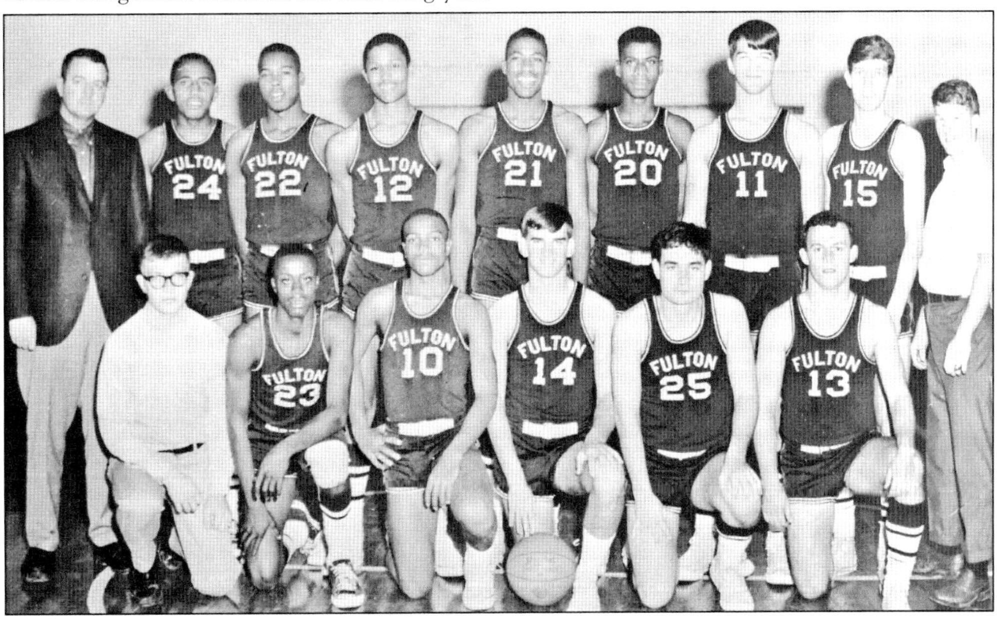

Fulton schools were integrated for the 1968–1969 school year under superintendent of education Wendell Brown. The East High School building was abandoned, and many of its teachers were integrated into the white public schools. Sports helped pull the town and students together, and the success of the integrated high school's athletic teams—such as this 1968 basketball team—aided in the transition.

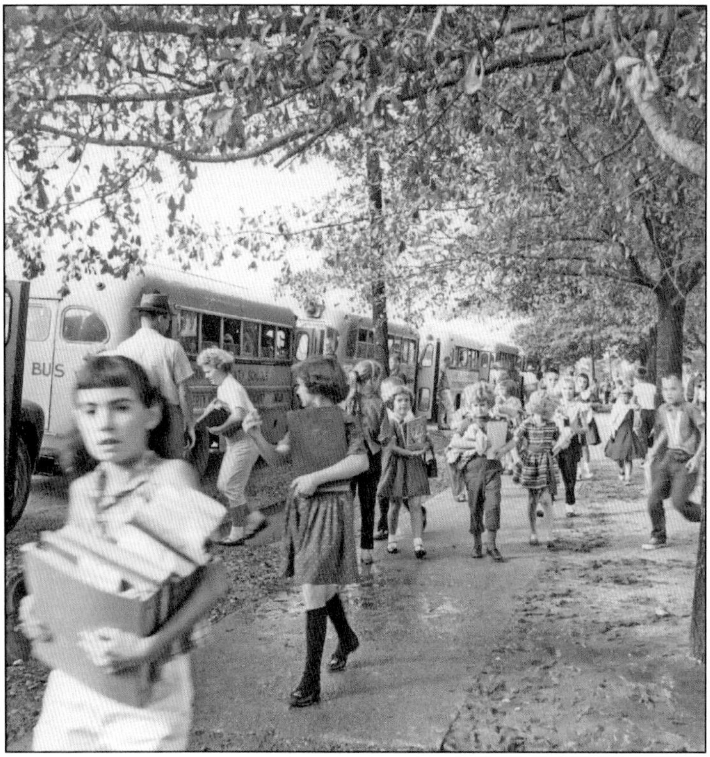

Sandra Thomas, far left, races for the bus in 1959 at the end of a school day at Fulton Grammar School. Most of the more than 500 grammar school students rode buses to school each day. Glenn C. Loden was principal at FGS from 1957 until 1970, replacing D.R. Raper and followed by Oren Wren.

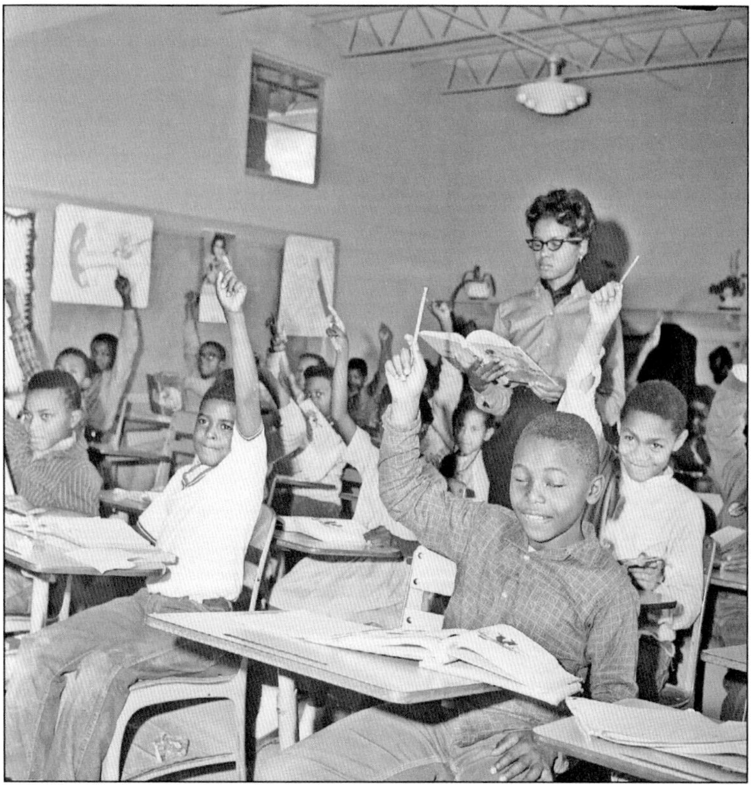

Eager students at East High School raise their hand in response to a question by Wilma Cummings, an Itawamba County native. Cummings did her practice teaching at the school in 1965.

Five

Fairs, Parades, and Other Fun Stuff

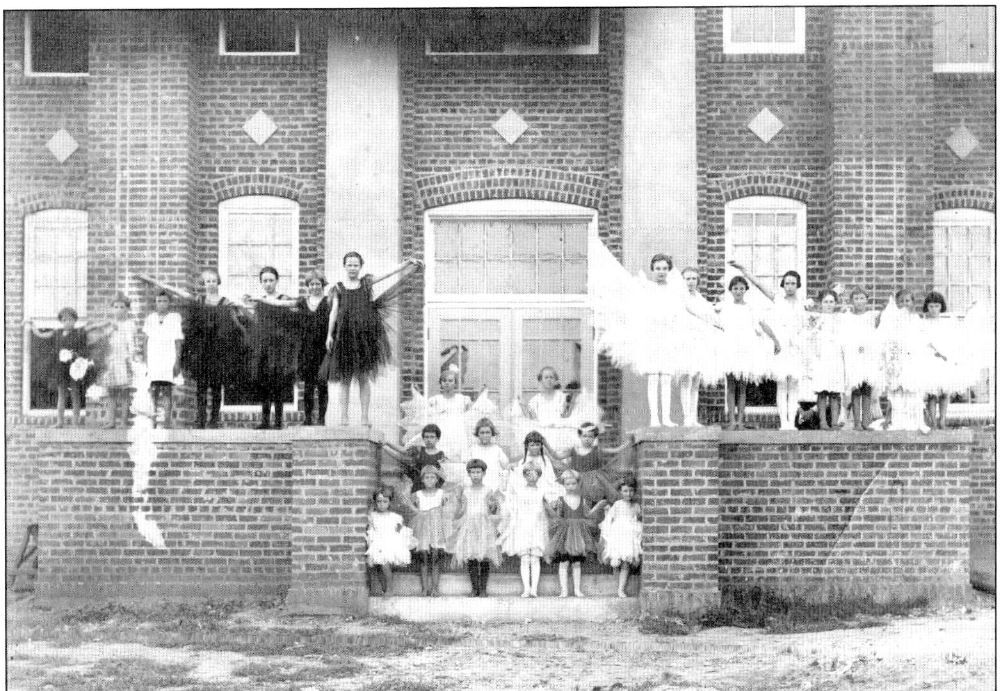

When the county's high school opened in September 1921, the first entertainment was provided by local Fulton girls performing "A Dream of Fairyland" for 25¢ admission to the new auditorium. The performers were Twila Pearce, Virginia Sheffield, Frances Dozier, Mary Belva Pearce, Helen Howard, May Ola Dozier, Lillie Mae Harden, Ruby Roberts, Blanche Reed, Annie Sandlin, Dessie Morrow, Frances Sheffield, Ruth Orr, Celia Frances Dulaney, Hortense Roberts, Ann Harden, Clara Nell Dulaney, Odell Pearce, Ruthellen Reed, Dessie Wayne Gaither, Lucy Nell Fain, Chloe Brown, Jennie May Gray, Corrine Reed, Euple Dozier, Jewel Fikes, and Stella Dulaney.

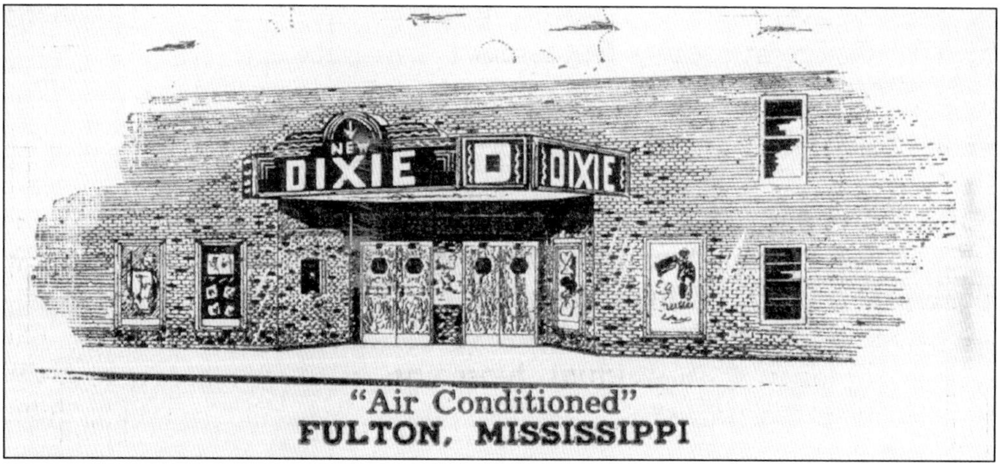

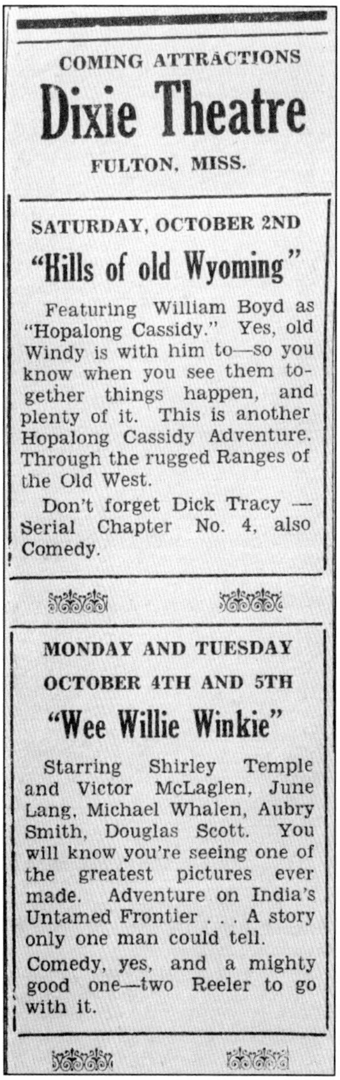

COMING ATTRACTIONS

Dixie Theatre

FULTON, MISS.

SATURDAY, OCTOBER 2ND

"Hills of old Wyoming"

Featuring William Boyd as "Hopalong Cassidy." Yes, old Windy is with him to—so you know when you see them together things happen, and plenty of it. This is another Hopalong Cassidy Adventure. Through the rugged Ranges of the Old West.

Don't forget Dick Tracy — Serial Chapter No. 4, also Comedy.

MONDAY AND TUESDAY

OCTOBER 4TH AND 5TH

"Wee Willie Winkie"

Starring Shirley Temple and Victor McLaglen, June Lang, Michael Whalen, Aubry Smith, Douglas Scott. You will know you're seeing one of the greatest pictures ever made. Adventure on India's Untamed Frontier . . . A story only one man could tell.

Comedy, yes, and a mighty good one—two Reeler to go with it.

Generations of Fultonians spent many afternoons and evenings at the Dixie Theatre. Built in 1923 by S.D. Johnson and later owned by James Milton Brown, future mayor of Fulton, the theater was originally located on Wiygul Street, with the art deco building facing north toward the courthouse. Brown sold the theater to Bonnie DeBow, who operated it for several years before selling to G.C. Pratt. In addition to showing movies, the building was used for events such as merchant fashion shows, cooking shows, and church services. In 1950, Pratt constructed a new brick building around the corner on Cummings Street, and the New Dixie Theatre opened in June with the latest equipment and furnishings. The theater closed about 1971, and in 1992, the vacant building was donated by the Bill Jamieson family to be used for an expansion of the Itawamba County Library. Advertisements such as the one at left from the September 23, 1937, issue of the *Fulton News Beacon* promoted the picture shows at the popular Dixie Theatre. (Both, courtesy of Itawamba Historical Society.)

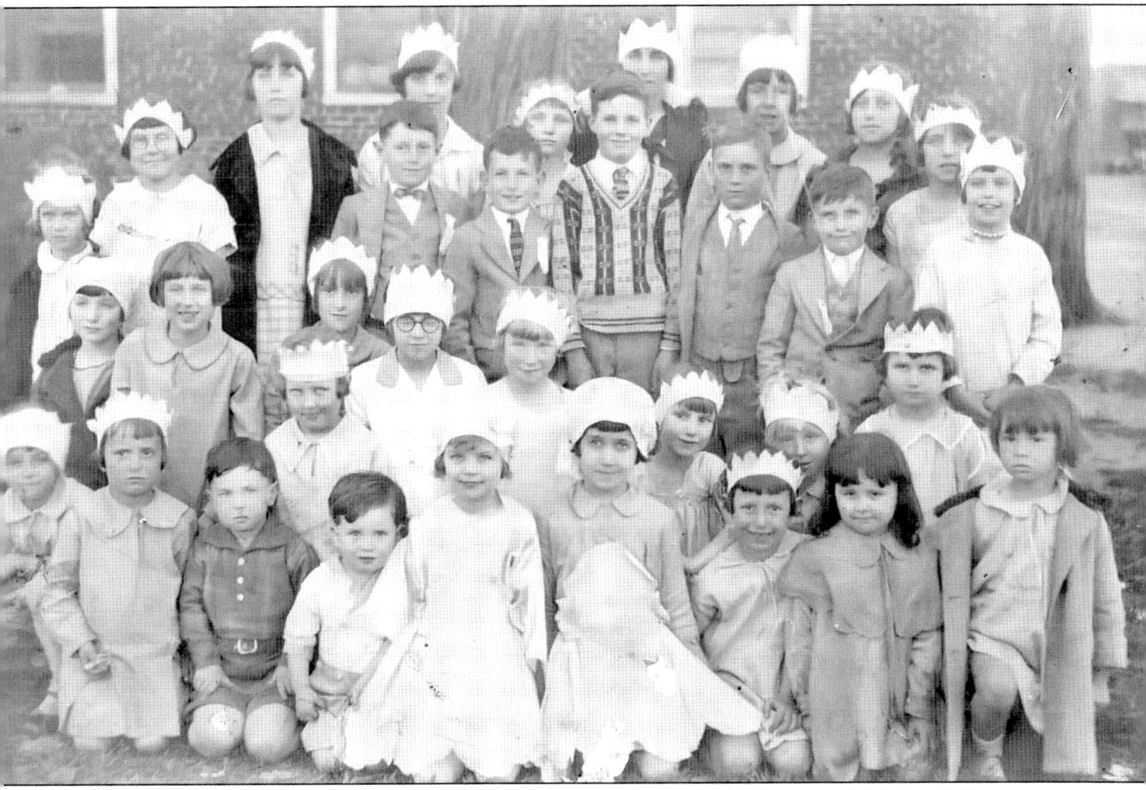

Gathered for a birthday party about 1929 are, from left to right, (first row) Mildred Gaither, Marguerite Senter, Hugh Brown Patrick, Bobby Stringfellow, Dorothy Kay (birthday girl), Corrine Reeves, Geneva Sheffield, Nell Cleveland, and Rose Wilson Patrick; (second row) Prebble McKee, Juanita McAdams, Rosalind Tandy, Madge Orr, Christine and Ernestine Haynes, Virginia Pate, Earline McAdams, and Mary Evelyn Brown; (third row) Muriel Reed, Ruth Sheffield, J.T. Bryant, Jimmie Brown, Wayne Senter, Dick Senter, Tyrus Gibbs, and Grace Gaither; (fourth row) Helen Howard, Dorothy Senter, Barbara Hawkins, Theresa McAdams, Faye Dulaney, Ruth Nanney, and Twila Pearce. (Courtesy of Itawamba Historical Society.)

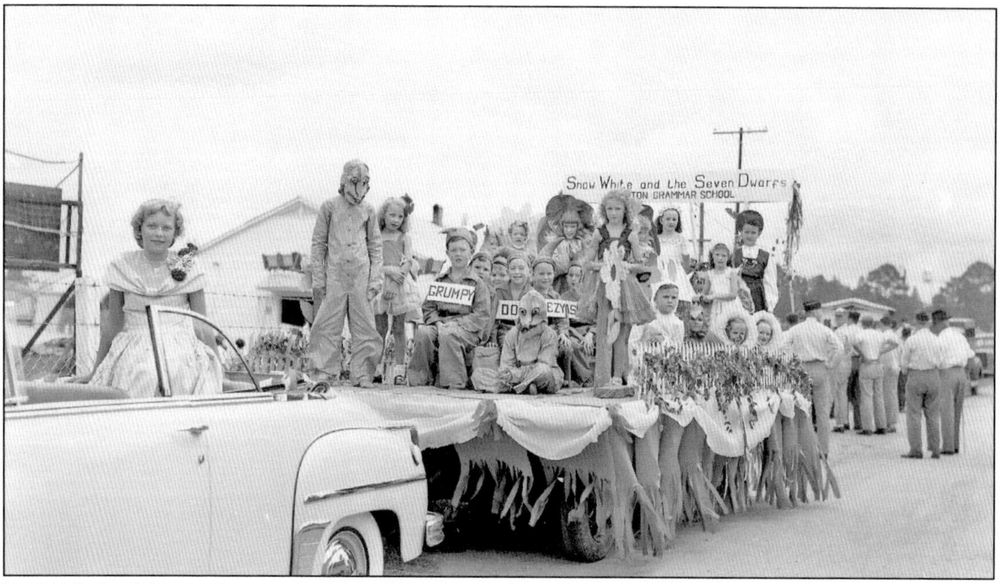

In 1949, this Fulton Grammar School float won first place in the Itawamba County Fair parade. Held each fall during the county's fair festivities, this was one of the largest parades during the year, complete with several marching bands, marches by 4-H club members, multiple floats, and beauty queens.

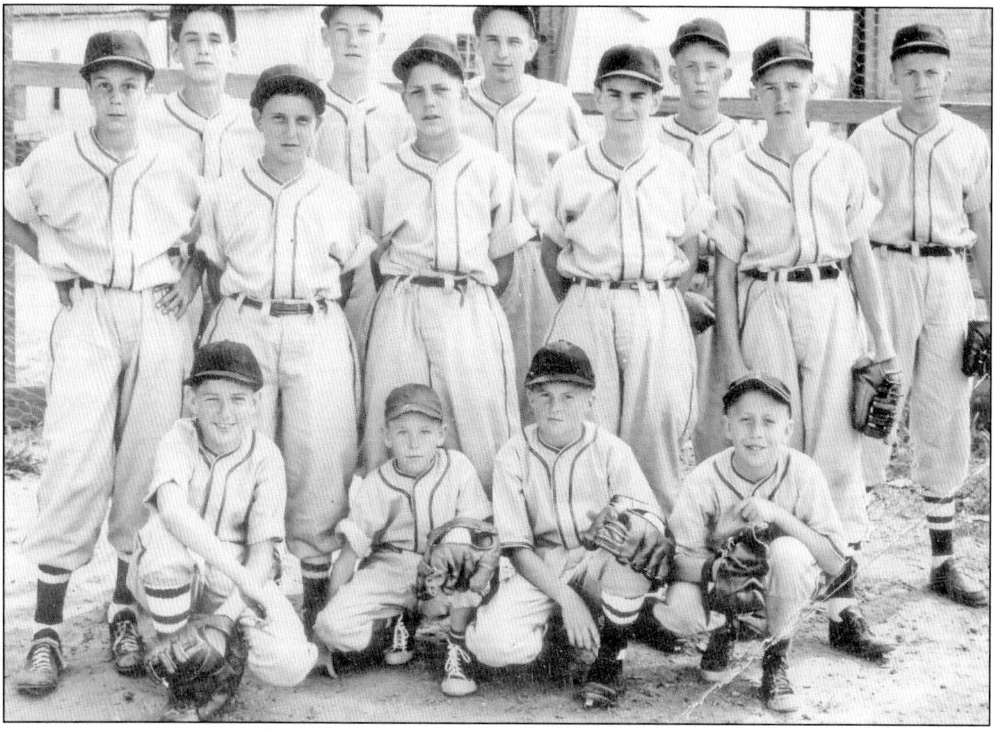

The Fulton junior baseball team displays their new uniforms in 1949. From left to right are (front row) Jimmy Staub, Johnnie Crubaugh, Don Atkins, and Jimmy Gibbs; (second row) Joe Davis, Kelly Wade Prestage, Dude Comer, Billy Raden, James Robinson, and Edward Holliday; (third row) Louie Yawn, Winifred Cooper, Travis Staub, and Huey Haynes.

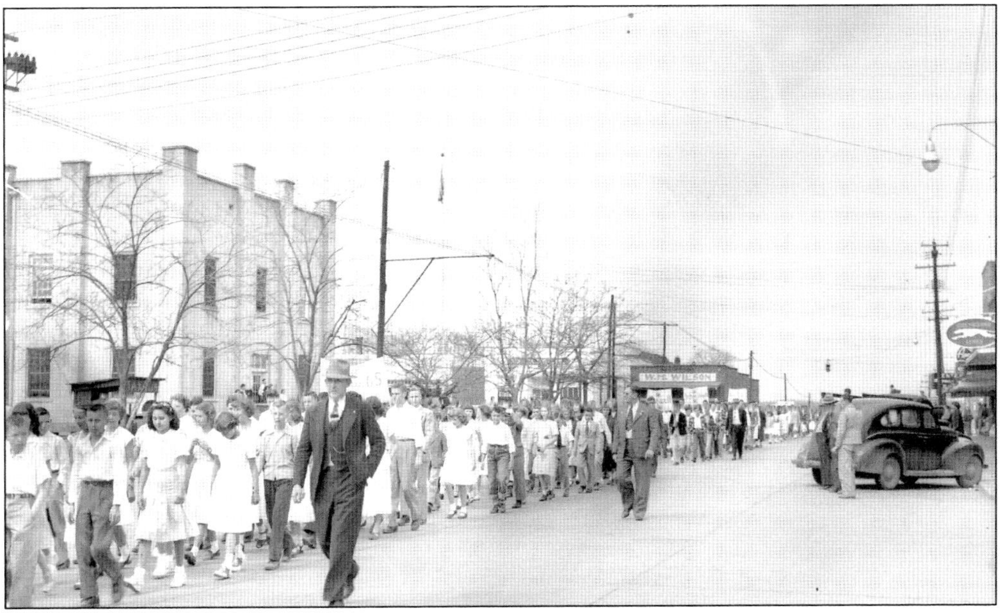

The 4-H club played a very important role in the lives of many schoolchildren in Fulton and across the county. Every spring, a 4-H club rally was held in Fulton, and hundreds of 4-H members paraded through town with banners, led by the Itawamba Agricultural High School and Itawamba Junior College Marching Band. Following the parade, the children convened at the high school's auditorium for skits and special recognitions. Here, the 1949 parade passes by the courthouse with W.H. Wilson Store and the Fulton Bank in the background. Note the Greyhound Bus sign at right.

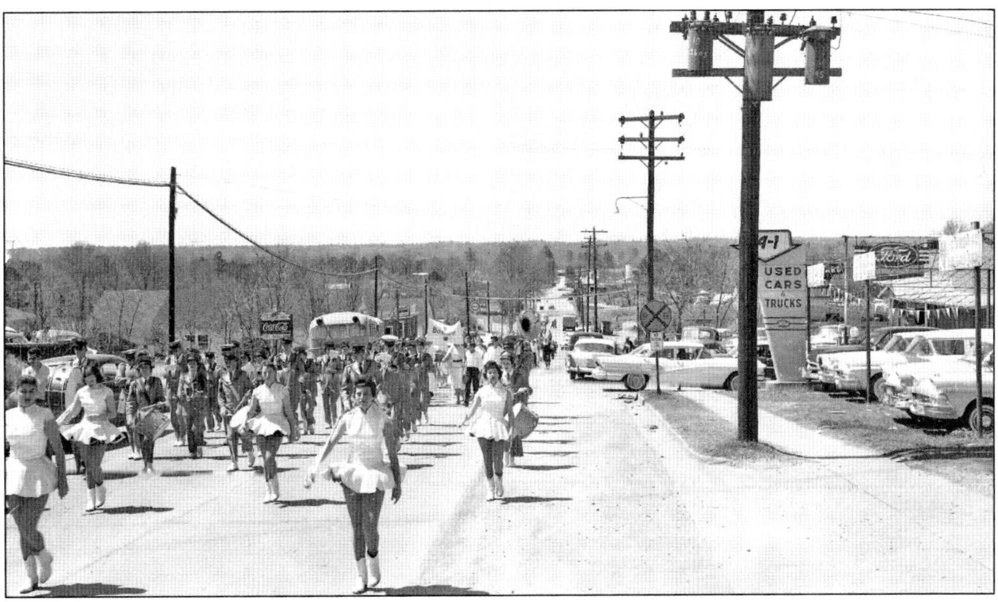

The 1958 4-H parade passes by the Ford dealership, at right, and College Inn Café, at left, as it marches up the hill from the high school campus toward the town square.

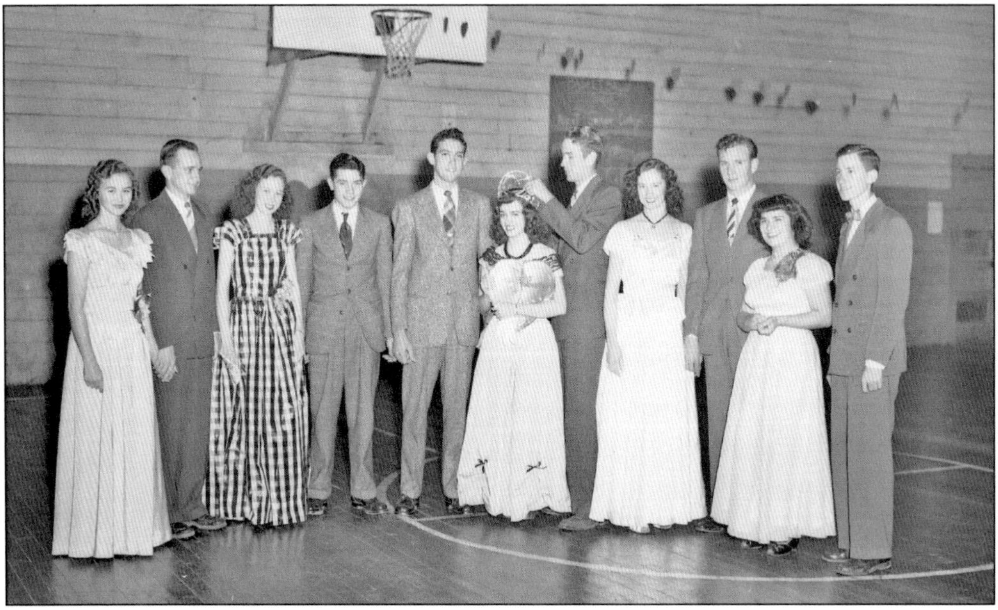

At the annual Sweetheart Party of both Itawamba Agricultural High School and Itawamba Junior College students in February 1949, Betty Jo Gilliland was crowned campus sweetheart. From left to right are Carrie Mae Graham and Travis Staub, Virginia Harris and Jimmie Pierce, F.G. Wiygul, Gilliland, R.D. Rutherford as master of ceremonies, Eva Mae Clayton and Joe Handcock, and Jeanette Loden and Wood Moore.

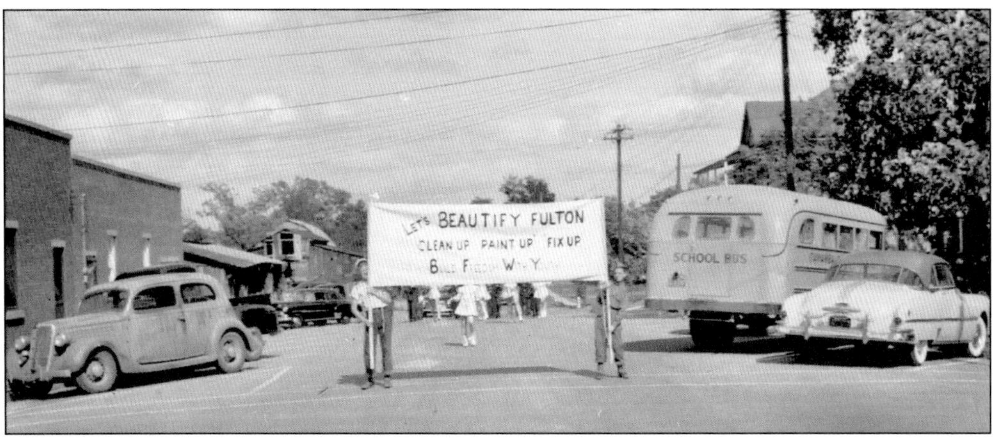

Fulton Civic Club sponsored a large number of community betterment projects in the 1950s with its Build Freedom with Youth program and won a $2,000 national third-place prize in 1952 for its efforts. The prize money was used toward the construction of a swimming pool for Fulton. Marching on Wiygul Street toward the court square, the youth parade passes by a mule shed on the left behind the brick building, and the top of the old Wiygul Hotel can be seen on the right. In the rear is a mule barn owned by Bob Senter on the lot behind the current post office.

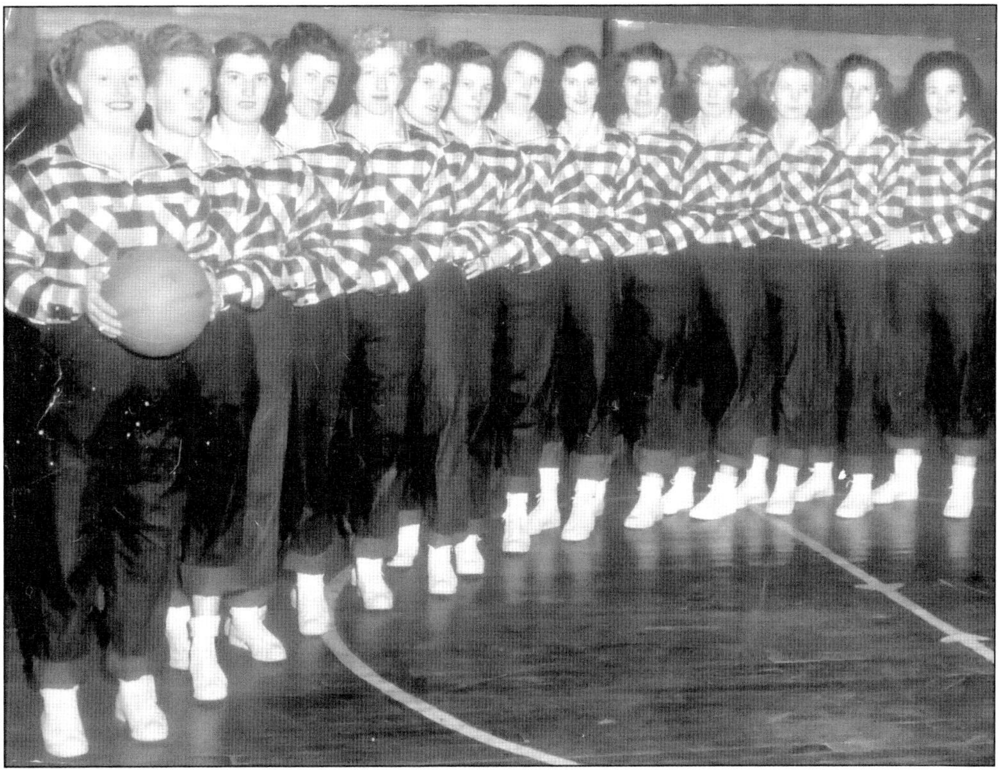

The local Blue Bell Garment Company plant sponsored a basketball team for its female employees, and the team enjoyed quite a bit of success. Newspaper accounts indicate that the Fulton Blue Belles were one of the leading independent basketball teams of the area. Squad members of the 1950 team are, from left to right, Annie Mae Gullick, Lizzie Cummings, Gladys Franks, Syble Clayton, Wilma Stovall, Mazell Oswalt, Ruby Cockrell, Aletha Pearce, Eva Mae Clayton, Earline Smith, Lois Hood, Etoile Grissom, Ruby Steele, and Mildred Gray. The team wore warm-up clothing made by other Blue Bell plants.

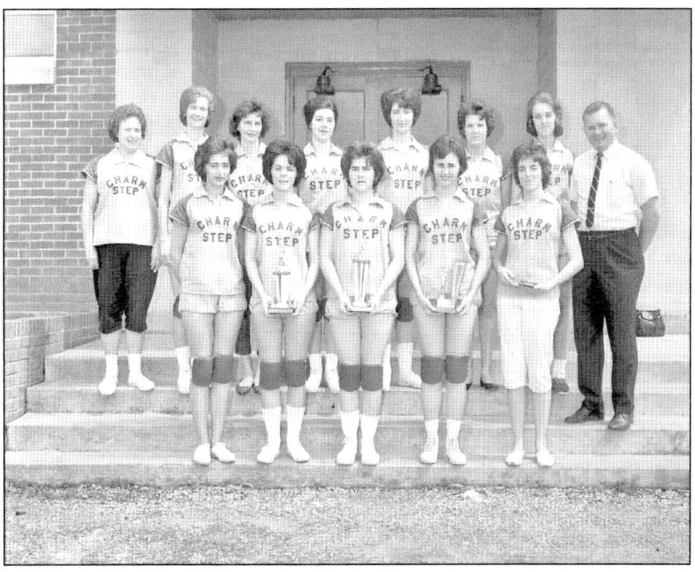

For the second year in a row, in 1964, the Charm Step ladies' basketball team won the Tupelo Industrial League tournament. From left to right are (first row) Jo Ann Gray, Betty Wilson, Helen Prather, Nancy Byrd, and Barbara Mayhall; (second row) Melba Dozier, Jo Ann Reynolds, Sally Dozier, Martha Roberts, Catherine Christian, Louise Chatham, Zereda Williams, and manager Floyd Drake.

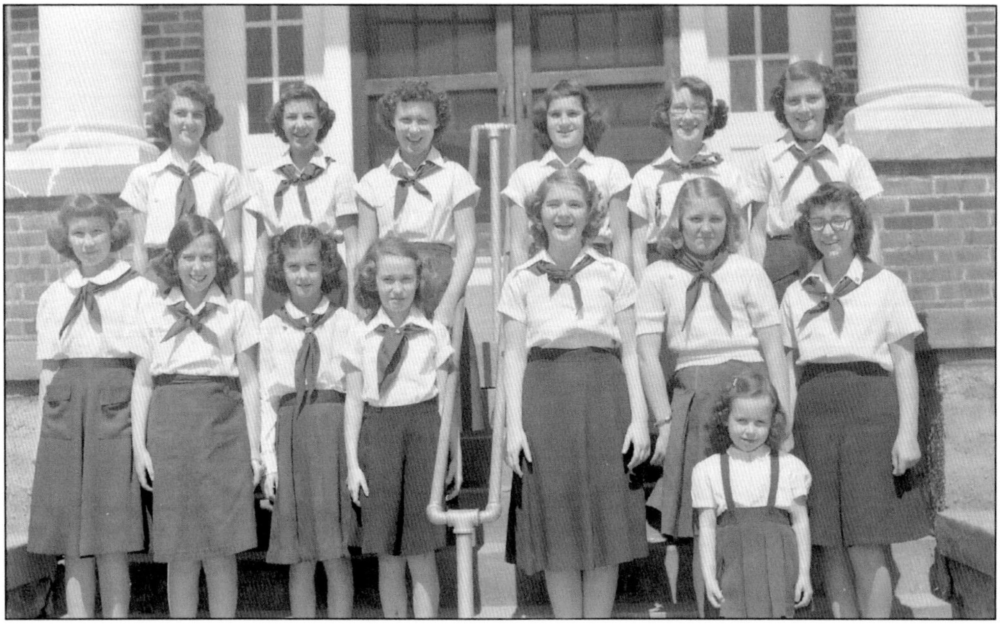

In 1952, the local Camp Fire Girls consisted of, from left to right, (first row) Patsy McKee, Daisy Holland, Mary Joe Sheffield, Rosemary White, Betty Stringfellow, Joyce Young, and Sarah Rushing; (second row) unidentified, Sarah McKinney, Nanette Holcomb, Jane Steele, Sherry Jane Whiteside, and Hilda Holcomb. Marie Holland was the adult leader for the group, and little Judy Holland (front) was the mascot.

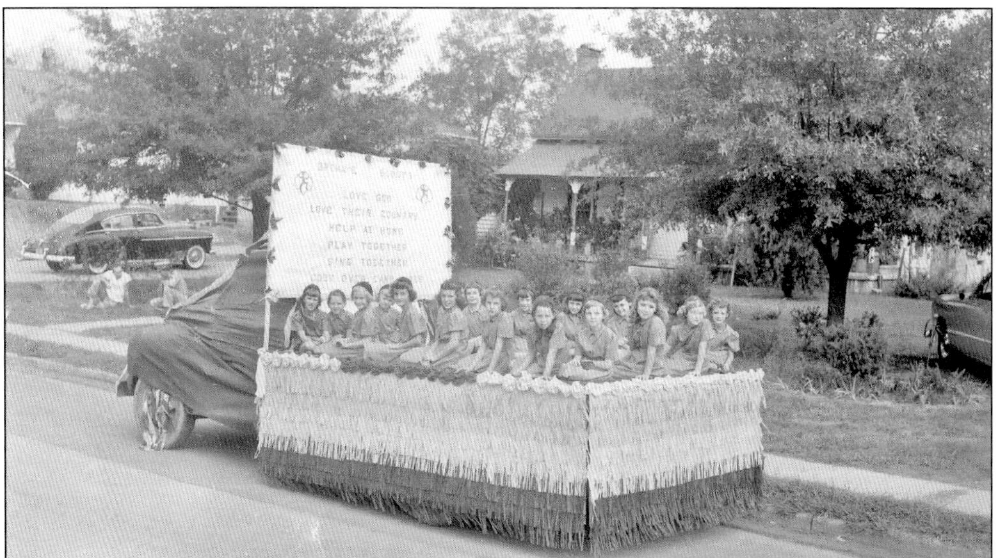

The Camp Fire Girls were not the only group having fun. In this 1955 photograph, Brownie Scouts enjoy participating in a parade as it passes in front of the Lee Phillips house on Main Street in Fulton.

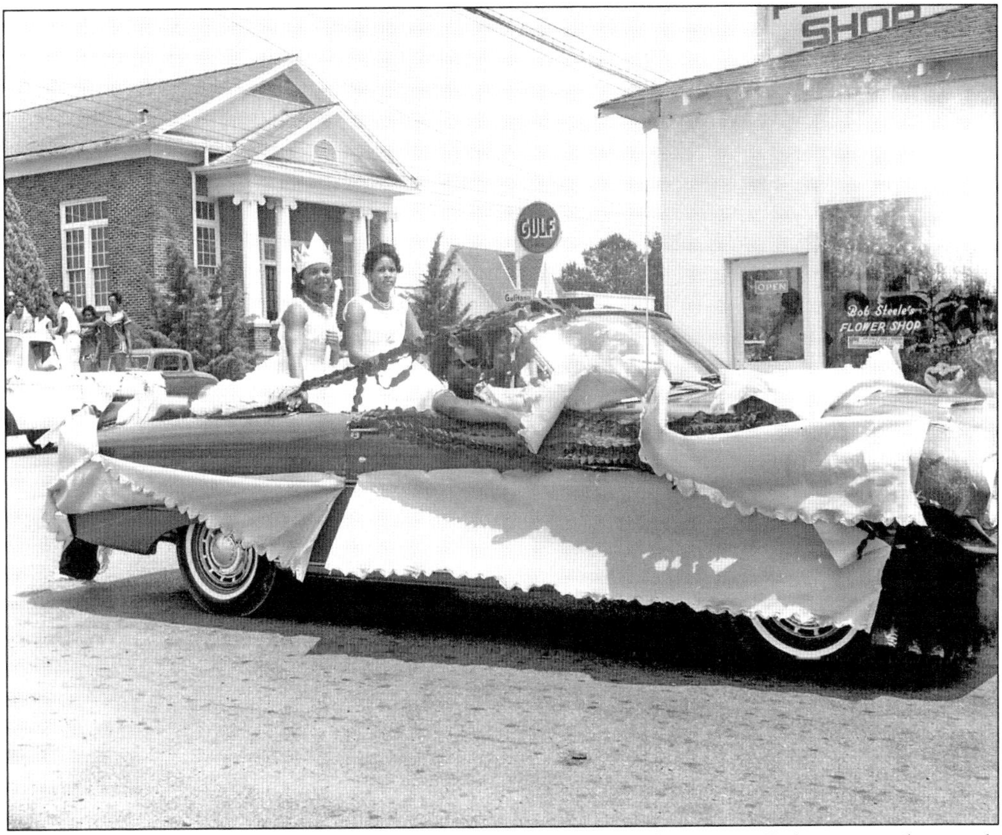

East High School held an annual May Day parade through downtown Fulton, complete with marching bands, floats, maids, and queens. In this 1963 photograph, a convertible carrying beauty queens Mae Celia Shumpert (left) and Delores Cummings passes by the former location of Bob Steele's Flower Shop.

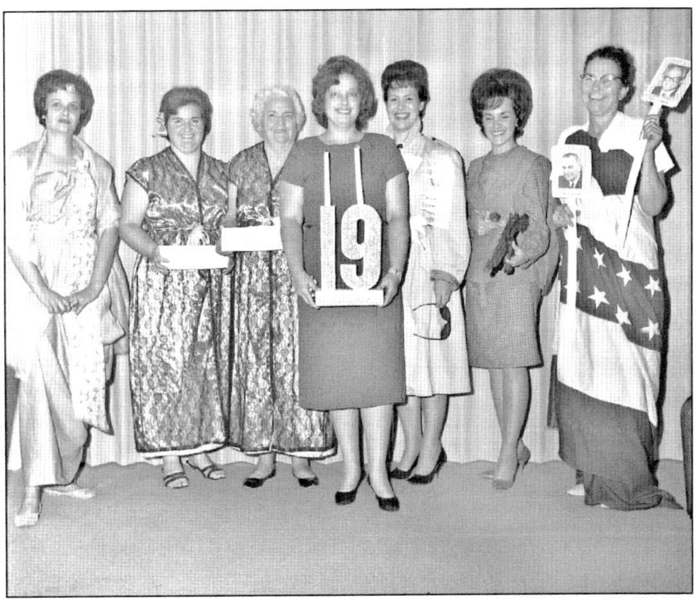

In 1964, Fulton Book Club celebrated 19 years of organization with a costume party. Members arrived dressed to represent a favorite book's title. From left to right are Nita Steele, Mrs. Wade King, Jettie Stringfellow, Mrs. Archie Sprayberry, Mitzi Lindsey, Carolyn Chatham, and Rubye Harden.

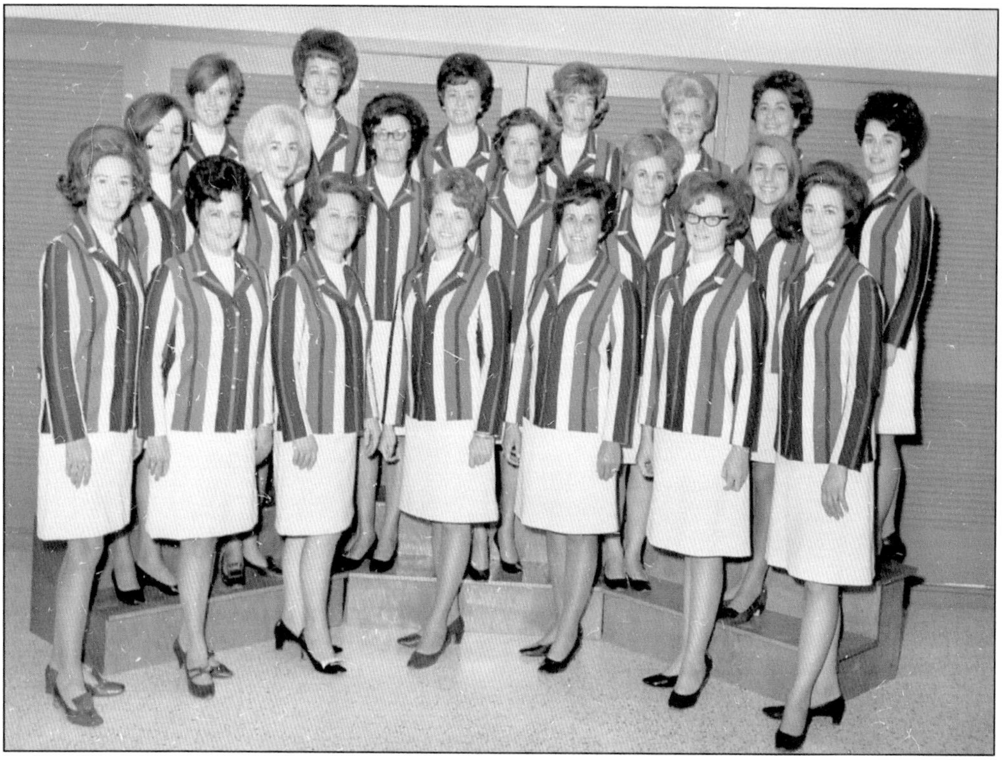

The Fulton chapter of the Sweet Adelines was organized in 1967 with members Ann Stubblefield, Janice Thrash, Marie Daves, Edna Todd, Ann Wheeler, Lenell Robinson, Julia Grimes, Sarah Cummings, Dorothy Mullins, Martha Davis, Bobbye Jones, Maxine Smith, Hilda Bishop, Lois Sullivan, Pat McCormack, Hazel Davis, Kathy McKinney, Jamey Suggs, Debbie West, Ruthie Pate, Linda Prestage, Carolyn Chatham, Adene Miles, Joan Barber, and Betty Senter.

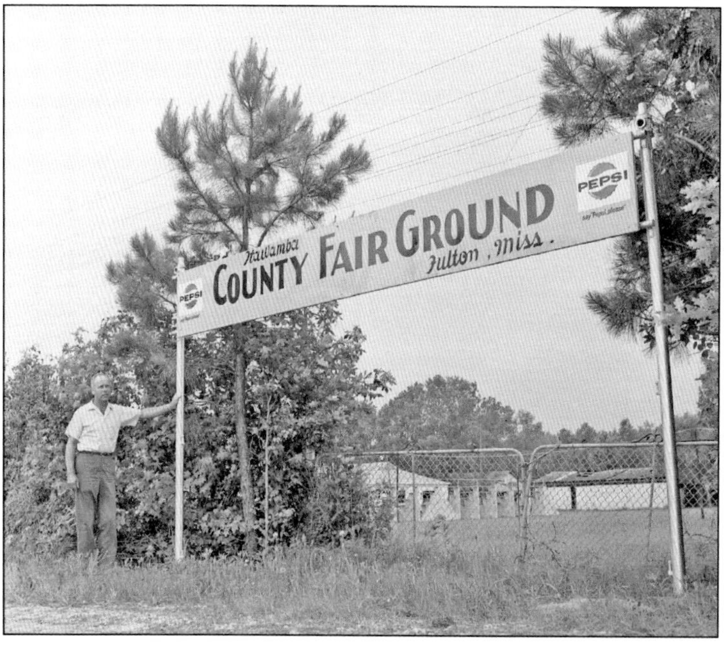

Buck Harrison, president of the Itawamba County Fair Association, is proud of the new sign at the entrance of the fairgrounds in 1966. The Itawamba County Fair was officially organized in 1942, and in 1949, it moved from the courthouse lawn to fairgrounds west of Fulton. Today, the old fairgrounds location is the site of the college soccer field.

Livestock shows, carnival rides, and exhibits were popular features of the fair, but competition was stiff for blue ribbons in the food categories. Here, in 1965, a group gathers in front of an exhibit of preserved foods. From left to right are home economist Janice Watson, Irma Estes, Mrs. G.W. Jobe Sr., Mrs. S.A. McDaniel, and Mary Ann Evans, daughter of John and Lucelle Evans.

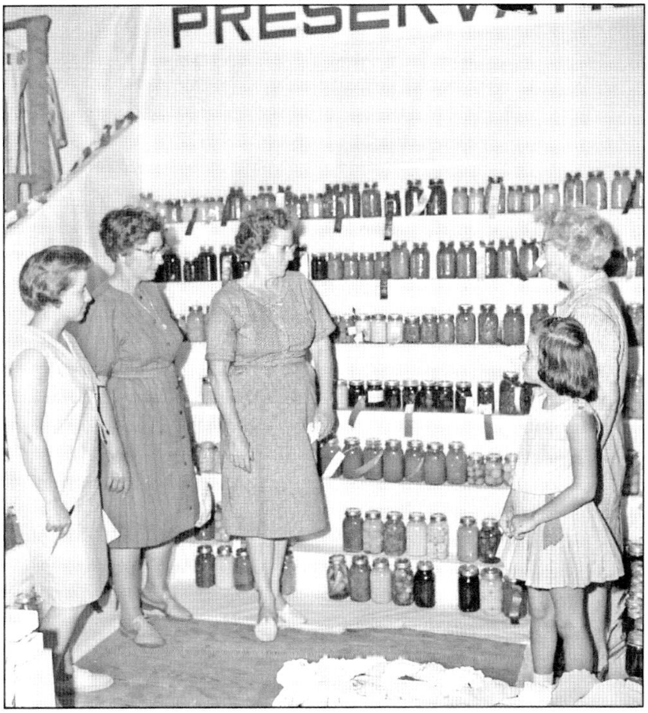

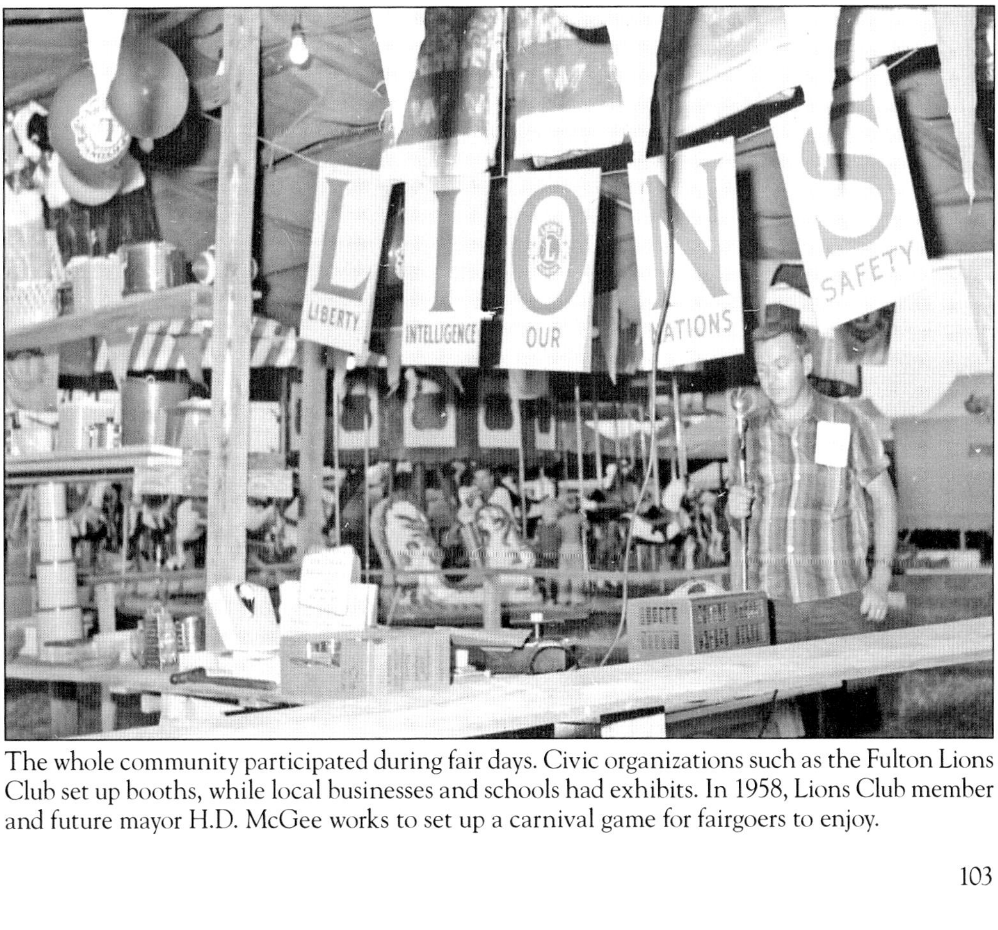

The whole community participated during fair days. Civic organizations such as the Fulton Lions Club set up booths, while local businesses and schools had exhibits. In 1958, Lions Club member and future mayor H.D. McGee works to set up a carnival game for fairgoers to enjoy.

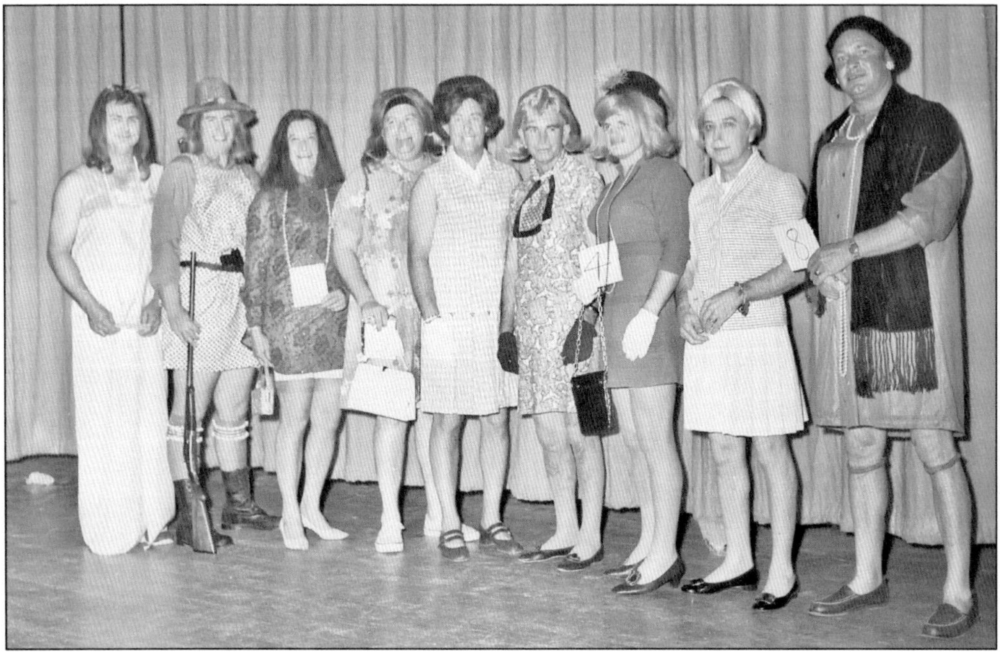

Womanless Beauty Revues were popular events among clubs and organizations, especially as fundraisers. In 1970, "Charlene" McCarthy, far left, won out over these other beauties. From left to right are McCarthy, "Donna" Sheffield, "Frances Gertrude" Wiygul, "Josephine" Barber, "Lucretia" Wheeler, "Nolanda" McKee, "Larrie Ann" Williams, "Ralphetta" Black, and "Cecilia" Abel.

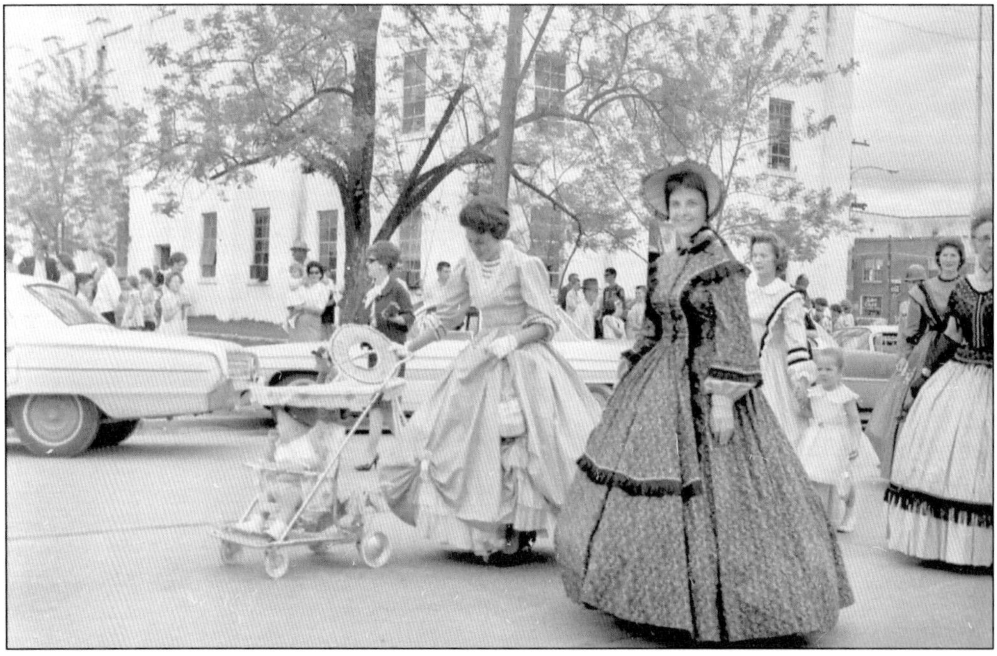

Confederate Memorial Day was commemorated in Fulton in 1964 with a costume parade and speeches on the courthouse lawn. Parading around the court square are, from left to right, Nancy Mattox pushing a baby carriage, Ann Stubblefield, Ann Walker holding the hand of her daughter Suzan, Gwendola Camp, and Vera Jane Mattox.

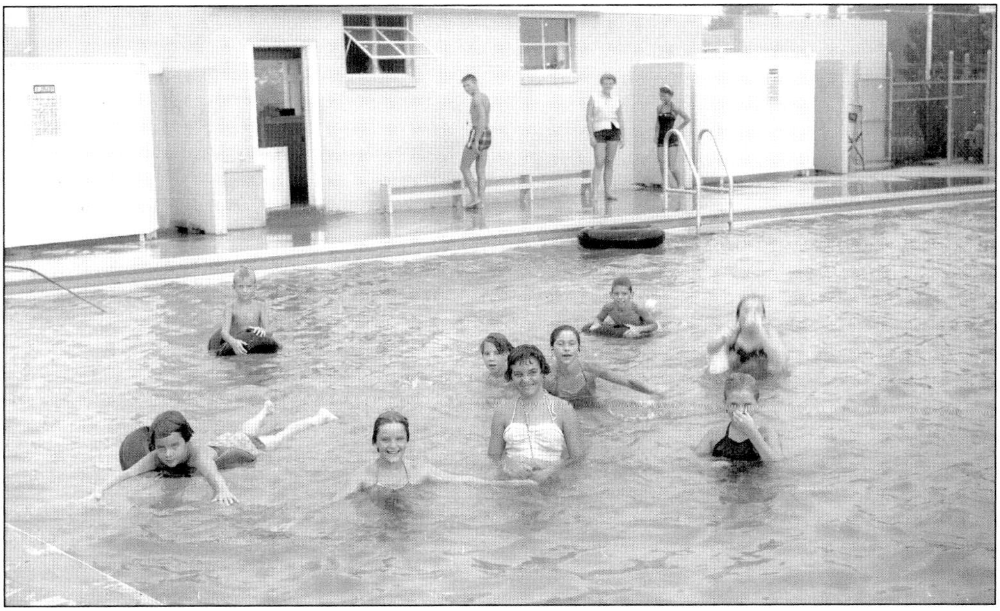

A swimming pool was built in 1953 on the community college campus using local money and prize funds won by the Fulton Civic Club for its volunteerism program Building Freedom with Youth. The pool was used for several summers until officials closed it during integration.

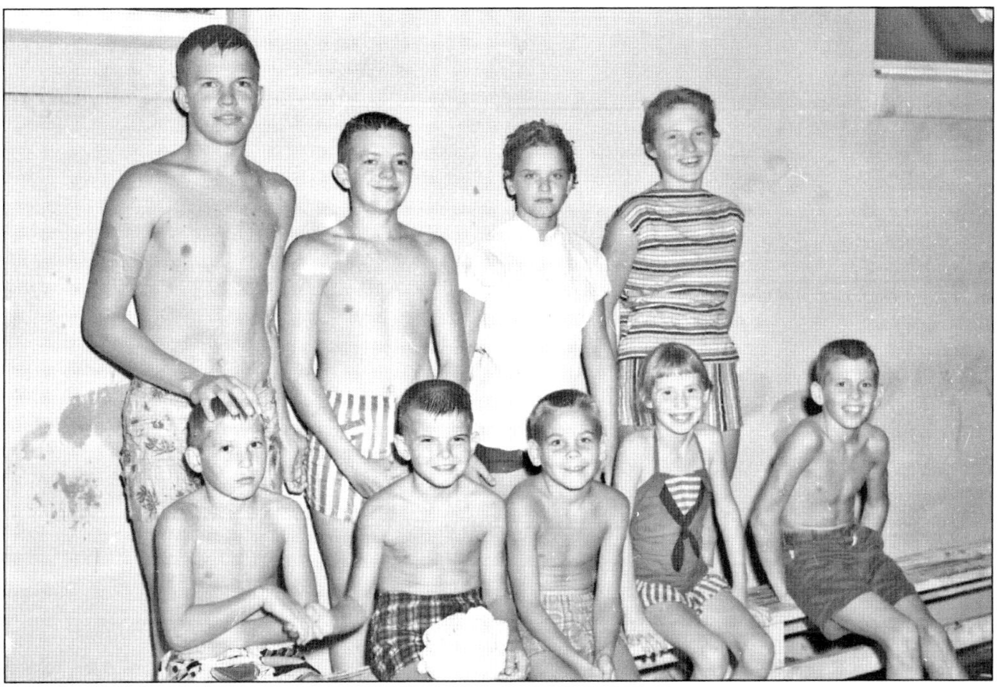

Following the installation of a community swimming pool, competitive swim clubs were organized that participated in regionwide events. In 1957, the swimmers had their picture taken following a swim meet; from left to right are (seated) Bob Garofalo, Gary Davis, Hollis Wiygul, and Nell Garofalo; (standing) Gary Walker, Bob Hawkins, Molly Haynes, and Emily Garofalo.

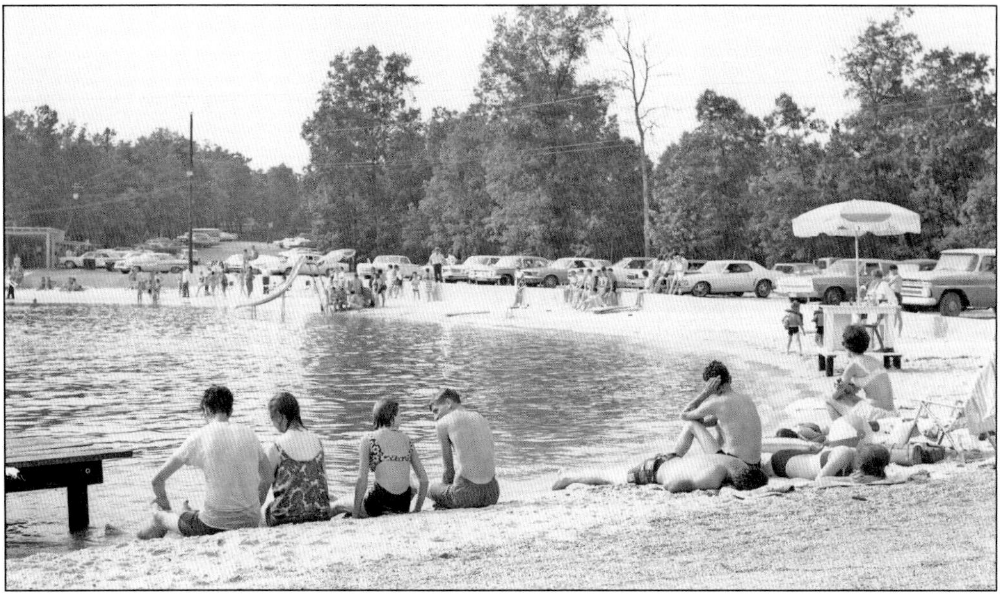

Nita Lake was a playground for Fulton and Itawamba County every summer. Opened by Paul Anthony about 1958, the resort was more than a swimming, boating, fishing, and skiing destination. Church groups and businesses hosted outings at the resort's pavilion, and many families held reunions at the facilities.

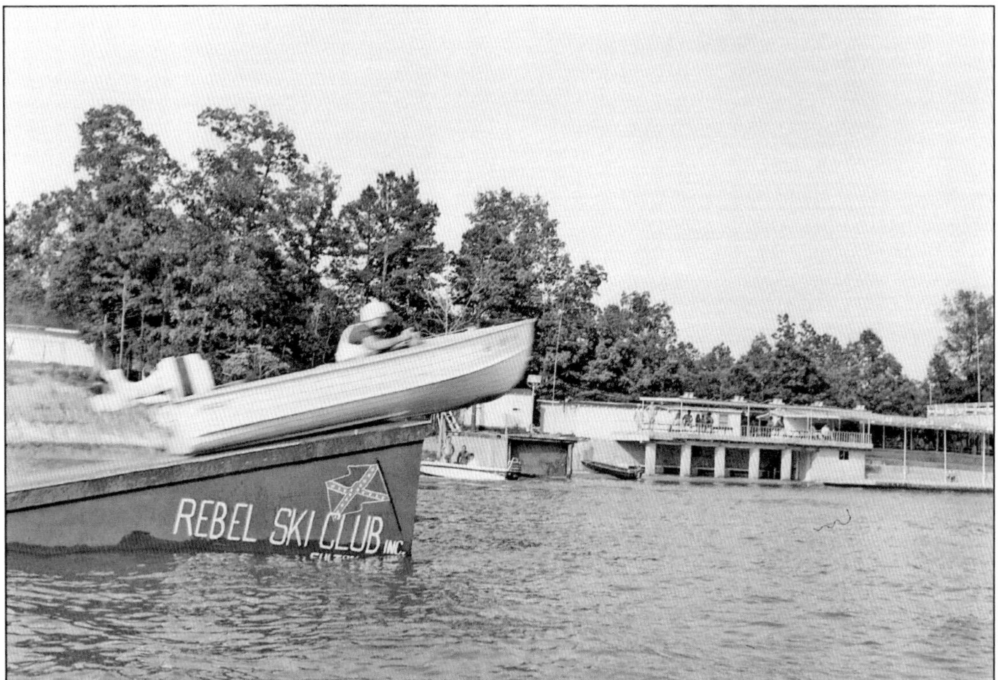

Rebel Ski Club, a local group, put on many shows at Nita Lake and around the state. In 1965, one of their biggest shows was a performance for the benefit of the new Itawamba County Library in Fulton. Daredevil stunts, such as Winford Green and his flying boat, thrilled the crowds.

Gatherings at soda fountains were not always fun occasions. Waiting for the Greyhound bus at Fulton Drug Store in 1960 were Army draftees, from left to right, Grady Tucker, Kenneth Adams, John Benson, Jimmy Senter, and Tommy Williams.

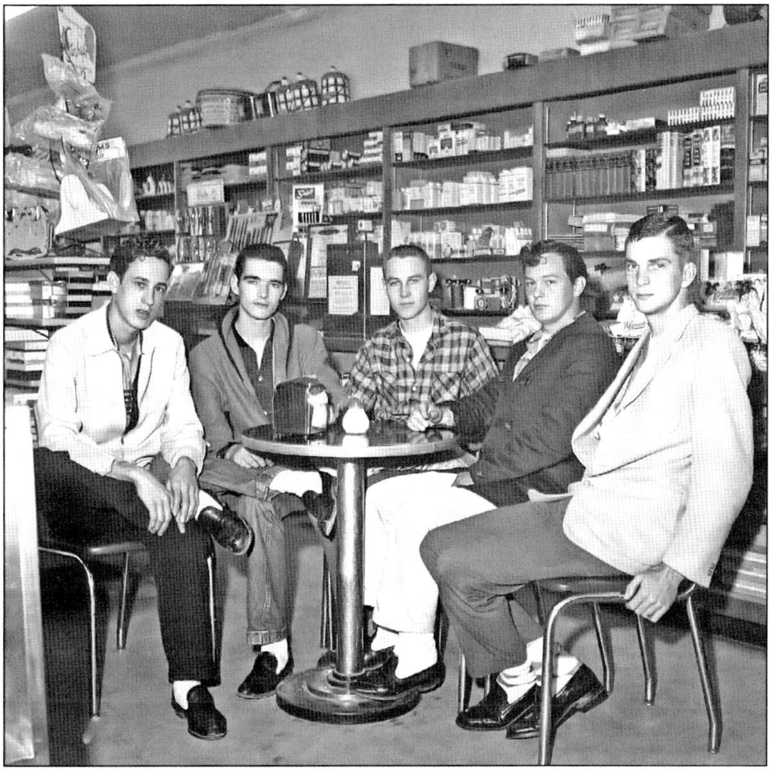

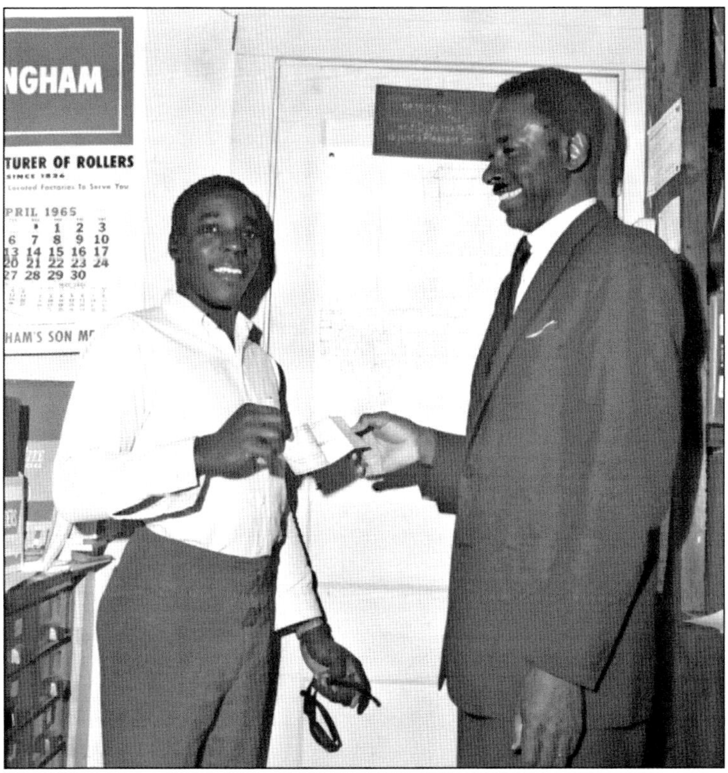

Agnew Cummings spent his extracurricular time competing in livestock judging contests. In 1965, he won second place in the competition for the northern half of the state and is being congratulated here by C.C. Cummings, the vocational agriculture teacher at East High School.

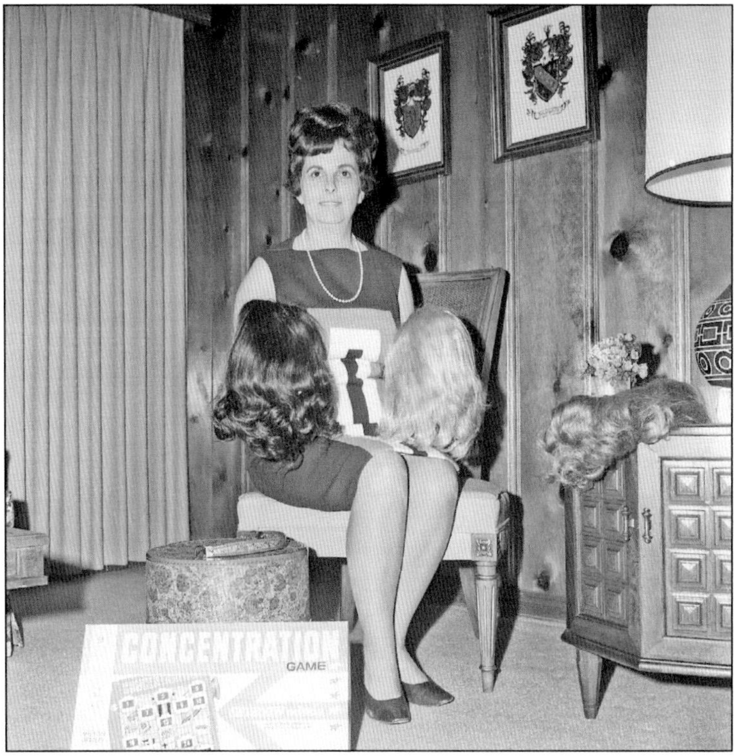

Ann Kilpatrick Stubblefield Gibbs, wife of Fulton mayor and businessman Malcolm Stubblefield, won more than $7,000 playing in the nationally televised game show *Concentration* in 1968, when she won four straight days of games. Here, she is pictured with the wigs she won on the show; other prizes included a trip to Las Vegas, a home workshop, and a boat.

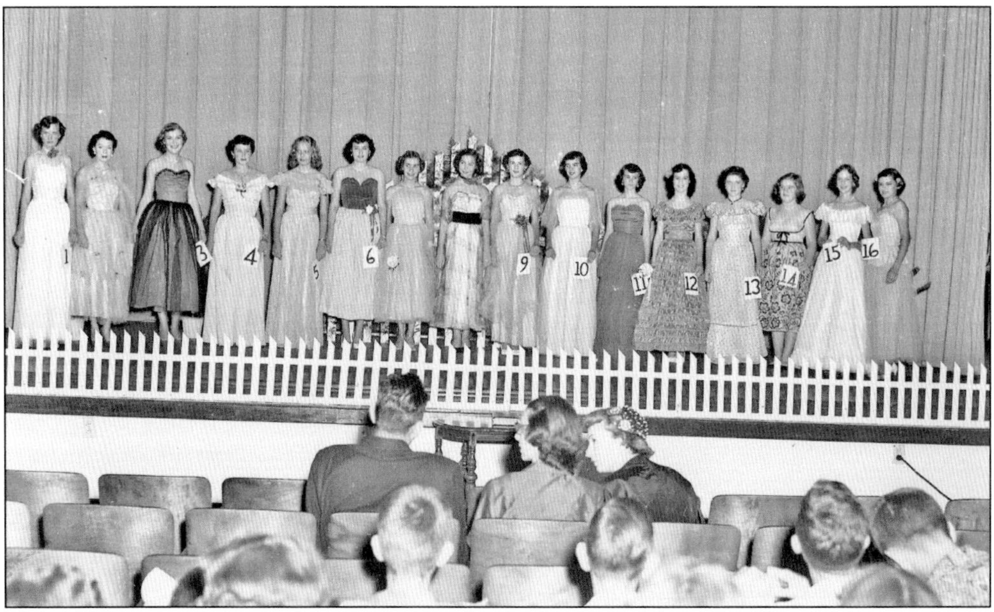

Participating in the Miss Fulton contest in 1952 are, from left to right, Tommye Dodson, Mildred Ann McCormick, Bettye McNeece (winner), Bettye Gilliland, Doris Dill, Glennie Sue Maske, Robbie Alverson, Sue Franks, Carolyn Wheeler, Mary Nell McKinney, Helen Holloway, Mitzie Brown, Hilda Holcombe, Bettye Stringfellow, Sara McKinney, and Joyce Gray.

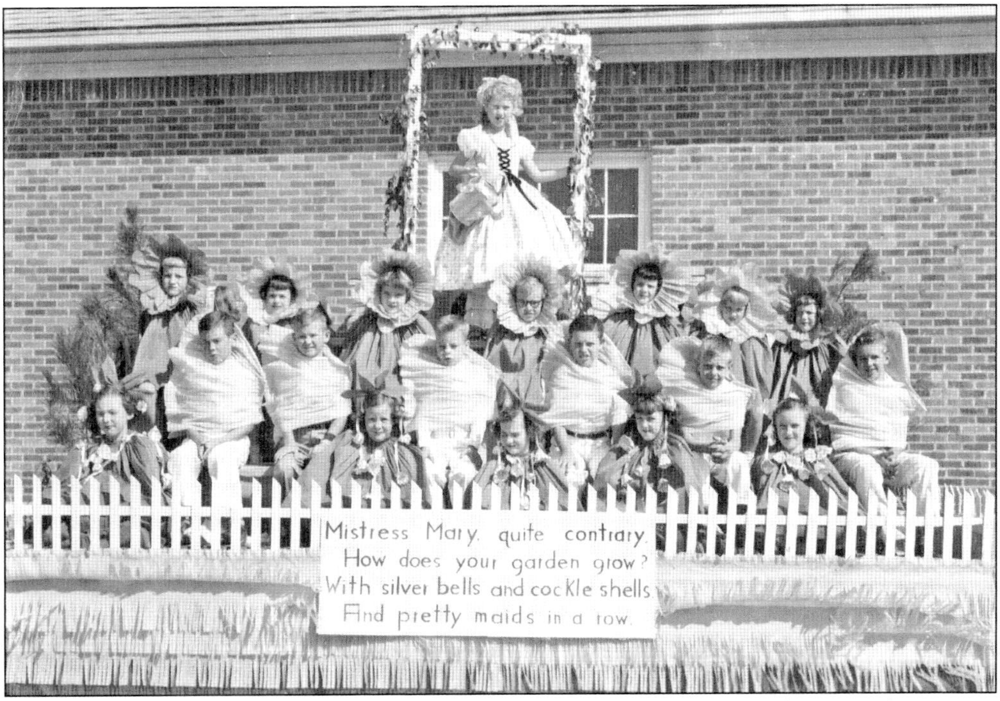

Fulton Grammar School provided stiff competition in the float division for the Itawamba County Fair parade held each fall. The school's entry in 1952 was no exception, winning first prize for its "Mistress Mary Quite Contrary" float.

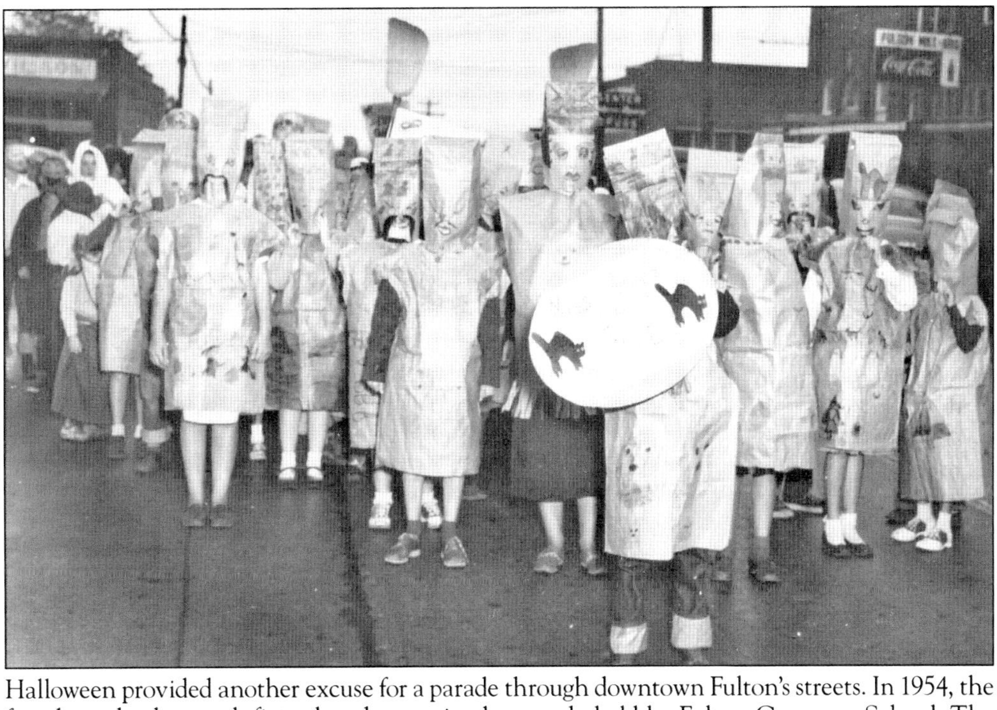

Halloween provided another excuse for a parade through downtown Fulton's streets. In 1954, the fourth-grade class took first place honors in the parade held by Fulton Grammar School. The students dressed in dry cleaners' sacks colorfully decorated with appropriate scenes.

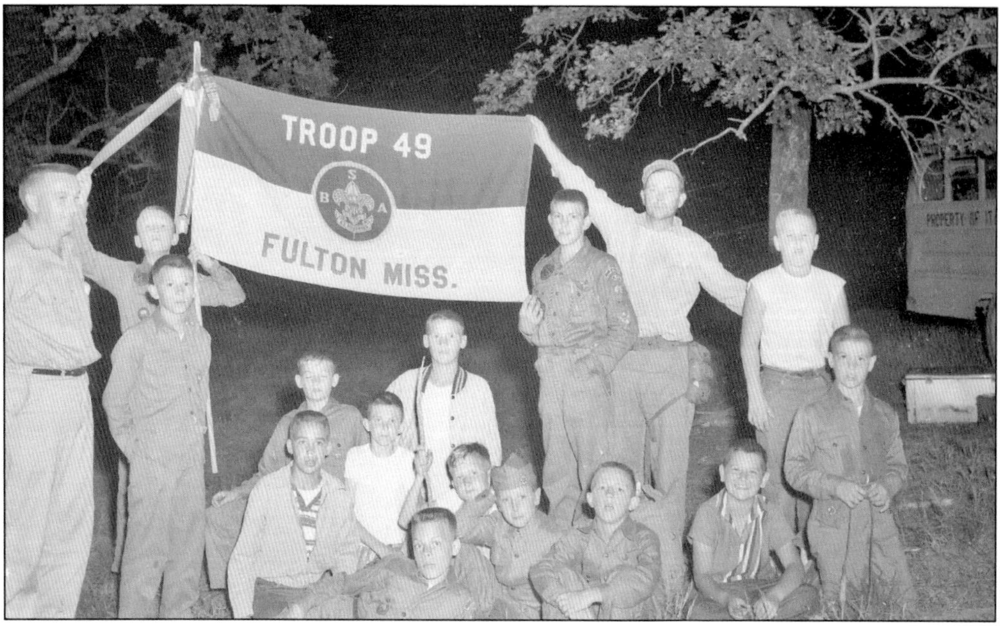

The Boy Scouts have had a strong presence in Fulton and Itawamba County for several decades. In 1957, Fulton Troop 49 raises its flag with troop leaders H.D. McGee (left) and Leonard Smith.

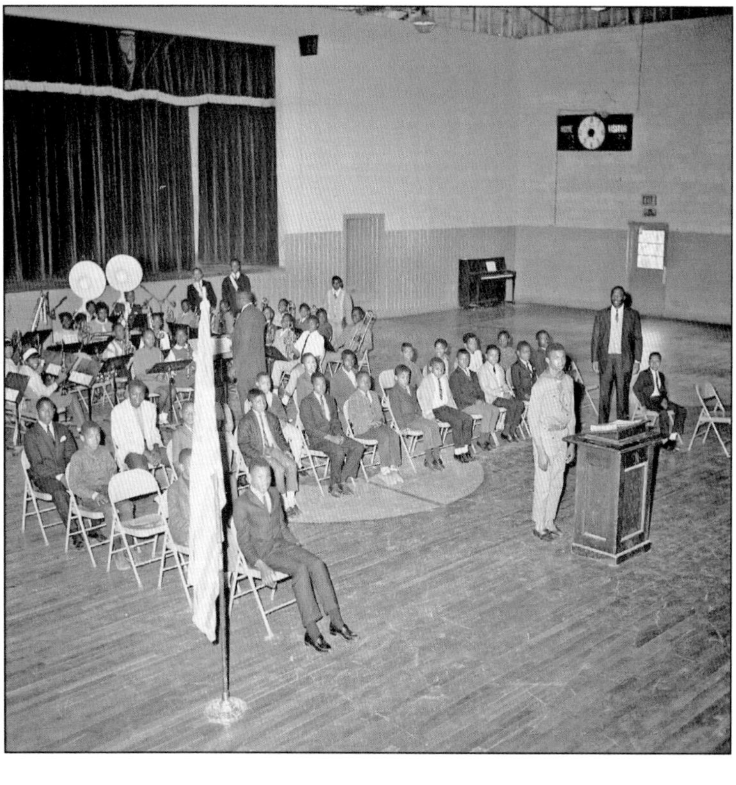

As part of the observance of Boy Scout Week in February 1968, Troop 151 held a special program at the East High gymnasium. Participating in the event was the safety patrol unit for the school as well as the school band. Presley Riley was scoutmaster for the troop.

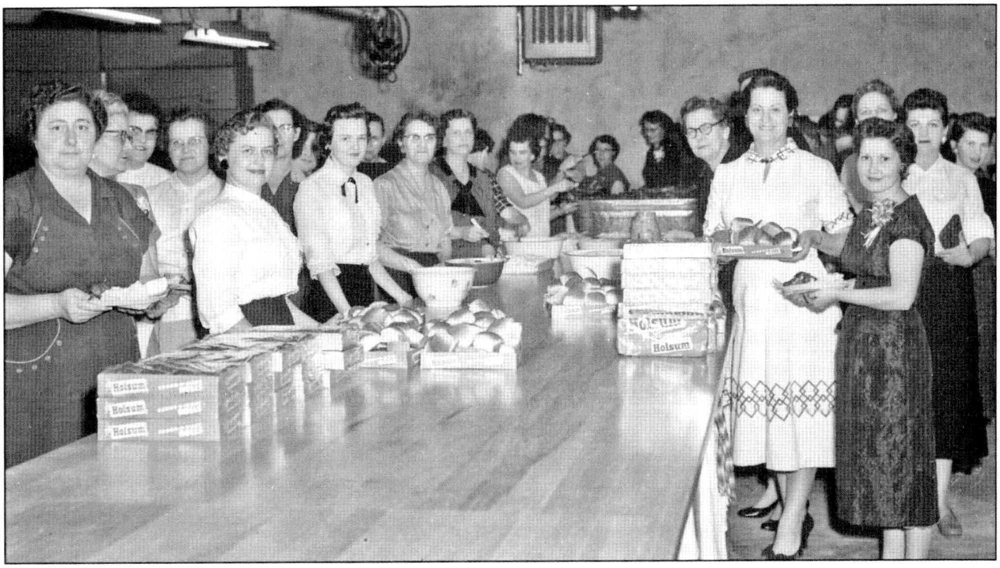

At many of the manufacturing plants in Fulton, workers felt a sense of family and community, a feeling fostered by picnics, athletic competitions, and other fun events such as annual Christmas parties. In 1957, these employees at Itawamba Manufacturing Company prepare for their Christmas meal.

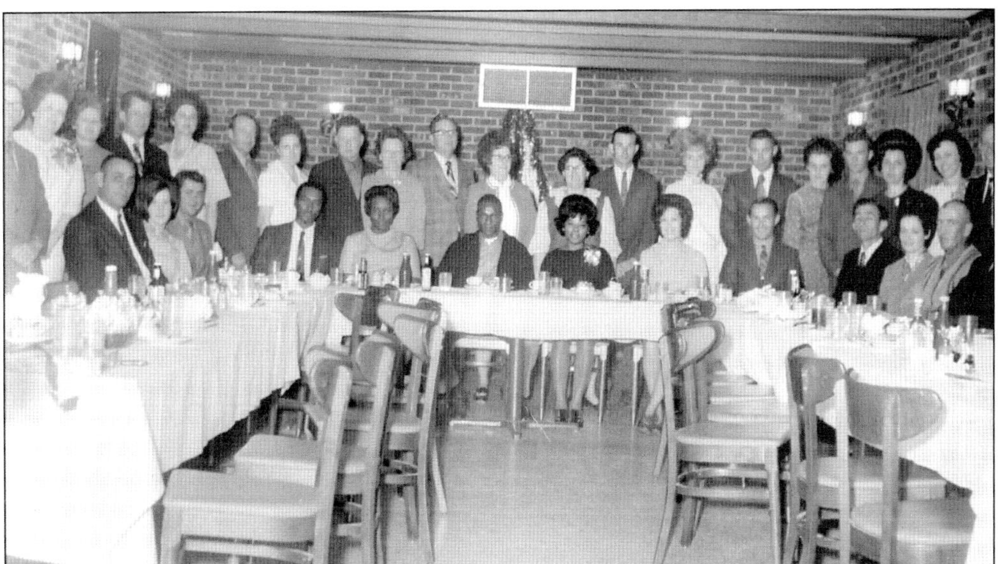

In 1970, the employees of the Fulton office of Tombigbee Electric Power Association held their annual Christmas party at the Wigwam Restaurant in Fulton. The Wigwam was opened in 1967 by Ben and Bobbye Jones and quickly became a popular hangout spot.

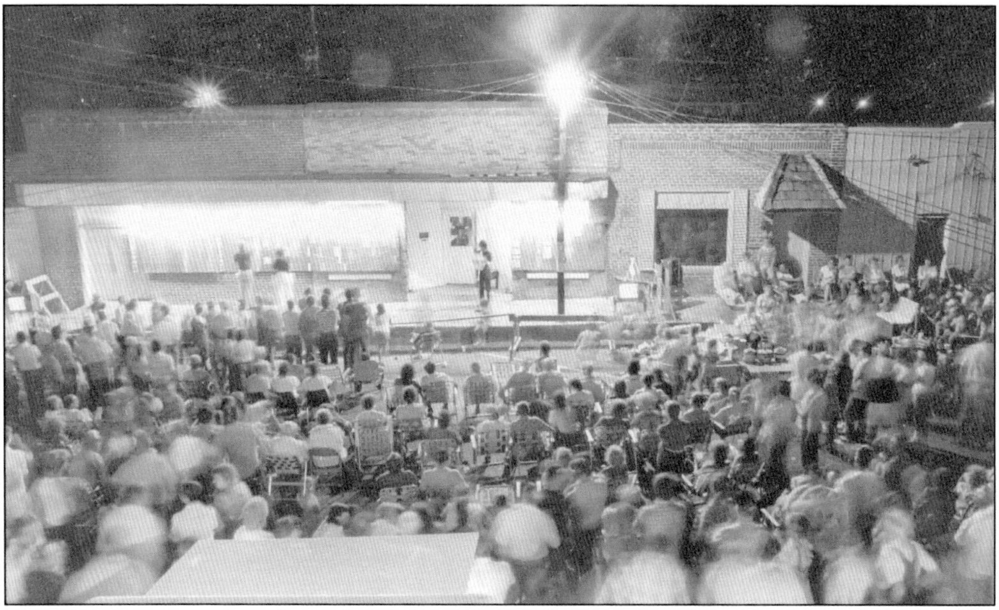

Election night was a special, late-night occasion in downtown Fulton as candidates and families gathered in front of the *Itawamba County Times* offices to watch as returns from county precincts were announced and then posted on the huge blackboard. The Times Election Party has become less of an event with the advent of electronic voting machines and social media. This election night scene is from August 1983.

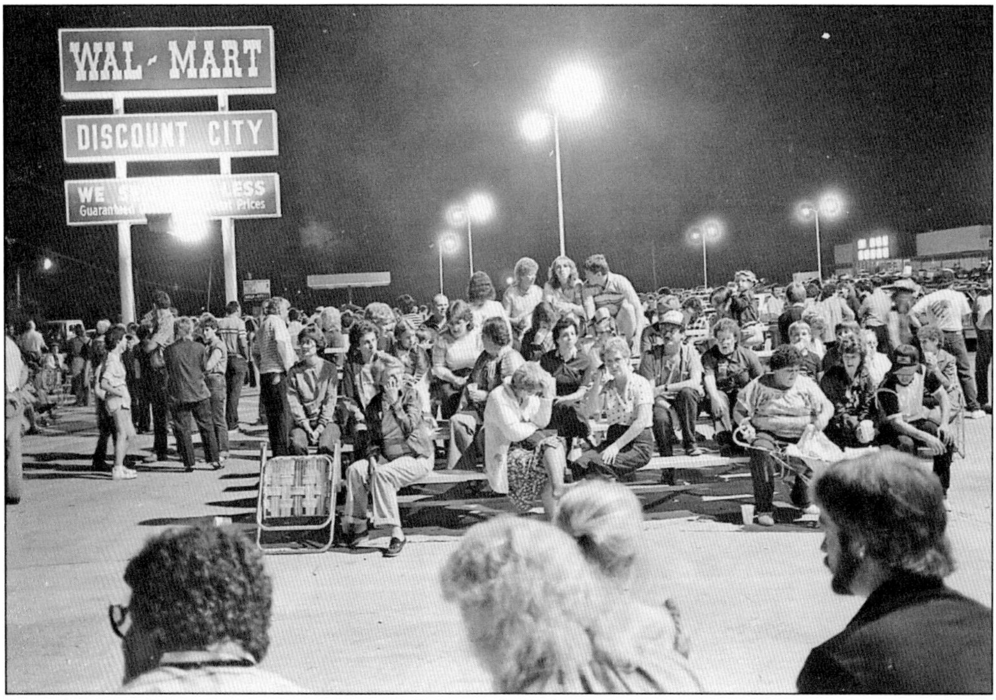

In 1984, the Olympic torch was carried through Fulton on its way to Los Angeles. Hundreds gathered along the route in the middle of the night to view the runner and the torch. Here, a crowd waits at the parking lot of the former location of Wal-Mart.

Six

FACES FROM THE PAST

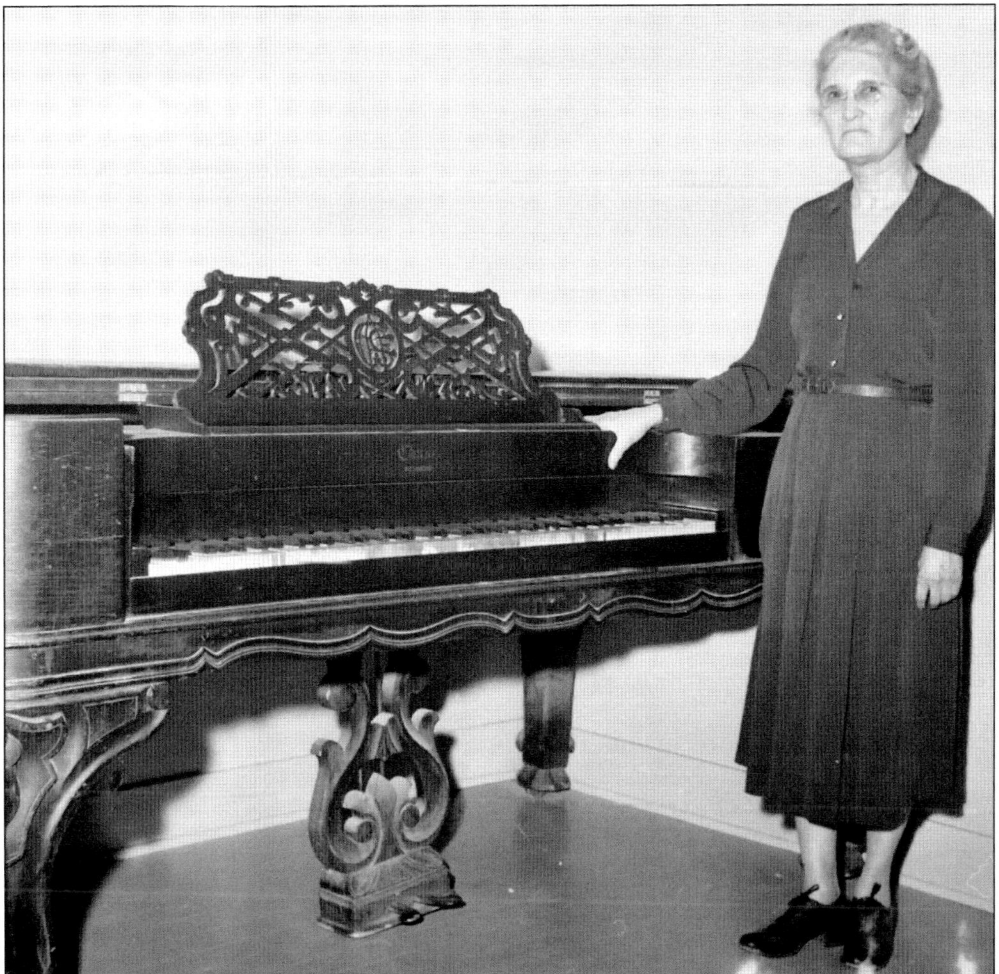

Zereda Greene, noted Itawamba County historian, was the daughter of local merchant James Alfred Howard Greene and Martha Jane Ward. She is pictured with an antique rosewood piano purchased by her father in 1903 from the J.P. Baldridge home.

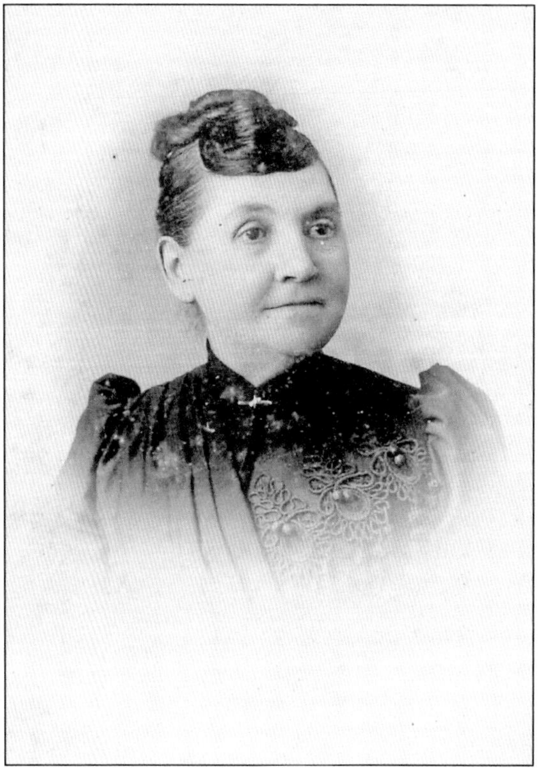

Desdemonia Wiygle Gaither was the daughter of Fulton settler Reuben Wiygul. She was born in Fulton in 1835 and died in 1919. She married Gilbert Burgess Gaither in 1850 and was the mother of Matilda Emmeline (who married John C. Cates), William Lafayette, Wiley Clifford, and Burgess Falls. (Courtesy of Danny Gaither.)

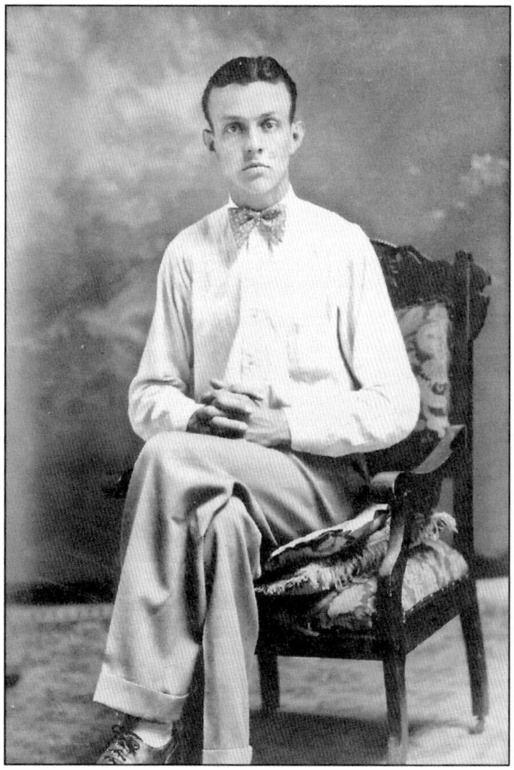

Homer Howard was the son of Sargent Prentiss and Lillie Albion Rosseau Howard of Fulton. The Howard family were residents of Fulton since the 1840s. The Howard home was directly behind the Fulton Bank, where S.P. Howard was president (currently the Haynes lot behind the Trustmark bank building on the town square). (Courtesy of Itawamba Historical Society, Benson Collection.)

Shadrack Newnan Cayce was born in 1844 in Fulton, the son of Judge Newnan and Matilda Gaither Cayce, early citizens of Fulton. Shadrack attended the Fulton Male Academy and served during the Civil War. In the later 1800s, he moved to Aberdeen, where he was an attorney, and later to Columbus, where he was a judge. He died in January 1912 in Columbus. (Courtesy of Evans Memorial Library, Aberdeen, Mississippi, F.S. McKnight Photograph Collection.)

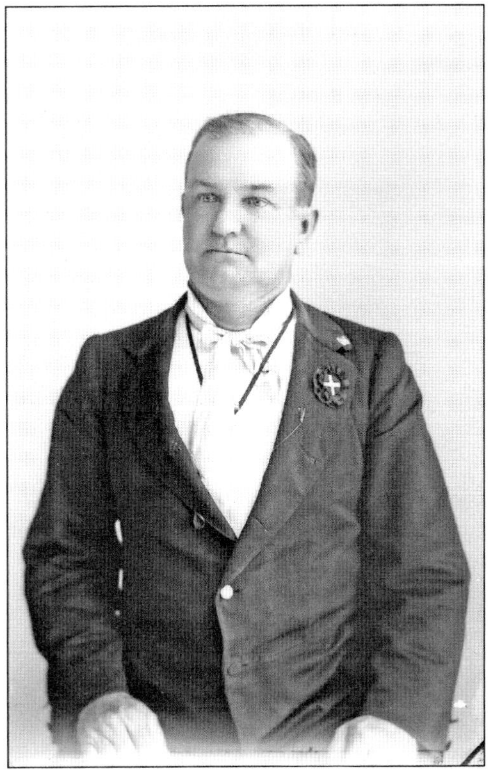

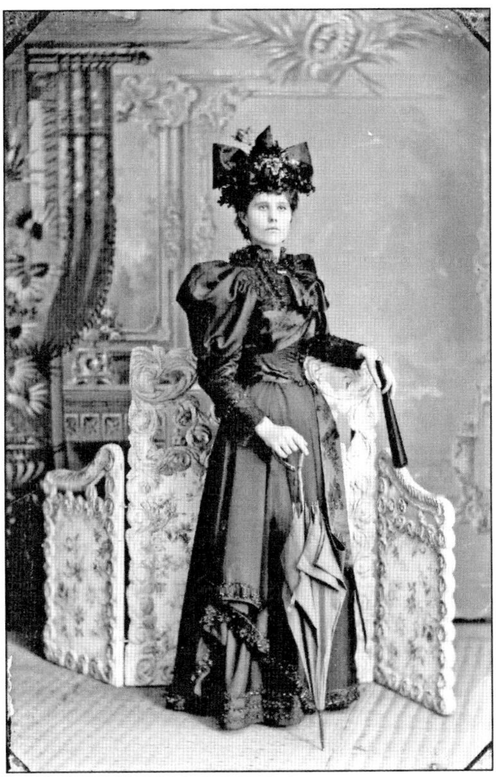

Julia Clifton was born in Fulton in 1855 in what was considered the finest home in Fulton in the antebellum years (near the present-day Fulton Church of Christ). She was the daughter of Fulton merchant and planter Wiley Daniel Clifton and his wife, Julia Oliver Clifton. Julia spent time between Fulton and Aberdeen with her Eckford cousins. (Courtesy of Evans Memorial Library, Aberdeen, Mississippi, F.S. McKnight Photograph Collection.)

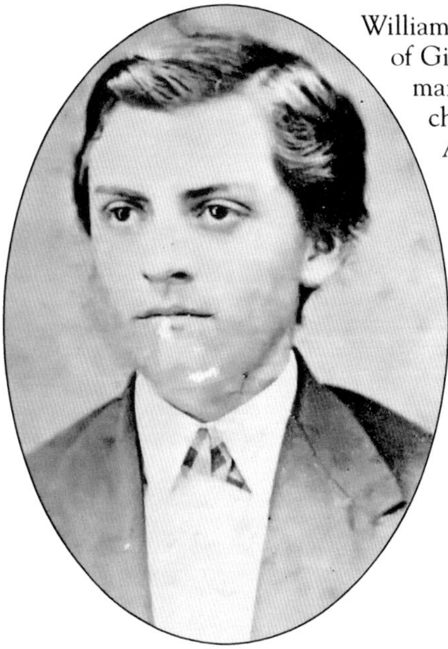

William Lafayette Gaither was born in Fulton in 1854, the son of Gilbreth Burgess and Desdemonia Wiygle Gaither. He married Alice Betts in 1881 and was the father of three children, Burgess and twins Eugene and Will. Following Alice's death, William married Annie Moore and had two sons, Grady and Wiley. William was a merchant in town and a large landowner. (Courtesy of Danny Gaither.)

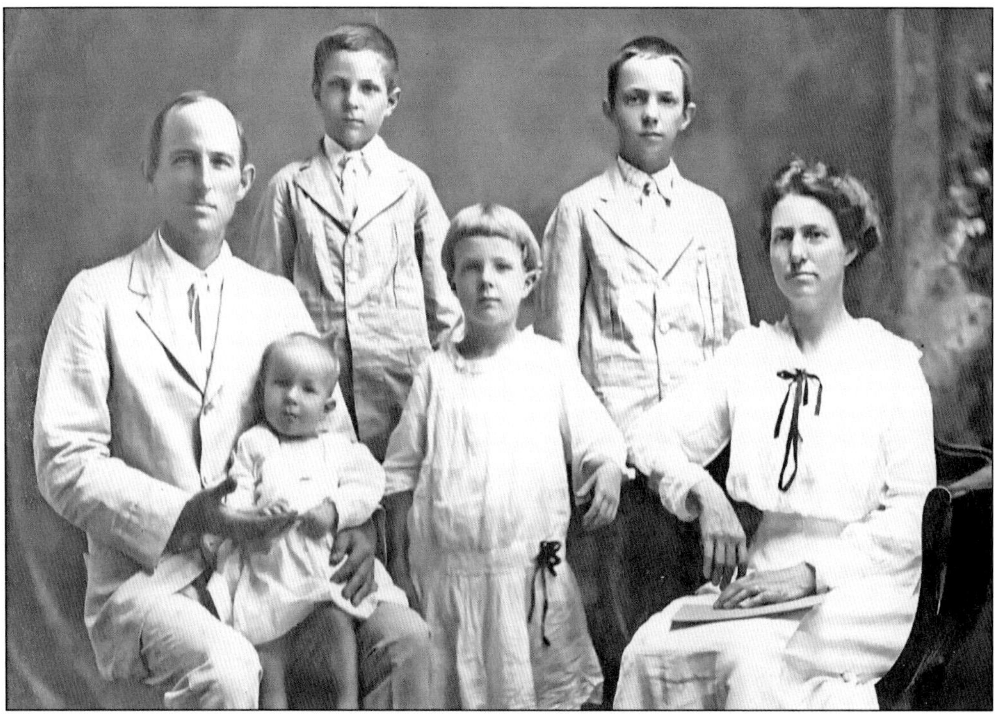

The Marcus Cidney Benson family lived in the old antebellum Keys Home just south of the Fulton town square (the present Fulton Police Department lot). Marcus Cidney Benson was born on November 9, 1873, in Itawamba County and married Daisy Burch. He was an attorney in Fulton and a partner in the law firm of Benson & Spearman, serving as the attorney for the Itawamba County Board of Supervisors, the Fulton Bank, and the Kentucky Lumber and Railroad Company. Marcus Cidney Benson died on September 19, 1921. (Courtesy of Itawamba Historical Society, Benson Collection.)

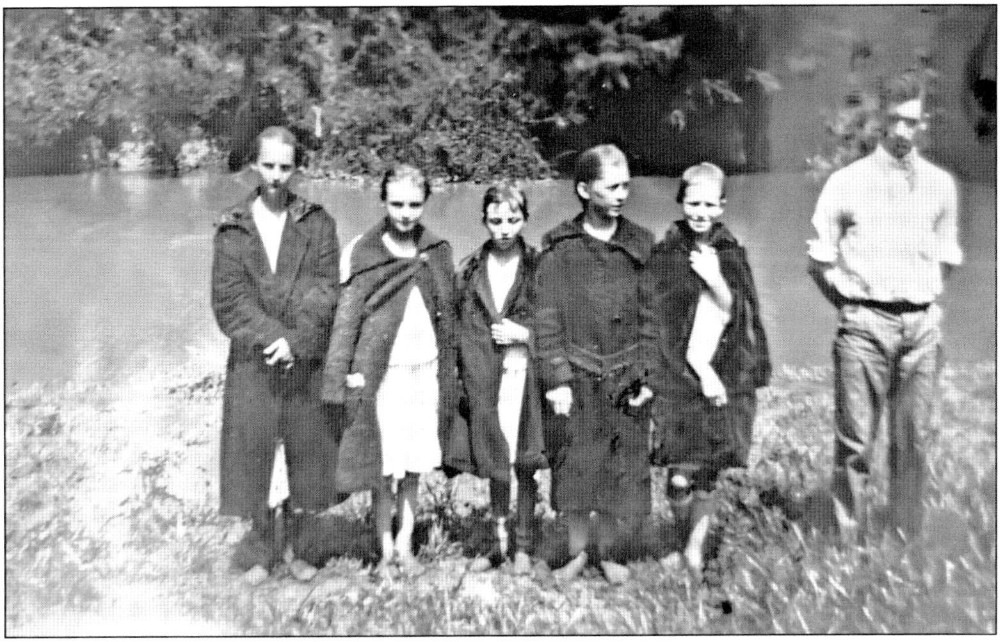

A group of Fulton youths gather on the banks of the Tombigbee River west of town about 1923. This appears to be a photograph of a baptism service. In the past, the Tombigbee River and area ponds were often used for baptisms. (Courtesy of Itawamba Historical Society, Benson Collection.)

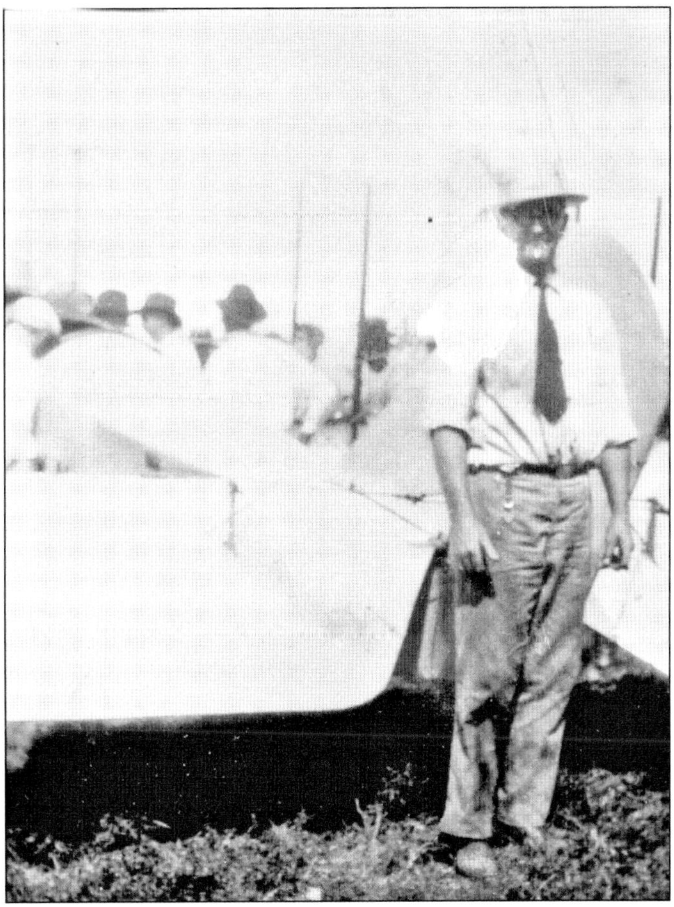

Escar Mattox was Fulton's first gasoline dealer. He is pictured here just after he gassed up one of the first airplanes to land in Fulton, probably in the 1920s. The airplanes took people up for $2 per ride, according to newspaper accounts.

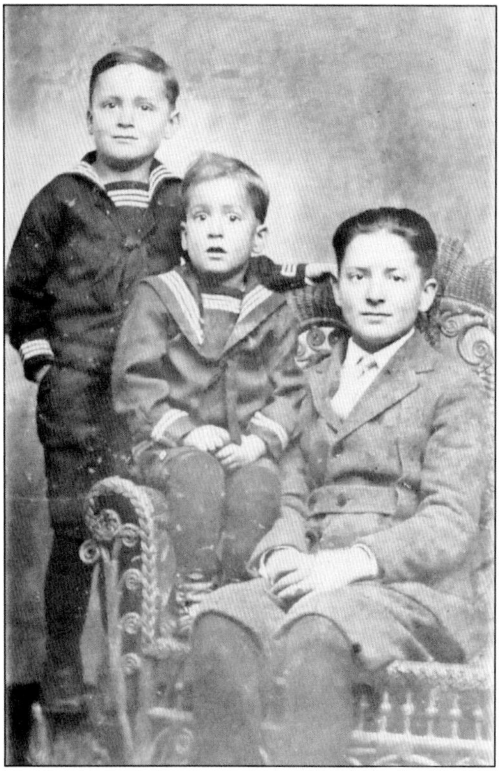

The Senter boys—from left to right, Graden, Frank, and Lyonel—were the sons of Dr. John Thomas Senter and Carrie Lee Sandlin Senter. Dr. Senter had a medical practice in Fulton and in 1921 opened J.T. Senter & Son, later known as Senter Drug Store, a Fulton landmark building featuring a large mural facing Main Street. (Courtesy of the family of Margueritte Senter Critz.)

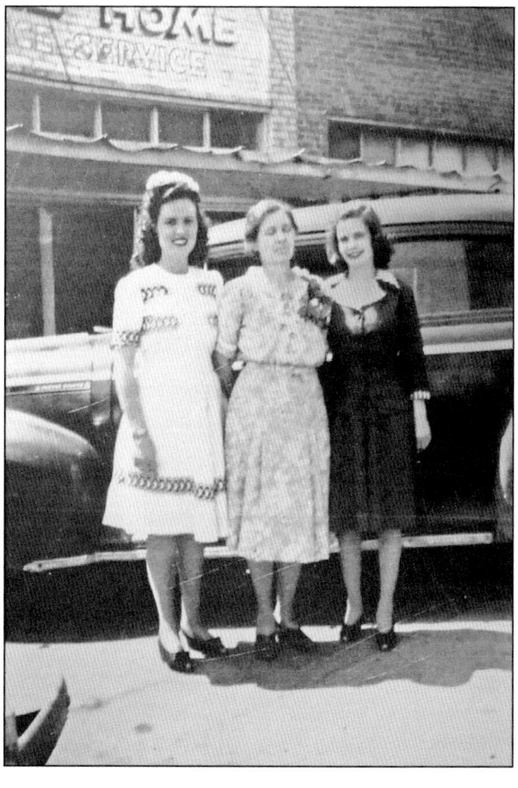

Margueritte Jane Senter Critz was the daughter of Dr. John T. and Carrie Sandlin Senter. She lived all her life in Fulton, the town that she adored. She married Frank A. Critz III of West Point and in 1949 opened Lee-Ann Ladies' and Children's Shop, a store she actively operated until her death in 2016. Margueritte, left, stands with friends in front of Senter Funeral Home on North Cummings Street. The funeral home occupied the south half of the building next to Senter Drug Company. (Courtesy of the family of Margueritte Senter Critz.)

Former slave Matilda Clifton is pictured in front of her home on Beene Street in Fulton. Matilda came with her owner, Harriett Caroline Pearce Johnson, wife of Stephen Johnson, to Itawamba County from North Carolina. Matilda, who had 12 children with her husband, George Clifton, died in 1939 when she was over 100 years old. (Courtesy of the Archives and Records Services Division, Mississippi Department of Archives and History.)

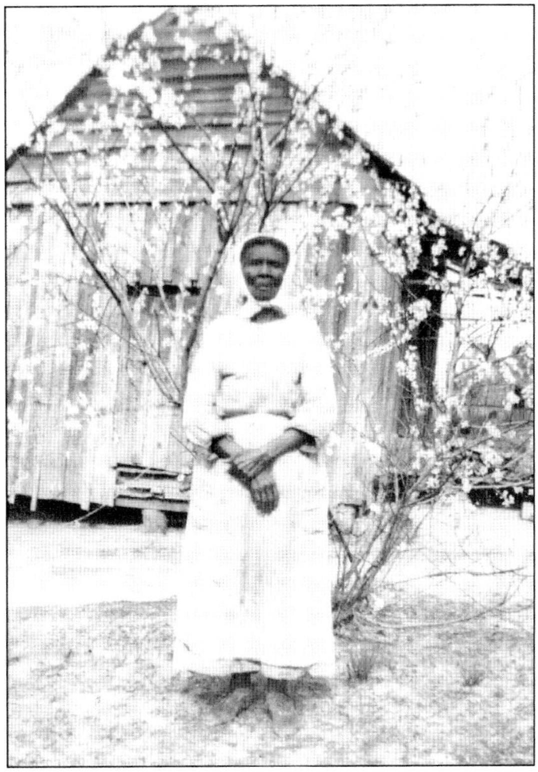

Madge Stubblefield sits at her desk at the *Itawamba County Times* in 1960. She wrote the weekly "What's Cooking" feature in which she interviewed people in Fulton, published their photographs and some of their recipes, and covered weddings.

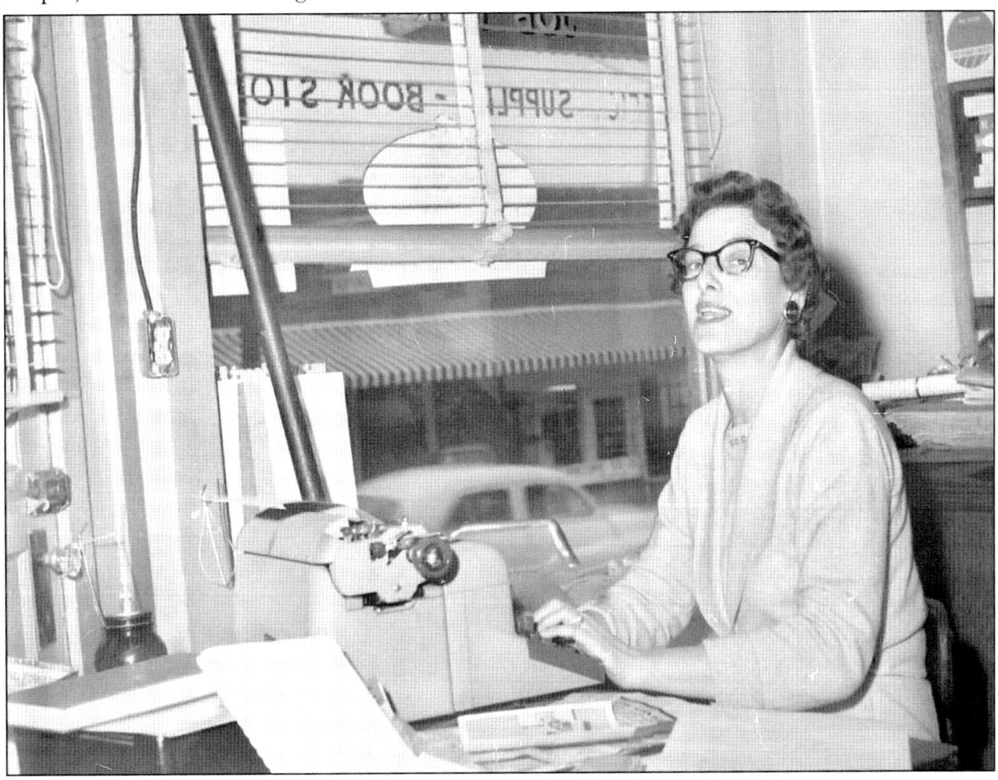

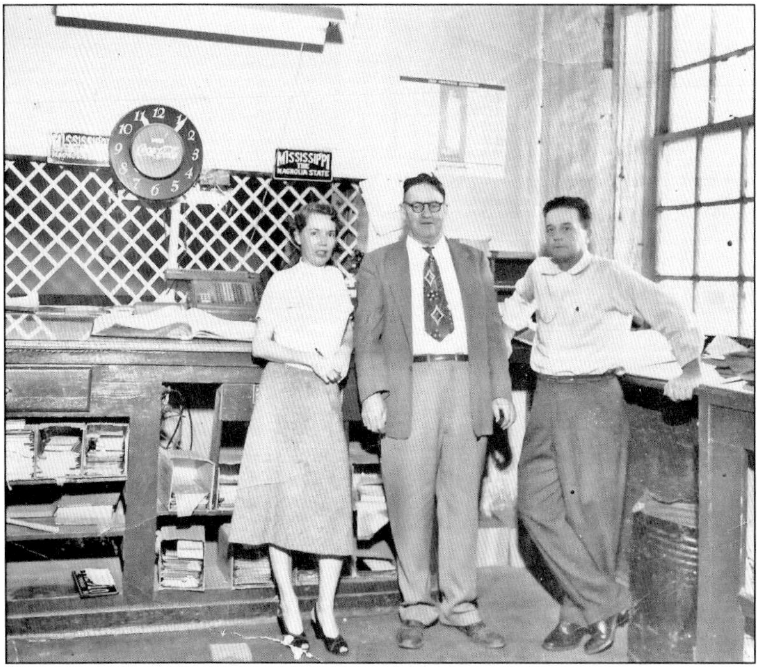

Pictured in the Itawamba County sheriff's office in the Itawamba County Courthouse in the early 1950s are, from left to right, Reba Gilliland, Otto Miller, and Sheriff Joseph Ezell "Jodie" Sheffield. Sheffield held office from 1952 to 1955 and from 1964 to 1968. During that era, the office of the sheriff collected taxes and sold automobile tags.

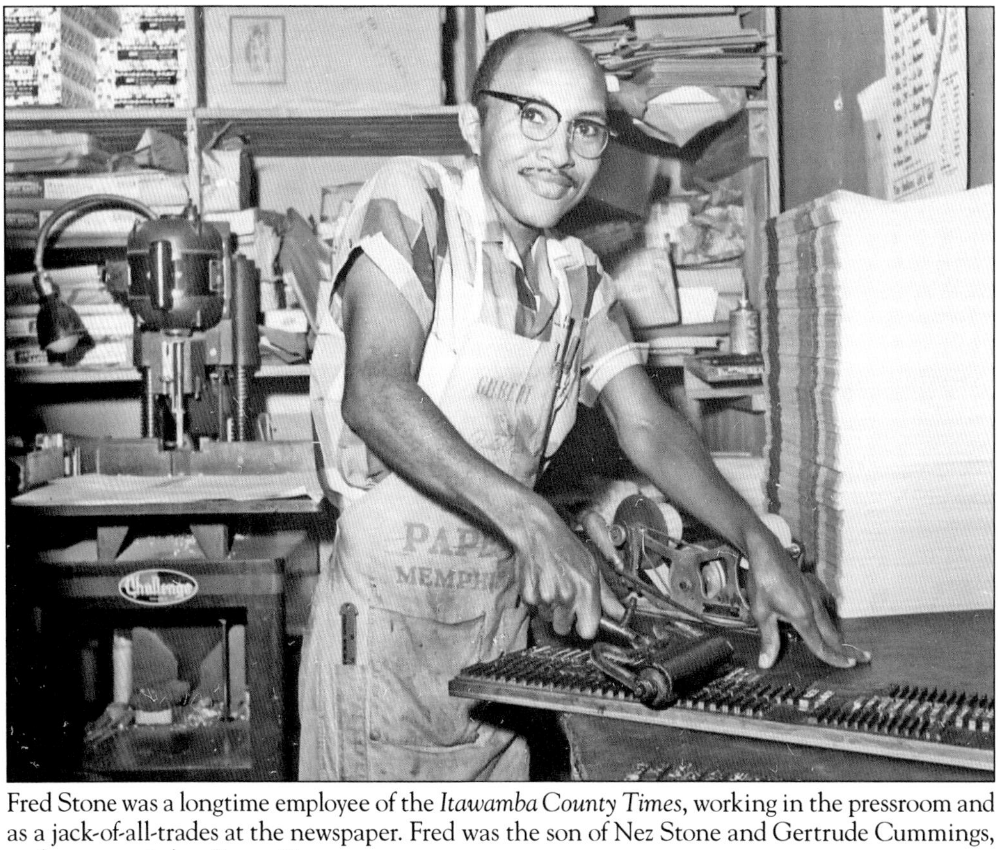

Fred Stone was a longtime employee of the *Itawamba County Times*, working in the pressroom and as a jack-of-all-trades at the newspaper. Fred was the son of Nez Stone and Gertrude Cummings, and was married to Peggy Casey.

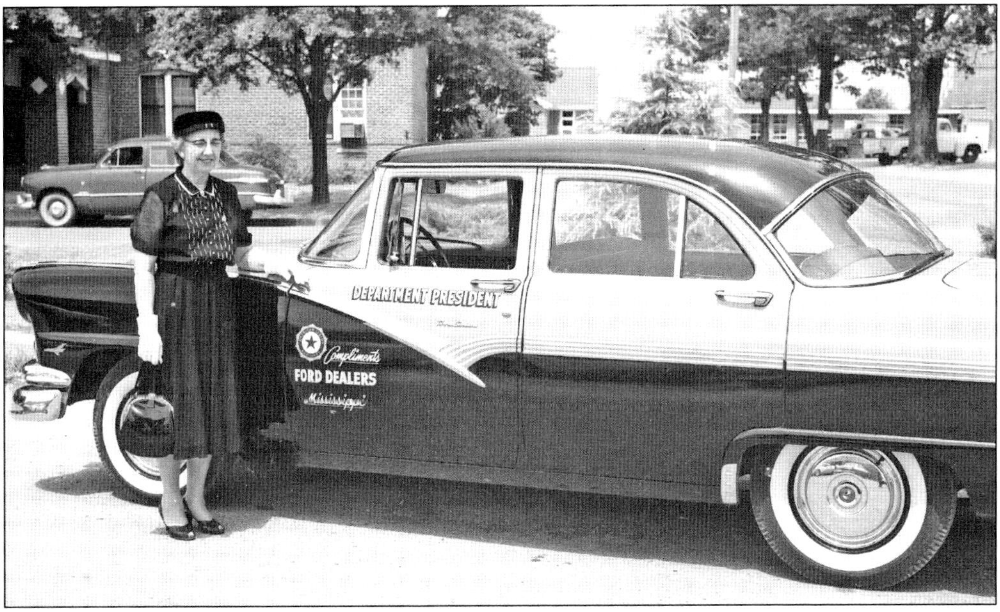

Vera Jane Whitesides of Fulton was the 1956 president of the Mississippi Department of the American Legion Auxiliary. She is posing on the Itawamba Junior College campus next to the car furnished to her by Mississippi Ford dealers for use in traveling around the state.

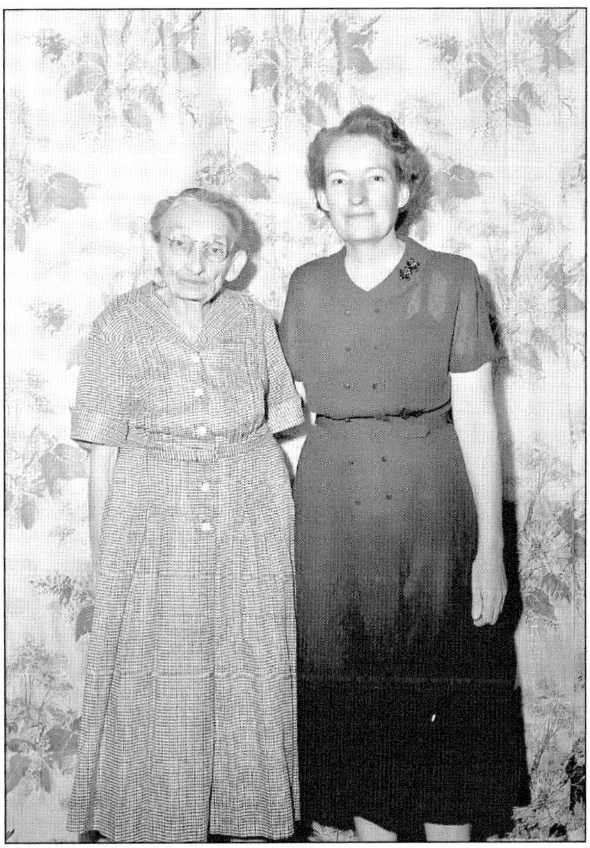

Euple Dozier, pictured at right with her mother, Miranda Dozier, was appointed interim US district attorney for the Northern District of Mississippi in 1961, only the second female in the country to serve as a US attorney and the first one in the South. In 1955, she became the first female assistant US attorney in Mississippi. Dozier and Nell May formed the first female law firm in the state of Mississippi.

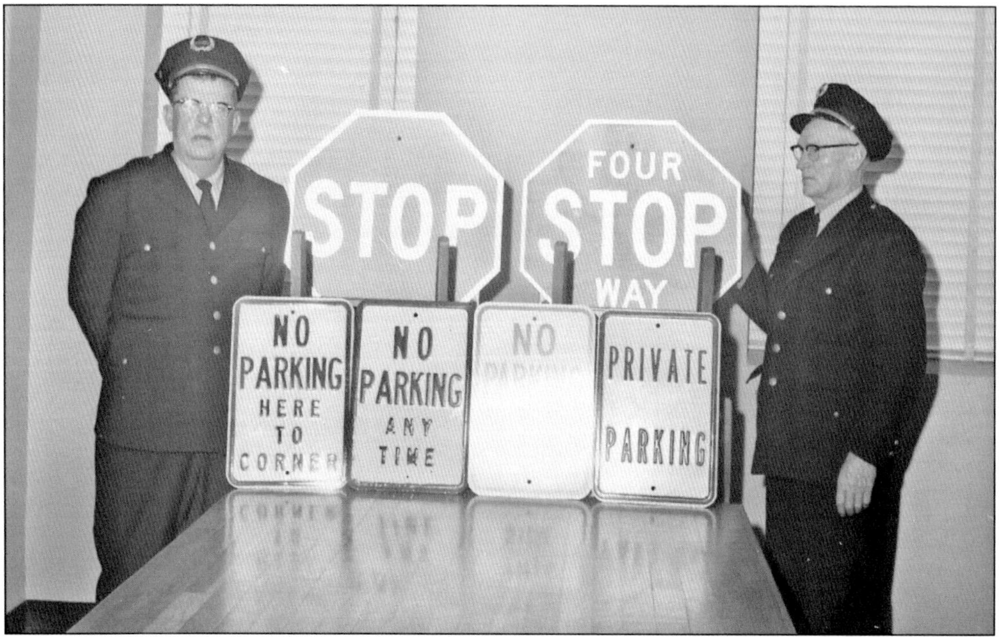

Policemen Newt Alexander (left) and J.O. "Bill" Shaw are pictured in 1962 with new signs for the city streets of Fulton.

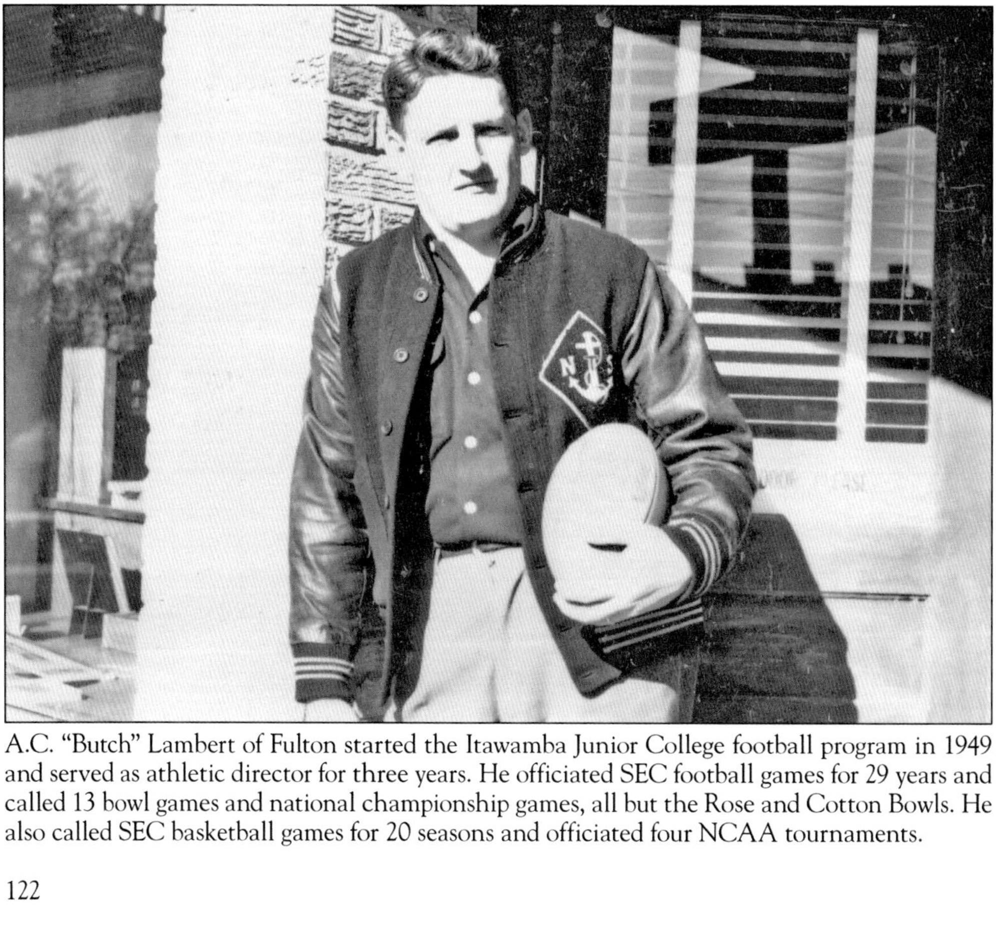

A.C. "Butch" Lambert of Fulton started the Itawamba Junior College football program in 1949 and served as athletic director for three years. He officiated SEC football games for 29 years and called 13 bowl games and national championship games, all but the Rose and Cotton Bowls. He also called SEC basketball games for 20 seasons and officiated four NCAA tournaments.

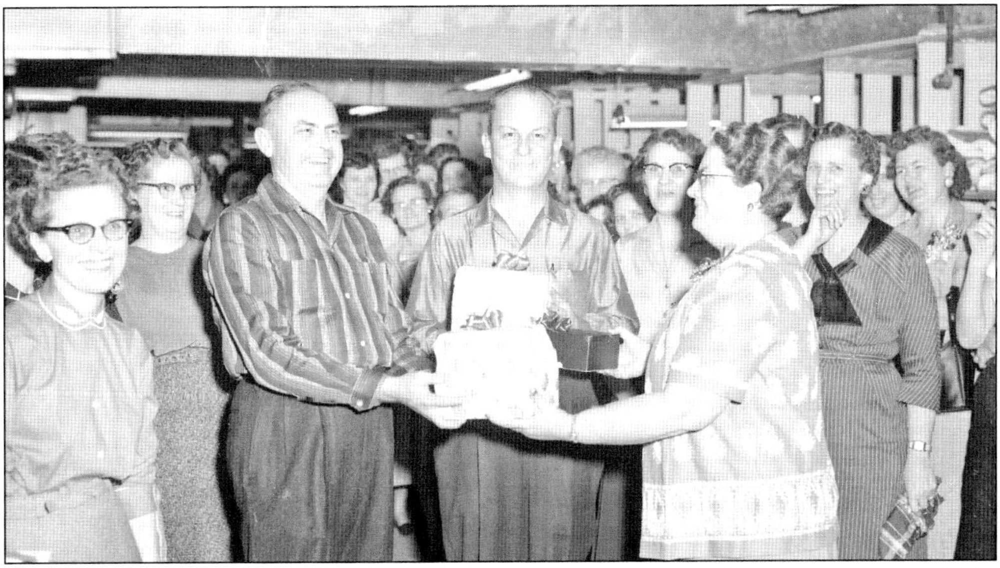

Elzie Hankins (left) and Rex Brown receive gifts at a company Christmas party in 1956. Itawamba Manufacturing Company, organized in 1948 by Hankins and Brown, was a leading manufacturer in Fulton for many years, making men's shirts, and was the first such company that was homegrown.

Basil Earnest (right) owned Earnest Hardware and Furniture Store. The store was originally located at the corner of North Cummings and Beene Streets but moved to West Main Street in 1961. Basil's father, O.E. Earnest, and Gaddis Prestage opened the business in the 1940s as a hardware and building materials store. After the death of O.E. Earnest, Basil took over the operation of the store. Pictured with Basil Earnest is Bill Wilemon, who worked at the store.

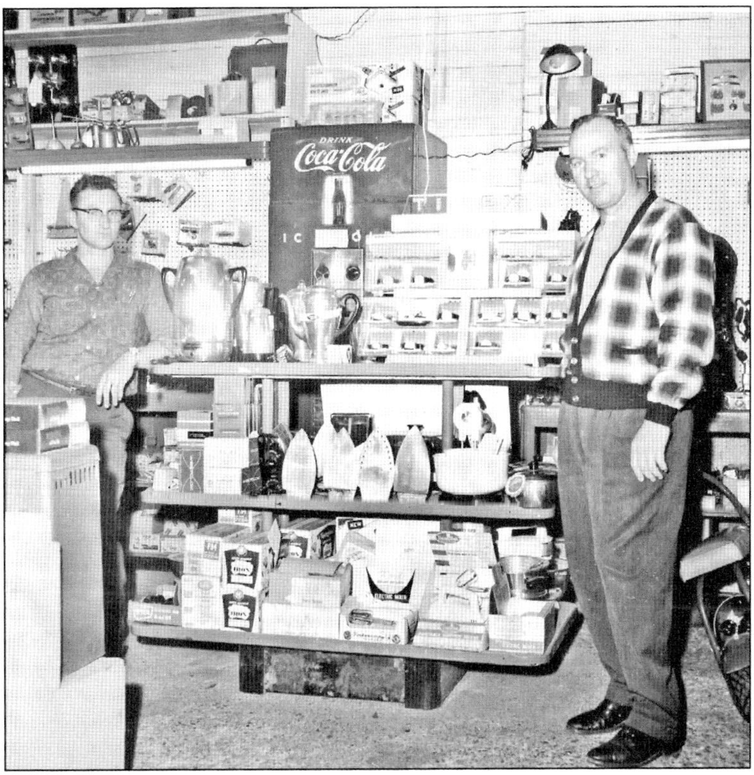

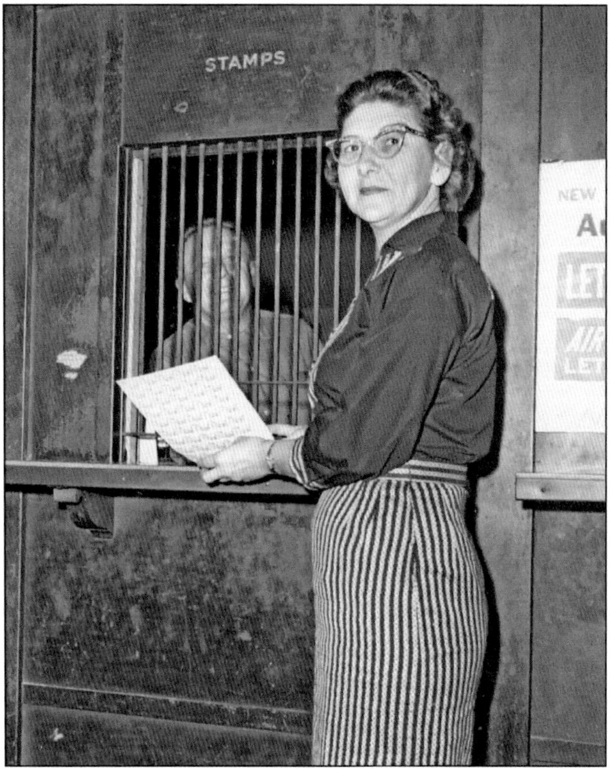

Charlie Mae Kilpatrick, president of Fulton Civic Club, purchases stamps from Shelby Gilmore at the window of the Fulton Post Office. Kilpatrick was a beloved teacher at Itawamba Agricultural High School and was involved in many community activities.

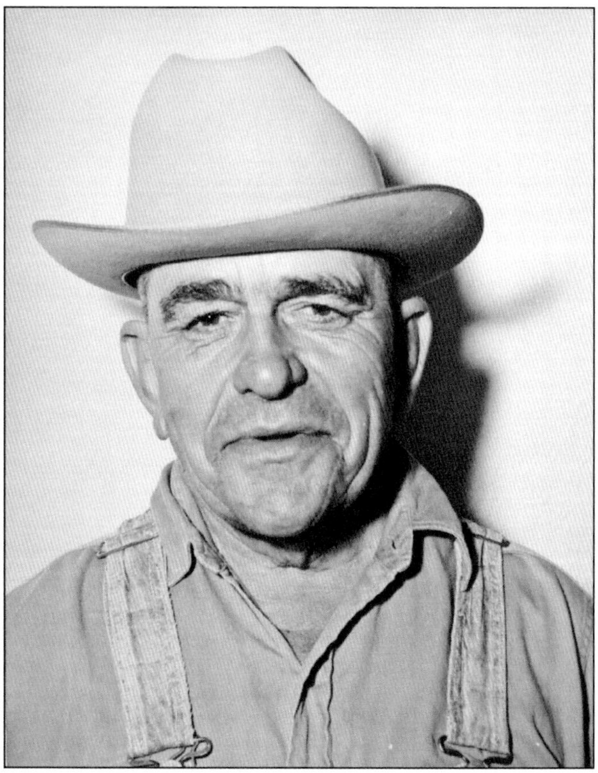

Bill Fields was for many years a fixture around the town square of Fulton. He was the son of G.R. and Minnie Fields. His family moved to Fulton, where his father was a mechanic in one of the local lumber yards. Many in Fulton fondly remember Bill, as well as his brothers Vardaman and Devoe.

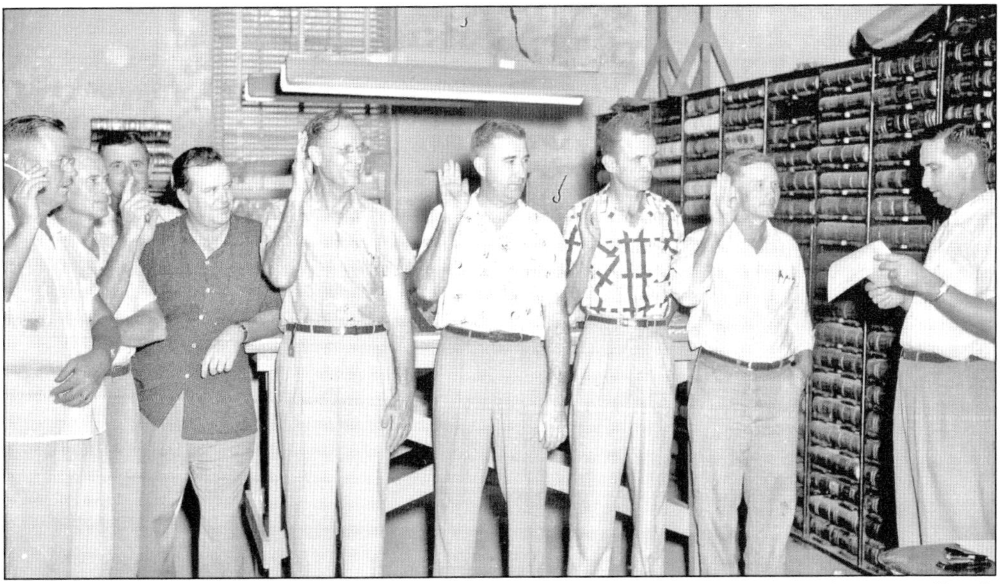

Chancery clerk Irsle Mills (right) administers the oath of office to newly elected Fulton officials in 1953. From left to right are T.B. Rushing and Hilton Holcomb (aldermen), Herman Camp (city attorney), J.M. Gibbs III (alderman), Mayor Jim Gilliland, Richard Harden and Paul Mize (aldermen), and police marshal J.O. Shaw.

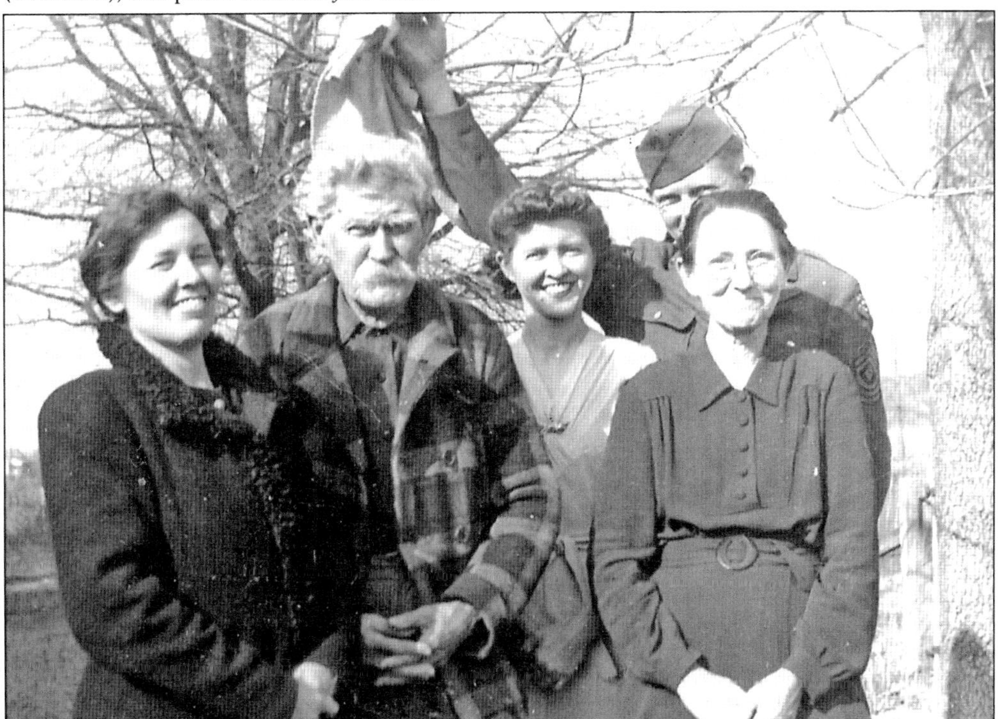

Joseph E. Sandlin (second from left) was an early educator in Fulton. He was born on February 4, 1859, and died in Fulton on July 7, 1952. Pictured with Professor Sandlin are his children and wife, from left to right, Lillian Gaither, Annie, and Mary Margaret Thorn Sandlin (wife), and in the back, Joseph Richard. (Courtesy of Danny Gaither.)

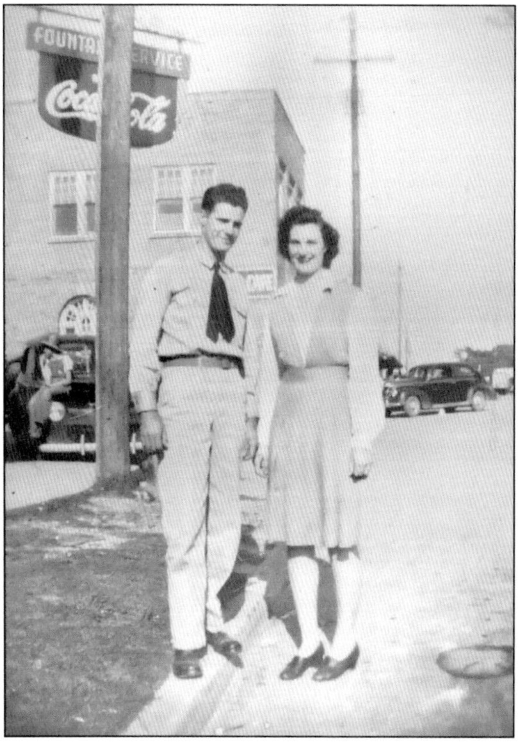

Frank and Mary Nell Leathers Senter stand at the corner of Main and North Cummings Streets next to Senter Drug Company. Frank was an avid fan of Itawamba Agricultural High School and Itawamba Junior College sports. Mary Nell was a champion basketball player at IAHS and operated the children's shop portion of Lee-Ann's Ladies' and Children's Shop on North Cummings Street. (Courtesy of the family of Margueritte Senter Critz.)

Billy Joe South (pictured) and Paul Summerford opened Bill and Paul's American Service Station in 1965 on Highway 78 just west of town; later, Finis Pearce replaced Summerford as partner at the Amoco station. South and Pearce were well-loved citizens of West Main Street.

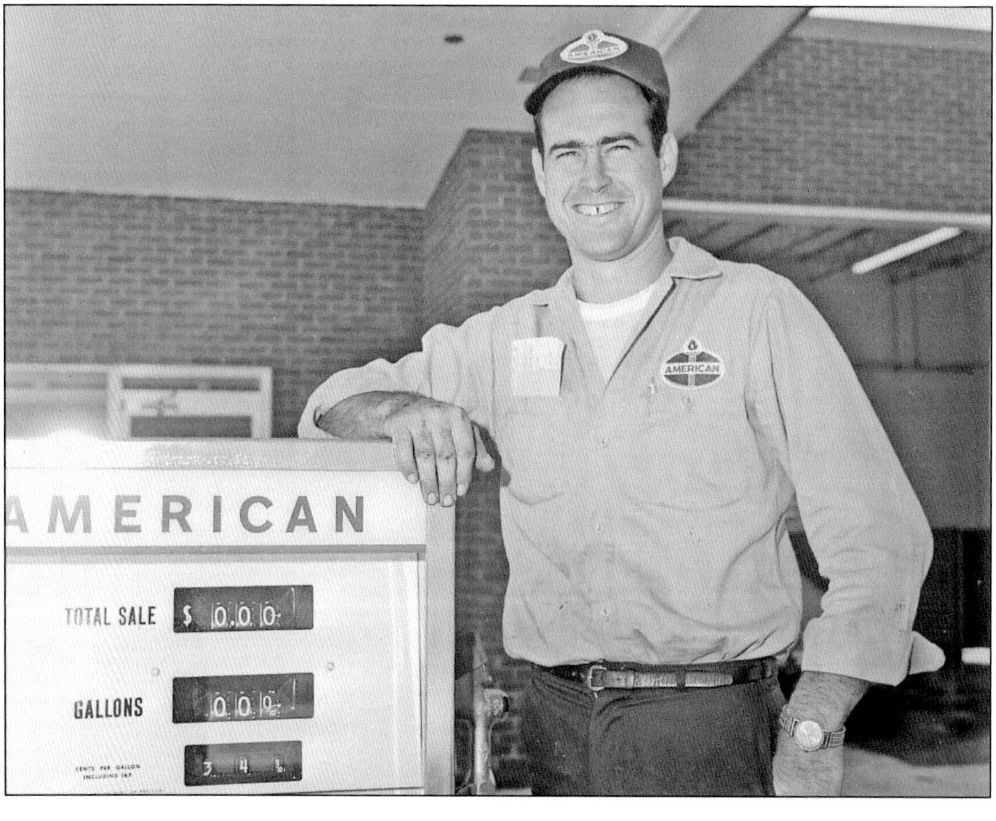

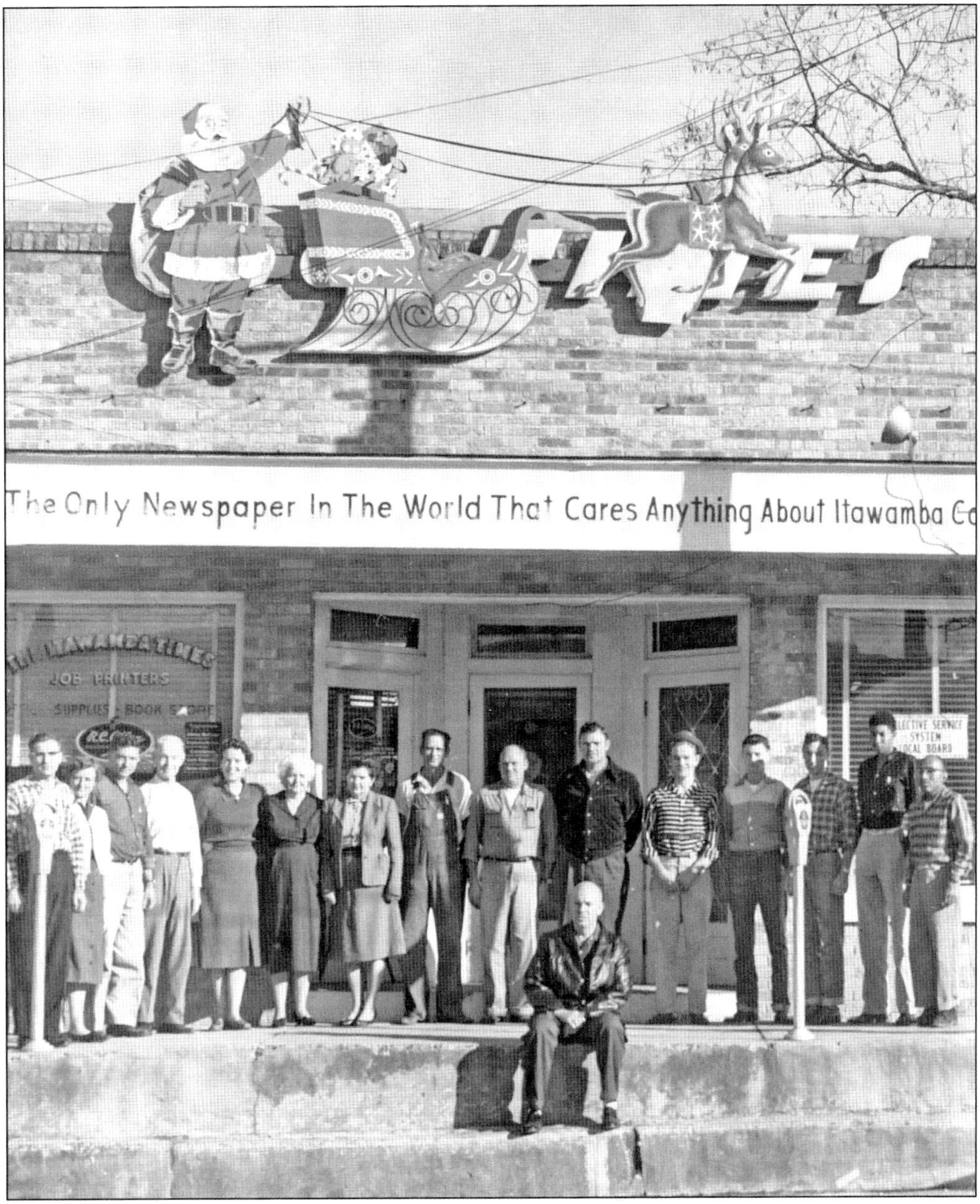

Longtime publisher of the *Itawamba County Times* Delmus C. Harden is surrounded by his employees in 1959 in front of the former location of the newspaper on North Gaither Street. Many of the photographs in this book came from the camera of Delmus Harden, who spent a lifetime capturing both special and everyday moments in his beloved Fulton and Itawamba County. Delmus and his wife, Rubye Jane Smith Harden, made important contributions to the growth and development of Fulton.